In Search of the
Real Dad's Army

In Search of the Real Dad's Army

The Home Guard and the Defence of the United Kingdom, 1940–1944

Stephen M Cullen

Pen & Sword
MILITARY

First published in Great Britain in 2011 by
Pen & Sword Military
an imprint of
Pen & Sword Books Ltd
47 Church Street
Barnsley
South Yorkshire
S70 2AS

ISBN 978-1-84884-269-4

A CIP catalogue record for this book is
available from the British Library.

Typeset in 11/13 Ehrhardt by Concept, Huddersfield, West Yorkshire
Printed and bound in England by CPI UK

Pen & Sword Books Ltd incorporates the Imprints of Pen & Sword
Aviation, Pen & Sword Family History, Pen & Sword Maritime, Pen &
Sword Military, Pen & Sword Discovery, Wharncliffe Local History,
Wharncliffe True Crime, Wharncliffe Transport, Pen & Sword Select,
Pen & Sword Military Classics, Leo Cooper, The Praetorian Press,
Remember When, Seaforth Publishing and Frontline Publishing.

For a complete list of Pen & Sword titles please contact
PEN & SWORD BOOKS LIMITED
47 Church Street, Barnsley, South Yorkshire, S70 2AS, England
E-mail: enquiries@pen-and-sword.co.uk
Website: www.pen-and-sword.co.uk

Contents

List of Illustrations

Acknowledgements

My thanks go to the following people, all of whom happily guided me to sources, or provided sources themselves. Writing this book was made much easier by the unfailingly friendly response I received from those I approached for help. I must thank Davy Orr, the historian of the Ulster Home Guard (UHG), who answered my queries, pointed me in the right direction, and provided photographs of UHG men. Davy Orr's history of the Home Guard in Northern Ireland is a model of its kind, and highly recommended. Ivor Ramsden, curator of the Manx Aviation and Military Museum, and the Museum of the Manx Regiment, provided me with a very warm welcome to the island on a very cold day, along with food and drink, and access to the museum's archives. Ivor also provided me with photographs of the Manx Home Guard, and put me in contact with Wendy Thirkettle of the Manx National Heritage Library, Douglas. Wendy found a range of important documents for this history. Both the Manx aviation and national museums are excellent, and the Island and its people are very welcoming. In this connection, too, I must mention Barry Quilliam, an enthusiastic collector of all things Manx military, who talked to me about the Manx Home Guard. In my research into the background of Lieutenant-Colonel Allsopp, Northamptonshire Home Guard, I was greatly assisted by my friend, Dr Philip Coupland, and by the archivist of Wellingborough School, Neil Lyon, who gave up one of his Saturdays to show me the fascinating collection of artefacts and documents that he has amassed at his old school. I must, too, thank Kate Swann, of the National Army Museum, for her help in identifying records there, and, of course, all the staff at the Imperial War Museum, who make it so easy to use the museum's vast archive. Thanks, too, to Andy Brockmann, of the innovative 'Digging Dad's Army Project', who provided me with an invaluable insight into that work; while Daniel Scott-Davies of the Scout Association provided me with a range of photographs of Scouts on War Service. My thanks, also, to Bryan Webb, of the Home Guard living history group, 'Men of Britain' (MoB), who provided photographs of MoB's re-creations of the force. MoB plays an important role in the process of remembrance, and is the founder of the Home Guard Association. In addition, the greatest of thanks to Bernard Lowry, for reading the draft of this book, for providing me with an informed insight into the topic; and for swapping images of twentieth century defence works with me. My thanks also to Rupert Harding at Pen and Sword, for his rapid responses to each chapter as it was written, and his encouraging remarks and support. Finally, and as always, my thanks to Mairi Ann, for her encouragement, and toleration, of my odd enthusiasms.

Part I

Background

Chapter 1

Defending these Shores

The Shield Wall

One August morning in the year 991, an English army, under Ealdorman Byrthnoth, faced a large Viking raiding force on the causeway that links Northey Island in Essex to the mainland and the town of Maldon. The subsequent battle, which saw the defeat of the English army and the death of Byrthnoth, as well as the withdrawal of the invaders, not only marked the first English defeat of the Second Viking Age, but also gave English literature one of its great early poems – *The Battle of Maldon*.[1] It is this poem, probably written very soon after the event, which tells us:

> *There against the fierce ones stood ready*
> *Byrhtnoth with his men. He commanded that with the shields*
> *They form the shield wall, and that the company hold out*
> *Firm against the fiends. Then the fight was near.*[2]

Byrthnoth's army which formed the shield wall, the *bordweall*, was made up of his aristocratic warrior *comitatus* drawn from a professional military elite, but also a host of other Englishmen – the *fyrd*. The *fyrd* was a part-time force, drawn from the towns and countryside, and designed to repel invaders and raiders. The parallels between the situation in Essex in 991 and Essex in 1941 are clear. In both years, a small professional army, supported by a part-time force of local men, faced invaders from the sea. There were, in fact, more than the obvious similarities, for, as one historian of early English warfare has argued, 'the Anglo-Saxon's preferred tactic for dealing with a raiding force [...] was to pin it between a land and a naval force'.[3] Nine centuries later, in a similar fashion, the Royal Navy was central to the defence of not only England, but also the United Kingdom. For example, in a War Cabinet discussion of 18 July 1940, Winston Churchill drew attention to the difficulties that would be faced by any German invasion force, and predicted that it would be trapped between British coastal craft, destroyer flotillas and the defenders on the beaches, both regular forces and the new Local Defence Volunteers, soon to be known as the Home Guard.[4] Some things, clearly, had changed in the intervening centuries. The navy that Churchill put so much hope in during the summer of 1940 was supported by a military arm, the Royal Air Force, undreamed of by the Anglo-Saxons. Nonetheless, there were constants – invasion, the sea, and the volunteer or amateur tradition of defending the country's shores, whether embodied in the *fyrd* of the tenth century, or the Home Guard of the twentieth century.

The Home Guard is of perennial interest, as is evidenced by the continued publication of local histories of the force. In recent years there have been some notable local and regional histories, such as David Orr's excellent history of the Home Guard in Northern Ireland, and Austin Ruddy's detailed account of the force in Leicestershire and Rutland.[5] The popularity of local studies is of interest because it reflects the very local experience of Home Guard service. The force was, literally, a territorial force, designed to protect 'hearth and home', or workplace, or school. Members of the Home Guard paraded and trained in their own localities. Their great strength was their local knowledge; their key role, as it developed in 1940–41, was to provide area defence. Hence, the force is the natural focus for local, and regional, historians. However, there is also a wider, national, UK, story to be told. A number of contemporary accounts of the force were written, and were widely bought, if their frequent appearances in second-hand bookshops are anything to go by. In particular, Charles Graves' valuable, *The Home Guard of Britain* (1943), John Brophy's beautifully illustrated and elegiac, *Britain's Home Guard* (1945), and John Radnor's history of the military amateur in Britain, *It All Happened Before* (1945)[6] all attempted the bigger picture. But it was not until 1995 that S P MacKenzie published 'a military and political history' of the Home Guard, one that is still a leading general history of the force.[7] It is the intention of the current history, *In Search of the Real Dad's Army; the Home Guard and the Defence of the United Kingdom*, to provide an overview of the force during the Second World War. This history will attempt to plug some of the gaps that are apparent, for example, in MacKenzie's *The Home Guard*. For instance, MacKenzie made little note of some of the unique aspects of the Ulster Home Guard, while no previous work covers the force on the Isle of Man, which lay in a strategically important position in the 'Western Approaches' to Britain. Both of these areas are covered here. In addition, a variety of sources, held by The National Archives, the Imperial War Museum, and the National Army Museum, are used, providing both a 'top-down' view of the Home Guard, as seen at War Cabinet level, as well as a 'bottom-up' perspective, with reminiscences of individual Home Guards, and contemporary personal records from the period. Finally, it has been possible to draw on the emerging academic and archaeological interest in the Home Guard to cover new insights into such vital topics as the Fifth Column, and the Home Guard and the historical landscape in the UK. The intention of this opening chapter is to provide an account of the historical background to the Home Guard in the modern period, showing how the force had a strong volunteer, amateur military tradition behind it. This was a heritage that helped propel the volunteers to the defence of the country, when government preparations for war had overlooked the probable need to defend these shores.

'They never charged anything but their glasses'[8]

In the modern period, Britain has periodically faced the possibility of large scale raids or invasion, and the volunteer tradition has waxed and waned with changing perceptions of the threat. The parallels between earlier volunteer movements and that of the Home Guard are often striking, and frequently highlight unreadiness on the part of government contrasted with popular demands for home defence to be supported by part-time, unpaid volunteers. In addition, many volunteers found that they were, at times, the butt of much popular humour aimed at their part-time and amateur status, but, occasionally, they discovered that the population's hope of salvation rested upon them. This was the case for the various volunteer forces that were, in part, responsible for the defence of Britain during the long French Wars of the late eighteenth and early nineteenth century.

At the start of the wars with France, the territorial defence of Britain was supposed, in part, to be in the hands of the militia, which the Militia Acts of 1782–3 had, in theory, revived and put on a firmer footing. However, this was far from being the case, and this element of the country's defence was of limited value. In consequence, volunteers began to form Associations to help defend the country from external threat, and from those Britons who were deemed to be sympathetic to the French Revolution. The first such Association was formed in March 1794 for the Parish of St George's, Hanover Square in west London.[9] Within a few weeks, the government passed a new Act, empowering counties and cities to raise volunteers for local, and, if necessary, national defence. The spontaneous action of the St George's Associators in 1794, had, as similar spontaneous action would in May 1940, provided the spur to government action designed to harness the enthusiasm of those who wished to defend the country at a time of crisis. And, in February 1797, it was Welsh Volunteers who played a famous role in defeating the French landings at Fishguard.

The French revolutionary government intended to mount simultaneous attacks on Ireland and Wales in December 1797, with the intention, at least, of distracting the British government from operations overseas. In addition, the French harboured hopes that sympathisers for the Revolutionary cause would aid French forces. In Ireland there was some hope of this, and the miscarried and ill-fated attempt at Bantry Bay, involved the famous Irish nationalist, Wolfe Tone, who hoped for a successful Irish rising against the British. The second prong of the French attack was aimed at mounting a large scale raid into south Wales, with the aim of destroying the docks in Bristol, before marching up the Welsh-English border and attacking Chester, then Liverpool. This large scale raid was led by an American named William Tate, who had fought against Britain and the Loyalists in the American Revolution, along with strongly Jacobin French officers who believed that Welshmen and women would rally to their political cause. Their army was made up of around 1,400 men released from French prisons and galleys. The force landed at Fishguard on 22 February 1797, and found themselves faced largely by Welsh volunteers, in particular, the Pembroke Fencibles, the Fishguard Fencibles, and local Yeomanry.[10] The Fishguard landing was a confused, haphazard, and poorly executed affair, and neither the American Colonel Tate, nor the ex-prisoner army he led, appeared to be over enthusiastic invaders. In addition, there was no Revolutionary uprising by Welshmen or women. In fact, the women of Fishguard were to the fore in defending their homes, lining a headland, wearing red clothing, to give the French the impression of British troops ashore. Although there was no set piece battle, lives were lost, and the French surrendered. The Welsh volunteers, despite confused leadership, had defeated what was, potentially, a serious raid, and dealt French prestige a blow. For the British government, the whole affair provided evidence of the effectiveness of domestic defence arrangements, and the value of the volunteers:

> The invasion had provided a massive test, under realistic conditions, of Pitt's home defence measures and the results were highly reassuring. There had been an effective 'closing up' of forces from as far away as Hereford and Gloucester, and some impressive performances by individual units. The New Romney Fencible Cavalry covered 61 miles from Worcester to Brecon in 5 hours, the Brecon Volunteers marched 20 miles to Llandovery in four, double the official rate of three miles in an hour and a quarter. The speed of communications, too, exceeded expectation.[11]

For the volunteers, the whole affair was an enormous boost to their morale and standing with the general public, and 'recruits poured in to the Volunteer forces, so often mocked in the past'.[12]

If the threat from France was real in the late eighteenth century, it was fear of France that led to the next outpouring of patriotic defence enthusiasm, and the emergence of the famous Rifle Volunteer Movement. By the 1840s, there was concern in some military and political quarters that Britain was open to invasion as a result of changing naval technology, the small size of the Regular Army and its extensive imperial commitments, and, from December 1851, the fact that France was under the modernising dictatorship of Louis Napoleon Bonaparte, Napoleon III. In addition, the British public seemed to be 'peculiarly susceptible to the phenomena of the invasion panic'.[13] This susceptibility was exploited by the press, with newspapers such as the *Morning Star, Daily News, Examiner,* and, above all, *The Times,* enthusiastically stoking fears that Britain was open to a rapid crossing of the Channel by French forces possessing temporary superiority in those narrow seas, and thereby able to land an army that would quickly overwhelm the defending British forces. Further, as would be the case later in the century, invasion fiction also played on fears of rampaging foreign soldiers destroying Britain and its place in the world. The fact that in 1850, for example, there were only some 37,000 regular soldiers stationed in Britain, whereas the French could call on 400,000 regulars and two million Garde Nationale,[14] seemed to lend credence to these fears. Added to this was the knowledge that, unlike many of Europe's main cities, London at that time was unprotected by fixed fortifications. This was the background to the invasion panics of 1846–47 and 1851–52. In both periods, there were calls for the creation of new volunteer forces that would defend the British homeland; calls that neither governments nor the military were keen to hear. However, the final invasion panic of the period was enhanced by new factors that did, finally, lead to the emergence of the great volunteer movement that would last for some fifty years.

In January 1857, Napoleon III appointed Dupuy de Lôme as the director of construction for the French navy. De Lôme was a renowned naval innovator, and, following the success of France's armoured floating batteries in reducing the Russian fort of Kinburn at the mouth of the rivers Bug and Dnieper during the Crimean War, began a programme to create the first ironclad fleet. The initial French ironclad in the programme, *La Gloire,* was an armoured frigate, laid down at Toulon in March 1858. Its very design made it clear that this ship was not a blue water warship, for 'its gunports were barely six feet above the waterline. This feature, and bunkers capable of carrying just 700 tons of coal, reflected the fact that the ship was designed not for traditional frigate duties but for line-of-battle service in European waters'.[15] This was taken, not unreasonably, to represent a threat to Britain in its home waters. Further, an earlier attempt on Napoleon III's life, by the Italian liberal nationalist, Felice Orsini, on 14 January 1858, in which eight people were killed and 142 were injured, led to popular outrage in France when it became clear that Orsini's bombs had been made in Britain, where the plot was also hatched by the Italians. The French military, in particular, was incensed by the attack on Napoleon III, and by Britain's harbouring of the terrorist and would-be assassin. The heightening of tension, and the threat posed by new naval technology, fed what became known as the 'Third Panic' in Britain, and finally brought success to the demands of the press and supporters of the volunteer cause.

The popular demands for the raising of volunteer corps for home defence were met on 12 May 1859, when the government authorised Lords Lieutenant to raise such units. Both government and the military were still largely unenthusiastic. Despite the government's reservations, 'the Volunteers had the over-riding advantage of satisfying public opinion at absolutely no cost to the Government'.[16] The corps were supported financially by public donation and subscription, with Volunteers providing their own uniforms and equipment. The details of service, training, and the actual role of the Volunteers were, at first, unclear, but enthusiasm for the force was undoubted. Even before the official founding of the Volunteers, some 60,000 men had come forward. Three weeks after the official announcement, there were 134,000 Volunteers;[17] and the movement was no flash in the pan. By 1863, for example, the Volunteers numbered 200,000 men,[18] and the typically grey-clad Volunteers became a social and military fixture of the Victorian age. In addition to providing rifle corps, the Volunteers also provided cavalry and artillery units, manned coastal artillery, and were later quick to take to new technological innovations like the bicycle and automatic weapons such as the Gatling gun and the Nordenfelt machine gun. In tactical terms, the Volunteers were envisaged, at the outset, as light troops, benefitting, as the Home Guard was expected to eighty years later, from local knowledge, and enthusiasm to 'hang with the most telling effect upon the flanks and communications of a hostile Army'.[19]

The Volunteer movement formed a popular and long-lived element in the Home Defence landscape of Britain. Further, Volunteers eventually saw action, but in Empire defence during the Boer War of 1899–1901, when Volunteer companies were raised for service in South Africa. This would prove to be the swansong of the movement, as the hard-earned lessons of the South African conflict led, eventually, to the military reforms of the Liberal government elected in 1906. The subsequent 'Haldane reforms' saw the passing of the Territorial and Reserve Forces Act, 1907, that brought into being the Territorial Force, which absorbed the Volunteers and the Yeomanry. This appeared to mark a new phase in the military history of the country:

> The birth of the Territorial Force appeared to mark the demise
> of the amateur tradition. Instead of spontaneously generated local
> corps of men, quite willing to accept government aid when needed

but nevertheless seeing themselves as essentially independent entities, there was from 1908 onward to be (in theory at least) a truly national and professionally administered part-time reserve force. The days of the volunteer corps, a more or less satisfactory method of local defence in time of emergency up to the mid–nineteenth century but now anachronistic, seemed over for good.[20]

However, the long history of volunteer home defence, combined with intense, and often exaggerated, public fears of invasion and occupation that were not shared by government, kept the idea of popular mobilisation for defensive purposes alive.

One of the main factors that underpinned the volunteer movement was the influence of the press and fiction in maintaining the fear that Britain was open to sudden invasion. This was certainly a key factor in the 'Three Panics' over the intentions of Napoleon III and the French military. By the late nineteenth and early twentieth century, this factor was, if anything, of even greater potency. Educational reforms in the late nineteenth century, largely driven by government fears that the United Kingdom was falling behind its industrial rivals in new areas of manufacturing like the chemical and electrical industries, created a newly literate population. The first of these reforms was the Education Act of 1870, which began the process of ensuring that a basic education was the norm for all Britons. This helped create a vast new market for newspapers, magazines, and popular fiction – and 'invasion fiction' had a notable place in that market. Today, the most famous book in this genre is *The Riddle of the Sands*, by the complex and tragic Erskine Childers, an enthusiastic British patriot who went on to be a noted Irish Republican, finally, and ironically, executed by the Irish Free State during the Irish Civil War of 1922–23.[21] However, Childers' book was not published until 1903, and was simply another highly successful book in a long line of popular invasion fiction.[22] The first invasion story best seller in Britain was published in 1871, and was a response to the defeat of Britain's old enemy, France in the Franco-Prussian War, and the emergence of a new dominant power on the continent in the shape of the German Empire. The novel, *The Battle of Dorking: Reminiscences of a Volunteer*, written anonymously by General Sir George Tomkyns Chesney, imagined the future in 1920, fifty years after a successful German invasion of an unprepared Britain. *The Battle of Dorking*:

> sounded a Last Post for the British Empire that alarmed the nation, angered the prime minister, astonished all Europe, and taught anxious patriots everywhere how to tell the tale of 'The

Next Great War'. More than that – it was the first short story to have an instant response throughout the world. By the end of 1871 there had been overseas printings in New York and Philadelphia; Toronto; Melbourne and Dunedin; and within months there were immediate translations into French, German, Danish, Dutch, Italian, Portuguese.[23]

Invasion fiction was popular in all the main European countries, but the difference, in the British public's mind, was that whereas Germany and France had vast standing armies, conscription and access to large reserve armies, Britain did not. The fear of Britain undefended on home soil animated many enthusiasts for volunteer based defence, just as it would during the great Fifth Column panic of the spring and summer of 1940. The growth of the German fleet was also taken as evidence that a lightening attack on the UK was planned. In many minds, such planning also included the use of German agents already in Britain; and the figure of the German spy as immigrant waiter or barber haunted many imaginations. The Haldane reforms did not change this. In fact, the creation of the Territorial Force, with its potential for overseas deployment, seemed to have weakened home defence as the Volunteers had effectively been disbanded. It was the continued, often pronounced fear of invasion combined with no dedicated home force that ensured that the volunteer tradition did not die in 1908. Indeed, in 1914, it was to re-emerge.

The aim of the 1908 reforms had been to create a Territorial Force that, unlike the Volunteers, was capable of being fully integrated with the Regular Army. The Territorials would, during wartime, supply garrison troops, resist enemy attacks on the UK, and, by voluntary enlistment, provide additional men for service with the Regular Army overseas. This latter element meant that the force had a much younger, and fitter, age profile than the Volunteers, and, in the event, would mean that almost all Territorials volunteered for service overseas with the British Expeditionary Force (BEF) in 1914. The BEF famously delayed the German army at Mons in 1914, as it attempted to seize the Channel ports, but that fighting retreat was costly, and increasing numbers of Territorials were fed into the frontline. In Britain, there was, from the outset of war, fear that, as had long been predicted, there would be a German landing on the east coast of England. The response was very much in line with the volunteer tradition. The letters page of *The Times* provided a forum for politicians and well-known figures like Sir Arthur Conan Doyle and H G Wells to call for the raising of local defence units, and within days of the outbreak of the war 'local "Town Guards" and dozens of other similarly named groups were making an appearance in a variety of locations' around the country.[24] Both the government and the army were unhappy about these initiatives, and acted quickly to forbid them, with the War Office issuing the notice that 'All unauthorised bodies to be at once disbanded'.[25] However, the London based committee – the Central Association – that had led calls for a volunteer defence force for London, consisted of influential political figures who continued to press for the right of citizens to drill and undertake weapons instruction. This was eventually permitted by the War Office, but still fell short of the demands to establish local defence forces. Finally, in November 1914, as it became clear that the UK would need to send as many of the young and active male population as possible into overseas service, the War Office permitted the Central Association, and its affiliated bodies, to form Volunteer Training Corps (VTC).

The function of the VTC was to enable those who wished to make a contribution to the defence of their local area to do so. Men who were eligible to join the Regular Army or the Territorial Force were not permitted to enrol in the VTC, although, later, those men who had 'attested' under the Derby scheme and were waiting for call up were permitted to join a VTC. In keeping with the volunteer tradition each VTC unit was responsible for its own uniform and weapons costs, paid for by members' subscriptions and public donations. The only uniform item the authorities contributed was a red armband bearing the letters 'GR' in black. Just as the Local Defence Volunteer armbands of 1940 would lead to various jocular interpretations of the initials 'LDV', so 'GR' was said to stand for 'George's Relics', 'Genuine Relics' or 'George's Wrecks'. By the end of 1914 there were more than 1,000 VTC units, with over a million volunteers,[26] and within a year 'volunteers were being employed to guard ammunition stores and other vulnerable points, were digging trenches, and were acting as an *ad hoc* Army Service Corps'.[27] The threat to the UK seemed to intensify, too, justifying the volunteers. In December 1914, the German navy made its heavy raids on Scarborough, Hartlepool and Whitby, while on 31 May 1915, London suffered its first Zeppelin attack, when LZ 38 dropped 3,000lbs of bombs on the East End. Both events highlighted the possibility of raids in force on the English east coast, as the need for manpower for overseas service continued to grow. These concerns led to the incorporation of the VTC into the armed forces, their reorganisation and the introduction of conscription to the force in early 1916. The VTC was reorganised into standardised volunteer battalions, service was for the duration of the war, and army style khaki uniforms were issued as opposed to the original grey-green VTC uniforms. In addition, volunteer battalions were given Regular Army adjutants, sergeant-majors and musketry instructors, while volunteer officers and NCOs could receive army training. Nonetheless, continued weaknesses in personnel, organisation, training and equipment led many to doubt the effectiveness of the force as a home defence army, and the War Office raised the possibility that volunteer numbers should be reduced to around a quarter of its total numbers, with only the more able volunteers remaining. Even then, it was felt that the volunteers were really only of use as guards and general labourers.[28] In February 1919, the volunteer force was stood down, and in October 1920 the force was disbanded. In the words of S P MacKenzie, 'the positive contribution of the volunteer battalions to victory as a military force was, to say the least, rather limited'.[29]

Preparing for War

The spectre that overshadowed home defence planning in the 1930s was not invasion, but the expectation of an overwhelming air attack. In the popular imagination, the fear of such an attack was encapsulated in the dramatic scenes of area bombing in Alexander Korda's film of H G Wells' *The Shape of Things To Come*. The film was released in 1936, and portrayed civilisation brought to its knees by area bombing, and the use of chemical and biological weapons on civilian populations. The fear of air attack was widespread, especially as the Spanish Civil War seemed to confirm the capacity, and willingness, of air forces to use mass bombing raids to instil terror among civilian populations. The Spanish Republican government was quick to utilise bombing atrocities committed by the Nationalists to boost international support for their cause. The famous images of children killed in Nationalist air raids, supposedly on the town of Getafe (but not its important airfield) in October 1936 were transmitted around the world by *aficionados* of the Republican cause. It was only recently that it has become clear that the raids did not, in fact, take place, but the powerful images helped reinforce the sense that the next war would, largely, come from the air;[30] a belief strengthened by the air attack on Guernica the following April. George Orwell, who fought in the Spanish Civil War, and was later an enthusiastic Home Guard, captured the underlying fear of civilian populations with regard to air attack in his pre-war novels, *Coming Up For Air* (1939), and *Keep the Aspidistra Flying* (1936). In the latter novel, Orwell's protagonist, Gordon Comstock imagines a future full of 'the reverberations of future wars. Enemy aeroplanes flying over London; the deep threatening hum of the propellers, the shattering thunder of bombs'.[31] It was an understanding of the capacity of air power that led the government to put much of its pre-war home defence planning into volunteer organisations designed to combat air assault on the UK. In particular, Air Raid Precautions (ARP), the

Observer Corps, the Auxiliary Fire Service (AFS), the Auxiliary Ambulance Service, and other elements of Civil Defence, such as the Women's Voluntary Services (WVS) were designed to counter air attack and its effects on the civilian population. Of these, the WVS was closest to the volunteer tradition, and, during the war, would be a vital prop for the civilian population, the regular armed forces and the Home Guard. By June 1943 there were 966,425 women volunteers in the WVS, with, for example, 27,253 volunteers providing canteen and hostel services for HM forces, 879 working with mobile canteens, and 8,237 women supporting the Home Guard.[32] The other organisations were, in contrast, organised by the authorities to take advantage of the volunteer spirit among the population. The Observer Corps, for example, with its origins in primitive attempts to track Zeppelins crossing the East Anglian coast (sitings were to be reported by post card), developed in the 1930s into an extremely effective air defence organisation. The force proved its worth during the Battle of Britain, as the radar defences of the country were ineffective under 500 feet and over land. Later, members of the corps accompanied the invasion flotillas, their recognition skills saving many Allied pilots from being shot down by their own forces.[33] In all these elements of home defence planning, however, there was no intention to create an armed, trained, and volunteer local defence force. The nearest thing that had existed in the post-Great War period was the almost stillborn National Defence Companies, created in 1936 to provide garrison guards from the ranks of ex-servicemen. However, not even the tiny establishment of 8,500 effectives was reached, and even in October 1939, the force could not be maintained, and 'in the following months the small number of active volunteers faded entirely from the consciousness of ministers and public alike'.[34] It would take the events of spring 1940 to shatter complacency and renew the volunteer spirit.

Phoney War to Blitzkrieg

The German and Soviet conquest of Poland in September 1939 was, to those more familiar with the slogging matches of the Great War, a stunning event. In the first few weeks of fighting, the German armed forces had, indeed, proved the effectiveness of what would soon become known as 'Blitzkrieg', or lightening war. However, the assault on Poland had not been an entirely one-sided affair. Polish forces valiantly defended Warsaw, inflicting significant casualties on 4th Panzer Division as it tried to batter its way into the Polish capital; and in the three day Battle of Kutno, the Poles destroyed the 30th Infantry Division; while individual garrisons, typified by that of the Westerplatte complex at Danzig, put up ferocious resistance.

Nonetheless, the combination of superior numbers, and new techniques of battle soon brought the Poles to near defeat. Matters were made worse by the failure of either France or the United Kingdom to mount any effective attack on Germany in the west, thereby showing that their guarantees to Poland in the days before the German invasion had, in fact, been hollow. Poland's fate was finally sealed on 17 September, with 'the Polish command system [...] disorganized and their defensive front shattered, it was clear [to Stalin] that the moment had come' to attack Poland from the east.[35] This development ended any hope of Poland surviving. The fighting continued until 5 October, and some 120,000 Polish troops managed to fight their way to Romania and Hungary, from where many were able to make their way to France, to continue their war.

In the UK, the declaration of war, on Sunday, 3 September, had not, as many had feared, led to almost immediate destruction from the air. In fact, in the months to come the British public began to suffer from what the French were calling '*la drôle de guerre*' – the Phoney War. Men were dying at sea and in the air, but there was little direct impact on the Home Front. There was, in fact, an increasing sense that all the Civil Defence preparations had been overdone. The press began to suggest that the fulltime members of the Civil Defence organisations were little more than overpaid army-dodgers.[36] Members of the Auxiliary Fire Service, who were paid for their work, also found that, like the ARP, they were seen as being unnecessary, or worse. One AFS member remembered:

> So bad did the feeling become in some places that Auxiliaries never wore their uniform (if they possessed one) in public, if they could avoid it. Not being thin-skinned the candid remarks so often heard about three-pounds-a-week men doing b***** all for their money didn't worry me at all, but quite a number of competent firemen gladly got themselves into one of the services, usually the Air Force, in order to get away from the cutting remarks of ignorant members of the public.[37]

Many members of the public chaffed at new regulations, whether it was carrying gas masks or identity cards, driving at 20mph in built up areas, or the evacuation of children from towns and cities. But the sense of anti-climax was shattered on 9 April 1940, when the Germans attacked Denmark, followed by Norway, in Operation *Weserübung*.

The tiny Danish armed forces, with only 14,000 men in the army, 3,000 in the navy, and an air force of fifty obsolete aircraft,[38] could offer little resistance to the German attack. But what was a sign of things to come was the use of airborne assault. The first parachute attack in history took place at 05:00 on 9 April, when German paratroopers seized the fortress of Madnesø, the airport at Aalborg, and the bridge between the islands of Falster and Fünen. The capture of airfields, bridges and the neutralisation of fixed fortifications by paratroopers, and glider borne assault soldiers, followed by the rapid insertion of reinforcements by air, were to be key features of subsequent German attacks in Norway, the Netherlands and Belgium, and the main motivation behind the creation of Britain's Local Defence Volunteers. Other aspects of Blitzkrieg were less apparent in the Scandinavian campaign, simply because the topography of Norway mitigated against the use of massed formations of armour and mechanized troops. Instead, Norway also experienced assault from the air, and the confused involvement of Norwegian traitors under Vidkun Quisling. The propaganda and psychological aspects of Quisling's opportunistic attempt to seize power in Oslo far outweighed any benefit to the invaders in real terms, and it was not until February 1942 that the Germans made Quisling 'Minister President' of Norway. In fact, members of Quisling's *Nasjonal Samling* (NS) party fought the Germans in 1940, with, for example, the gunner credited with firing the torpedoes from the coastal defence battery at Oscarborg that sank the German heavy cruiser *Blücher* being a member of NS. Nonetheless, the assault on Scandinavia saw the emergence of the perception that not only did the German armed forces possess large numbers of highly trained airborne troops, but that they were also able to benefit from organised Nazi sympathisers and agents within countries that they attacked, made up of native fascists and German spies. This perception gained even more strength in May 1940, when the Germans turned their attention to the Netherlands and Belgium.

Both the Dutch and the Belgians had significant armed forces, and extensive field fortifications. In addition, the Dutch believed that their defensive situation was greatly improved by the water defences that criss-crossed the country. The Belgians also believed that the lessons of 1914, when their army had dramatically slowed the German advance, could be replicated. The Belgians possessed the world's strongest fortress, at Eben Emael, lying behind the Albert Canal on a key invasion route into the country, which could be expected to stall any German attack, allowing the French and British to reinforce the Belgian front. But none of this planning took account of air power, especially close army-air co-operation, and airborne assault. On 10 May, the Luftwaffe attacked Dutch and Belgian airfields, and then German airborne units attacked. In the Netherlands, battalion strength parachute forces seized bridges at Moerdijk, Dordecht and Waalhaven. The paratroopers were quickly reinforced by air landed infantry, and the bridge-heads that they had opened up were exploited by the tanks of the 9th Panzer

Division. The myth of the Fifth Column also received a boost during the invasion, when German special forces soldiers wearing Dutch Army uniforms escorted German 'deserters' onto bridges before revealing that it was a *ruse de guerre* and opening fire on the Dutch defenders. However, this trick only worked at Gennep, but that opened the way for the 9th Panzer Division.[39] But this event was sufficient to subsequently greatly stoke fears in Britain that German paratroopers would come in many guises – including, infamously, as nuns. In Belgium, Eben Emael fell in a masterly air assault by glider borne troops landing on and around the Belgian fortifications, capturing and holding the fortifications until relieved by German infantry. The allied reaction to all this was too slow and too confused and the initiative stayed with the Germans. The Dutch surrendered five days later, and Belgium became a trap for the French and British forces that had entered the country to support the Belgians. Within days, it was apparent that the allies were on the back foot, and defeat in France was likely. One of the reactions in the United Kingdom to these rapid developments was akin to that of earlier times when the country was faced with invasion threat.

Volunteer stirrings
Even at the outset of the Second World War, there were voices calling for a new home defence volunteer force. Perhaps unsurprisingly, one of the earliest calls came from Winston Churchill, who, as the new First Lord of the Admiralty, wrote to Sir Samuel Hoare on 8 October 1939:

> Why do we not form a Home Guard of half a million men over forty (if they like to volunteer) and put all our elder stars at the head and in the structure of these new formations. Let these five hundred thousand men come along and push the young and active out of all their home billets. If uniforms are lacking, a brassard would suffice, and I am assured there are plenty of rifles at any rate.[40]

This, and some other stirrings of the old volunteer spirit, came to nothing in the period of the Phoney War, but the events of May 1940 transformed perceptions of the threat to the UK. The shock of the German advance across northern and western Europe, the fear of the Fifth Column, which rose to levels close to hysteria in the early summer of 1940, and the belief that the Germans had large numbers of paratroopers ready to descend at any moment on the country, all concentrated minds on home defence. Once again, the press agitated for a volunteer defence force, with articles in the *Sunday Express* and the *Sunday Pictorial* on 12 May, and in the *Daily Mail* on 14 May.[41] And, as in the days of Napoleon III, the letters page of *The Times* reflected popular anxiety about home defence:

> I have spent this Sunday in my village in Sussex. An air troop carrier landing on the Downes [sic] – indeed a handful of German parachutists – could take possession of the village and of the look-out posts on the cliffs. [...] Some dozens of able-bodied men and myself, armed with rifles, could handle this situation with at least some measure of success. But as things are we should be obliged to stand by helpless and do nothing. A similar situation might arise in hundreds of other villages and towns from Land's End to John o'Groats within the next few months. Ought we not to anticipate it by arming – and swiftly?[42]

Other similar letters poured into newspaper offices, army headquarters and to Members of Parliament. The British Legion called on the government to mandate the creation of local defence units in co-operation with the ex-servicemen of the Legion. The pressure on the government grew, as did the pressure of events on the continent. The debacle in Norway, where British, French and Polish troops were unable to prevent the occupation of most of the country, brought down the Chamberlain government, and saw Churchill ushered in as the new Prime Minister. By 12 May, plans emerged for a new home defence force, and on 14 May, the Secretary of State for War, Anthony Eden, made his famous radio broadcast. His message to the British people was:

> I want to speak to you to-night about the form of warfare which the Germans have been employing so successfully against Holland and Belgium – namely the dropping of troops by parachute behind the main defence lines [...] in order to leave nothing to chance, and to supplement resources as yet untapped and the means of defence already arranged, we are going to ask you to help us in a manner which I hope will be welcomed to thousands of you. Since the war began, the Government has received countless enquiries from all over the kingdom, from men of all ages who are for one reason or another not at present engaged in military service and who wish to do something for the defence of the country. Now is your opportunity. We want large numbers of such men in Great Britain who are British subjects, between the ages of fifteen and sixty-five, to come forward now and offer their services in order to make assurance doubly sure. The name of the new force which is now raised will be the Local Defence Volunteers. This

name describes its duties in three words. You will not be paid, but you will receive uniform and will be armed. In order to volunteer, what you have to do is to give your names at your local police station, and then, as and when we want you, we will let you know.[43]

It was a somewhat low-key announcement of the birth of the most significant volunteer home defence force in the United Kingdom's history.

Part II

The Home Guard and the Defence of the UK, 1940–44

Chapter 2

Time of Crisis; May 1940–June 1941

New fears and a new force

Even before Sir Anthony Eden had made his famous broadcast appealing for volunteers for the new Local Defence Volunteers (LDV), groups of concerned citizens had begun to patrol their neighbourhoods. It was not the first time, of course, that Britain had faced the possibility of invasion, and neither was it the first time that British civilians had spontaneously tried to organise local defence,[1] but in the early summer of 1940, the fear of invasion had some dramatic new aspects to it. The stunning successes of the German military in their invasions of Denmark, Norway, and the Netherlands had already alarmed the British government and population, even before the onslaught on Belgium and France. In particular, the role of German para-troops, and, apparently, of their allies in the 'Fifth Column', led to a feeling that nowhere in the United Kingdom was safe from sudden attack or invasion. It was against this background of fear of new forms of airborne assault, and of an enemy within that the LDV was formed. Planning for the creation of the LDV was extremely limited and rapid, and its role was far from clear.[2] In addition, the government was surprised by the rush to volunteer, with 250,000 men registering for the LDV within twenty-four hours of Eden's broadcast on the 14 May, rising to a total of 1,456,000 by the end of June 1940.[3] The task facing the government, the army, and the new volunteers, was to organise and equip the LDV, but also to establish its role in the defence of the UK. This chapter examines the changing perceptions of the threats to the UK, and the role that the LDV/Home Guard had in countering those threats, in the first year of its existence. By drawing on Cabinet level discussions, and the memories and records of volunteers the story of how the force developed to combat airborne assault, the 'Fifth Column', work places, and defence lines is told. In addition, the force's place in planning for post-invasion resistance, and its contribution to national morale, will be examined.

The 'parashots'

On 11 May 1940, three days before the creation of the LDV was announced, a high level meeting of ministers and military chiefs, led by the new Prime

Minister, Winston Churchill, considered the threat of parachute attack, and ways in which it might be met. During the German invasion of the Netherlands, the German 1st Parachute Regiment had seized bridges, airfields and key points in advance of German mechanized forces. In addition, they took the Hague, and, supported by the 22nd Air Landing Division, took the vital port of Rotterdam. The German airborne troops faced some stiff opposition, especially from Dutch marines defending the Maas bridges at Rotterdam, but the paratroops and airborne troops were the key to the conquest of the country, which took a mere five days. The flexibility and potency of German airborne assault was confirmed by the brilliant attack on the Belgian fort complex of Eben Emael by a small assault force under Hauptmann Koch. The fall of Eben Emael, which opened the way for Allied defeat in Belgium and France, took place the very day that Churchill and his key ministers and chiefs of staff were considering the parachute threat. With much of the army in Europe, options were limited. One element that was in place across the UK was searchlight units, and it was decided that these could provide a focus for locally raised anti-parachute volunteers:

> It has been decided that the best way of dealing with this matter [the airborne threat] was to utilise, as a nucleus of the organisation required, the existing searchlight organisation. This organisation already comprised small detachments suitably armed and spaced at intervals over the country. To these searchlight detachments should be attached bodies of local volunteers. [. . .] General approval was expressed to the preparation of a scheme on these lines. The Chief of the Imperial General Staff was invited to initiate action and report progress on Monday, the 13th May.[4]

The thinking at this stage was that the British Legion would organise small groups of ex-servicemen for attachment to the searchlight units. They would act as observers, watching for paratroopers or troop carrying aircraft, and reporting back to their searchlight units if any were spotted. This plan was rapidly overtaken by events, increasing press and public pressure for local defence, government concerns that spontaneously created defence groups would increasingly spring up, and the realisation that much more was needed than small, localised auxiliary groups attached to searchlight units. In his history of the Home Guard, S P MacKenzie outlined the confused and hurried background to the creation of the LDV, noting that two separate plans were developed by the War Office and by GHQ Home Forces.[5] A meeting of the War Cabinet on Monday 13 May, the government made the decision that: 'A corps of local defence volunteers should be formed. This Corps would be placed under the Commander-in-Chief, Home

Forces'.[6] Insofar as there was a design to this new creation, it was that of
General Sir Walter Kirke, the Commander-in-Chief Home Forces, and it
was expected that he would make the announcement to the British public
after the BBC's nine o'clock news broadcast on 14 May. However, Eden, as
the new Secretary of State for War, was not to be deprived of an opportunity
to make his mark, and he made the call for volunteers for the new Local
Defence Volunteers instead.

The immediate impetus behind the creation of the LDV was fear of
airborne assault by parachute and glider, backed by troop carrying aircraft,
and aided by the 'enemy within'. However, the precise delineation of the
LDV's role was unclear. There appeared to be an overlap with roles that
were within the remit of the police. By mid-May 1940, around 10,000 full-
time police officers and thousands of part-time Special Constables were
'employed in guarding vulnerable points against sabotage', points such as
bridges and police stations.[7] There was a shortage of weapons for the police,
and it was estimated that an additional 12,000 rifles and 10,000 revolvers
would be needed if the already overstretched police forces were to continue
these types of guard duties. Sir John Anderson, the Home Secretary, was
concerned that the police were being called upon to extend their role beyond
their capacities. In a memorandum dated 23 May, he suggested that the new
LDV could take on some of the functions that he felt were not those for
armed police. Anderson suggested tasks for the LDV:

> Overpowering formed parties of parachutists. This it is suggested
> is a matter for the military authorities or the Local Defence
> Volunteer units. Protecting points of importance other than police
> stations which might form primary objectives for parachute parties
> and are not now scheduled as vulnerable points for specific pro-
> tection, e.g. railway stations, local telephone exchanges and many
> power stations. This appears to be a task to be undertaken
> primarily by units of Local Defence Volunteers.[8]

The focus was clearly on defence against airborne raids or large scale
invasion, but, as suggested by the Home Secretary's memorandum, the list
of potential targets was long. Further, there was an immediate problem
associated with a scarcity of weapons available for the new force. By 5 June,
the War Cabinet listened to Anthony Eden, as Secretary of State for War,
explain that while some 300,000 men had enrolled in the LDV, only 94,000
rifles had been issued to them.[9] The Canadian government had promised the
rapid despatch of another 80,000 rifles, but there was a pronounced shortage
of ammunition even for those weapons that had been issued. Further, in the
immediate aftermath of the evacuation of the British Expeditionary Force

(BEF) from Dunkirk, there was little prospect of the LDV receiving priority for arms, ammunition or equipment. In this light, it was apparent to many members of the LDV, and the general public, that, in the defence against airborne assault, the 'parashots' as the force had been dubbed by the press, would be able to do little more than report enemy landings to regular army units (in all probability searchlight, anti-aircraft or balloon units) and then keep out of the invaders' way. This led to it being claimed that LDV actually stood for, 'Look, Duck, and Vanish'.

By early June, therefore, it was reasonably clear, in the authorities' mind, at least, that given the new, untrained, and poorly armed nature of the LDV, it had two main roles:

> The Local Defence Volunteers are neither trained nor equipped to offer strong prolonged resistance to highly trained German troops, and they will therefore best fulfil their role by observation, by the rapid transmission of information, and by confining the enemy's activities. They will also act as guard at places of tactical or industrial importance.[10]

But the LDV themselves were keen to extend their role, the government, and, in particular, the Prime Minister, were keen to maintain LDV morale by encouraging the volunteers in their obvious keenness, and there were other functions that they could carry out. One of these was taking part in the capture of downed enemy airmen. Sporadic air attacks began to take place early in June, and continued throughout July, and then increased dramatically in early August, which is commonly seen as the beginning of the Battle of Britain. For many downed German aircrew, their first meeting with armed defenders was with volunteers from the LDV. One of these was the seventeen-year-old Colin Cuthbert, and his sixteen-year-old school friend, Roy Addison, both members of the Margate LDV in the early summer of 1940. While on night observation duty overlooking the sea, a Heinkel 111 bomber flew very low over the two and crashed into the sea between Walpole Bay and Palm Bay. The two volunteers ran down to the beach, just as Margate's searchlight unit reacted to the crash:

> The searchlight came on with a dramatic click, because there was a searchlight right on Foreness point, and it swept around the sea, and it gradually came back towards the land where we were, then back towards the bay. And there, illuminated, was the great tail fin of the Heinkel 111, with the rest of the plane in front of it, and the big swastika on the back of the tail. Well, we thought the war had really started. We ran down to the water's edge, and we dug some

pretty quick holes, and we split up. Roy got one side and I got the other, and the idea was that we'd catch them in cross fire if it got going, a bit rough. Because [laughing] we were full of enthusiasm, we thought we could handle this [laughing].[11]

The two watched as the searchlight illuminated the Heinkel crew as they inflated their dinghy, and began to paddle slowly to the shore. A short distance from the beach, the airmen stopped paddling and put up their hands in surrender. Colin Cuthbert then ran into the sea, and pulled the dinghy and the crew to shore, while his friend kept the Germans covered with his rifle. There then followed an exchange that seemed, in Cuthbert's view, to somehow illustrate cultural differences between the two groups of young men:

They got out [of the dinghy], they stepped out, and we frisked them for guns. And they just stood there. And the pilot asked me if he could comb his hair, and I said, 'yes'. And he was a very young, blond German, very, very smart. [Later] in the war, I flew with Bomber Command, and I would say that a great feeling of camaraderie existed between us, but, certainly, we didn't dress up as smart as the Germans did. They were immaculate, and everything about them was new, their flying gear was perfect. [. . .] So we got talking to them, and when they saw that we weren't going to cut up rough with them, shoot them, or that sort of thing, one put his hand inside his jacket and pulled out another revolver, which rather shook us because we thought we had all their guns. Then the [LDV] C/O came down, and the police came down, and everybody descended, and they were taken away to the police station.[12]

The next day, Cuthbert's LDV commander, a Major Farman, who was the president of the local rifle club, and, as Cuthbert remembered 'was a red hot man on guns as his hobby', went out to the Heinkel to examine the machine guns on the aircraft. By this time, the cliff tops were lined with local people. The next thing that happened was that Major Farman 'unfortunately pulled the trigger of a machine gun and sprayed the cliffs, and everybody ran, for miles. It amused us greatly!'[13] But there was a less amusing find yet to be made, for when Cuthbert swam out to the Heinkel, he discovered that one of the crew had attempted to bail out before the aircraft crashed, only to be hung by his parachute, which had caught on the tailplane. The surviving German bomber crew spent the rest of the war in a prison camp in Canada, while Cuthbert went on to serve in the RAF.

After the war, Cuthbert and his German pilot captive corresponded with each other for many years.

Colin Cuthbert's account is of interest in that it illustrates one role of the LDV in the summer of 1940. The extreme youth of the two volunteers is of interest, as is the fact that, probably because they lived in an area that was most threatened by invasion, the two boys were armed with rifles. In fact, Cuthbert did not seem to have to share his rifle with other volunteers, as many did at this time. He remembered how he used to make use of his LDV issue rifle, as well as developments as the force became better equipped:

> I used to keep my gun behind the shop door here, and I also used to lay on the workshop roof and take pot shots at anything that was flying over [laughs]. Then the LDV got more organised, and we started to get proper uniforms [. . .] and remember the first Tommy guns [sub-machine guns] coming from America. That, of course, was of great interest to a boy, to have a go with a Tommy gun.[14]

Cuthbert's memory of his boyish excitement in the arrival of the powerful Thompson sub-machine gun – the Tommy gun of Chicago gangster and Hollywood fame – has a link with an idea floated in the war cabinet in June 1940 that illustrates the way in which the scope of the LDV's role was far from clear. A war cabinet meeting held at 10 Downing Street on Monday 17 June discussed the UK's defence against invasion. To add urgency to the discussion, it was during the course of the meeting that the British government learnt that their French counterparts had agreed to a ceasefire. The assumption made at the meeting was that there was a possibility 'that within the next few weeks this country would be faced with an attempted German invasion, whether on a larger or smaller scale'.[15] In discussing German military successes, it was agreed that one key element was the use of 'Storm Troopers', both in the Great War and in 1939–40. The cabinet minutes do not reveal exactly how the war cabinet defined German storm troops, and there is a sense that the memory of First World War German storm troopers, which were particularly effective in Germany's final, spring offensive on the Western Front in 1918, might have been in the minds of the Churchill and his ministers. Nonetheless, it was noted that there were 500,000 volunteers in the LDV, and that 'most of them were very keen'.[16] As always, the desire was to capitalise on that keenness, and the apparent example of dedicated, reckless German storm troopers was raised as a model for the LDV, especially, as it was noted that the arrival of the first batches of personal weapons from the USA, including Thompson sub-machine guns, meant that they would be armed in the near future. This idea, which does not appear to have surfaced again, was an indication of the uncertainty surrounding the possible use of the LDV beyond its original anti-airborne role. Nonetheless, it is hard to imagine that the typical LDV volunteer of June 1940 provided the best material for the creation of some kind of assault soldier, even if the weapons and training had been available.

Fifth Column fears

Notwithstanding eccentric suggestions as to the possible role of the volunteers, their main task in 1940 remained, in the words of *The Home Guard Training Manual*, to counter 'the new methods of invasion used by the Nazis'.[17] Their anti-parachute and anti-airborne role was seen to mesh closely with another threat that loomed large in the imaginations of the government, army and population – that of the 'Fifth Column'. The concept of the Fifth Column emerged during the Spanish Civil War, when the nationalist General Mola announced that in addition to four military columns advancing on Madrid, there was a fifth column inside the capital poised to rise against its defenders. Although, in the peculiar circumstances of a civil war, there were plenty of Francoist sympathisers in Madrid, the main impact of the Fifth Column was to create a potent myth of organised and directed opposition lurking within the ranks of a defending force. In Spain, this fear had fuelled killings of those suspected of being 'fascists', and internecine fighting among rival groupings on the Republican side. Although some contemporary commentators, like the experienced war journalist, and later Home Guard enthusiast, John Langdon-Davies, realised that the concept of a 'Fifth Column' was essentially a psychological weapon, the idea implanted itself in many minds as a description of reality.[18] In the UK, the Fifth Column fear took on a new, and even stronger, in the spring of 1940 when an 'ill-assorted hotchpotch of aliens, native fascists, communists, pacifists, and religious dissenters under Nazi control, [...] were deemed responsible for the collapse of the dominoes following the blitzkrieg in western Europe'.[19] In the UK, the Fifth Column fear resulted from incomprehension at the speed of German military successes, the desire of Britain's secret security services to extend their own role, press hysteria, particularly on the part of *The Daily Express* and *The Daily Mail*, German radio broadcasts designed to convince the population that a Fifth Column was, indeed, operating in the UK[20], fear of the real, and apparent foreign links of the British Union of Fascists (by 1940 known as British Union) and the Communist Party of Great Britain (CPGB), along with apparent evidence of Fifth Column activity in Norway, the Netherlands and France. The result was that in the spring of 1940, it was widely believed that there was 'a vast conspiracy' at work in the UK, designed to guarantee the success of any invasion of the country.[21]

Cabinet minutes from the period give a clear picture of the nature of the Fifth Column fear in 1940, and the emergence of a role for the LDV/Home Guard in combating that apparent threat. On 10 May 1940, the War Cabinet was presented with a report, 'Seaborne and Airborne Attack on the United Kingdom', drawn up by the chiefs of staff committee in collaboration with the Ministry of Home Security, in the guise of the Joint Intelligence Committee.[22] The report was a revised assessment of the threat to the UK 'in the light of the situation created by the German invasion of Denmark and Norway'.[23] There were six conclusions, one of which stated:

> Enemy 'Fifth Column' activities will be designed to play a dangerous and important part in any operation which Germany may undertake against this country. The degree to which aliens [in the UK] can be controlled by the authorities and the adequacy of the legal powers which exist to deal with such aliens should be examined and any steps considered necessary to improve the situation should be taken immediately.[24]

The threat here was seen to come from 'aliens' already in the UK, but also those arriving as a result of German conquest in Europe. Although a large proportion of those 'aliens' were Jewish refugees from the Nazis, their likely attitude to their persecutors seemed not to be uppermost in the authorities' minds, at least, not at this stage in the war. However, the threat from 'sleepers' and agents within the 'alien' population was not deemed to be the only source of potential Fifth Column activity. In an appendix, the report went on to note:

> The main features of 'Fifth Column' activity with which we are confronted in this country appear to be as follows:
>
> (a) the presence of 73,000 non-interned enemy aliens and 164,000 non-enemy aliens. In addition, there are recently naturalised British subjects of German origin from selected groups and possessing special qualifications;
> (b) the British Union of Fascists (8,700 subscribing members, organised in 188 districts, each of which has a leader);
> (c) the Communist Party of Great Britain (well organised, with 20,000 pledged subscribing members. The *Daily Worker* circulation is 90,000);
> (d) the Irish Republican Army (strength in the United Kingdom unknown);
> (e) miscellaneous organisations and individuals and crews of ships.[25]

The details of the BUF and the CPGB seem, with hindsight, to be a little inaccurate, while the strength of the IRA was, in Northern Ireland at least, reasonably well known, while point (e) seems to be something of a catch-all, which, if the apparent experience of Belgium was to go by, would include 'horticulturalists and florists'.[26] The report's authors acknowledged difficulties in intelligence gathering, saying that 'direct evidence is difficult to find', yet still stated that it was 'probable that the enemy has an organisation drawn from members of the above categories which would act in his support at the appropriate moment, as in other invaded countries'.[27]

If the security services and the cabinet were convinced of the existence of an organised Fifth Column under the control of the Germans, what was to be the solution to that threat? Before the end of May 1940, a Home Defence (Security) Executive was set up under Lord Swinton (who had executive control of MI5) 'to co-ordinate action against the Fifth Column'.[28] The perception that 'aliens' and refugees, and members of 'subversive organisations' (for example, the BUF and the CPGB) represented the most serious potential Fifth Column threat led to the Chiefs of Staff Committee to recommend to the war cabinet that 'the most ruthless action should be taken [. . . including] internment of all enemy aliens and all members of subversive organisations, which latter should be proscribed'.[29] A week earlier, at a war cabinet meeting of 18 May, the Home Secretary, Sir John Anderson, had 'regretted that we had already undertaken to receive another 100,000 refugees, but he hoped that this number might be cut down'.[30] At the same meeting, Anderson had also noted the difficulty with regard to interning members of the BUF, or proscribing the movement, was an 'absence of evidence which indicated that the organisation as such was engaged in disloyal activities'.[31] However, the increasingly bad news from France, and pressure from the security services, meant that Churchill's view was that it was 'important that a very large round-up of enemy aliens and suspect persons' be carried out.[32] In the event, this is what happened, and by July 1940, some 27,000 people had been interned. In addition, over 1,000 members of the BUF were interned, and the movement was proscribed.[33]

Although the government felt that it had taken important preventative action with regard to 'aliens' and the BUF, there was still a pronounced fear that a Fifth Column organisation existed, ready to act in conjunction with airborne attacks.[34] It was here that the LDV was seen to have an important function, just as it did with regard to parachute and glider borne assault. And, in the fevered atmosphere of the early summer of 1940, it was a role that many LDV were only too keen to carry out. During that period, many people, civilians and service personnel, found themselves stopped and questioned by LDV members keen to establish that the Fifth Column was everywhere. People were arrested, and worse, by the volunteers. One victim was Francis Codd, who had joined the Auxiliary Fire Service (AFS) in 1938, during the build up to war. Codd was in the River Service of the London Fire Brigade, and took part in the evacuations from Dunkirk on the fireboat, *Massey Shaw*. The fireboat had returned from one trip to Dunkirk, and some of the crew were given twenty four hours leave before they returned to the evacuation. Codd decided to take the bus home to Ramsgate to see his mother, but, instead, he met some keen anti-Fifth Columnists from the LDV. Codd's problem was, he thought, that, with his blond hair, and AFS uniform, he looked too Germanic. He remembered:

I looked a bit extraordinary. I remember that I was wearing the reefer jacket of the Auxiliary Fireman, and the dark trousers. I had an open-necked, white tennis shirt, and my cap, and I'd got white plimsolls. Now, I was extremely sunburnt, and my hair, being fair, almost bleached, almost white, and was a bit long and unruly. When I got to Sandwich, on my way back to Ramsgate [. . .] I thought, well, I must have a walk round in the hour I've got to wait between buses; walk around the town, and have a look at the churches. And there is one big church, I'm not sure if it is called St Clement's, a particularly fine church. So, I walked towards it, and stood in the church yard, looking up at the old flint tower, and admiring it on this calm, beautiful summer evening, and suddenly I was pounced on by two enormous men, and I didn't know what had happened. They didn't seem to be hurting me, but their obvious enmity towards me was a bit off-putting. They said, 'Feel him for guns!' Anyway, they frisked me, the only time in my life I have been frisked. They looked in my pockets – nothing incriminating. They said, 'We have a lot of German spies, you know, and we're not satisfied'. And I said, 'I'm not a German spy'. They said, 'Well, we think you might be. You look German!' And said, 'I don't. This is my standard uniform, I've been to Dunkirk'. They said, 'Well, that's your story!' Anyway, I argued and remonstrated with them for some time. I said, 'I've got a bus ticket'. But, they said, 'Come along to the police station'. Well, they were the first I'd heard of the Home Guard in action. And they were just enthusiastic, local Sandwich Home Guard people. Thought they'd trapped a German descended on them by parachute, and out to take all sorts of notes about church towers and points of advantages for troops due to arrive.[35]

Codd's adventures were not entirely over, as the local police were also suspicious. They telephoned the headquarters of the London Fire Brigade to find out if there really was an AFS man in Sandwich, but, such was the Fifth Column fear, the police would not tell the fire brigade what Codd's name was. In the end, Codd was taken by police car to the London Fire Brigade headquarters, before he returned again to Dunkirk.

Francis Codd was able to see the 'comic side' of his 'arrest' by Sandwich LDV men, but, for others in the summer of 1940, the anti-Fifth Column mentality of the LDV was to prove fatal. For example, on the night of 2/3 June, four people were shot dead in separate incidents by the LDV.[36] On 22 June, two motorcyclists and their passengers were killed and wounded in separate incidents in Scotland and northern England, while 'in Romford, a noisy exhaust prevented a car driver from hearing a [LDV] challenge; four passengers were killed outright and a fifth seriously wounded'.[37] RAF crew, baling out of stricken aircraft, also found themselves the target of LDV riflemen, and this problem became more severe as foreign volunteers in the RAF, particularly Poles and Czechs, became more common. These types of incident added to concerns about the lack of discipline among the new force, something that the War Cabinet discussed on 17 June:

> There had been a good deal of criticism in the press and among Members of Parliament of the lack of organisation and discipline among the LDV's. It was no doubt difficult to reach a very high standard with men who gave part-time service only, on an unpaid basis. On the other hand, the LDV's were now some 500,000 strong and most of them were very keen.[38]

The keenness of the LDV was something that was much valued, not least by Churchill, but there was clearly a need to strengthen discipline among the volunteers, and to put the whole force on a more regularised footing. At the same meeting, Anthony Eden noted that:

> The organization of the LDV's had now become too heavy a task to impose on the existing staffs of the Home Defence Forces. It was proposed to reorganise them under separate Central and Local Commanders of their own. The whole organisation would, however, remain under the orders of General Ironside.[39]

This new force, the LDV, had quickly made its presence felt, but it highlighted the need for increased weapons and equipment production for home defence, and illustrated the limits of army organisation in the summer of 1940. Nonetheless, the LDV was 'keen', and it had a role – defence against airborne attack, and a guarantee against the Fifth Column.

The main problem with the LDV's anti-Fifth Column role was that, fairly quickly, the government began to realise that the Fifth Column was something of a myth. As early as 17 May, the War Cabinet heard a report by the Home Secretary on the Fifth Column's role in the defeat of the Netherlands. It was widely believed that it was in the Netherlands that all elements that made up a Fifth Column, including Dutch civilians, had given widespread help to German airborne forces. Yet, Sir John Anderson reported:

> I have had the advantage of a long interview with the Dutch Minister of Justice, a civilian official of that Ministry, and two Dutch military officers. While it is clear that the German troops arriving in Holland, whether by parachute or by troop-carrying aircraft received invaluable assistance from persons resident in the country, my Dutch informants were very emphatic that for the most part this help was given, in accordance with a pre-arranged scheme, by Nazi Germans resident in Holland. They had no evidence that such assistance had been given by the refugee element in the German population, and they said that comparatively little help had been given, at any rate until a late stage, by Dutchmen who were members of the NSB (the Dutch Fascist Party).[40]

From the Dutch point of view, then, it was clear that they saw the key, if not the main, element of Fifth Column activity as being 'Nazi Germans' already in the Netherlands. Further, refugees, and, to a slightly lesser extent, native fascists, were not seen to be part of the threat. In fact, even the Fifth Column activity that was identified in the conversations with the British Home Secretary was, in reality, very limited. The most significant actions came when German troops dressed in Dutch uniforms to give the impression that other German soldiers were captives, allowing them to get close to bridges in the early stages of the assault. This was not Fifth Column activity, but a classic case of *ruse de guerre*, and one, furthermore, that was not entirely successful.

The War Cabinet continued to receive information that the Fifth Column threat might not, in fact, be all that the security services, or general sentiment feared that it was. This information included a report from the Minister of Information, presented on 15 June 1940, which denied the existence of the Fifth Column. The source this time was Adolf Hitler. The German dictator had been interviewed on 11 June by a well-known American journalist,

Karl Henry von Wiegand. The interview included the following, which was presented to the War Cabinet:

> I touched upon the Fifth Column which seems to have fired the imagination of many countries. With a cough of sarcasm Hitler said, 'So called fifth column conveys nothing to me because it doesn't exist except in the imagination of fantastic minds or as a phantom created by unscrupulous propaganda for obvious purposes by incompetent governments who drive their peoples into war and then experience pitiable collapses. It is understandable they prefer to shift responsibility elsewhere'.[41]

It might be observed that there was a good deal of truth to Hitler's comment, and it was a view that it gradually became clear, through the summer of 1940, was accurate. The British government had established a Security Intelligence Centre (SIC) to examine anti-invasion security. It held fourteen meetings about countering the British Fifth Column, but 'it could find no evidence for the existence of an organized British fifth column'.[42] The idea, and the fear, of the Fifth Column would linger on, especially in the minds of the press and public, but it was no longer a major concern of the government.

Defending the workplace

At the beginning of July 1940, the government issued a public information leaflet, *If The Invader Comes*. The leaflet covered a range of topics designed to inform the public about how they should respond to invasion. One of these was outlined under the heading, 'Defence of factories', and included current thinking with regard to the defence of the UK's economic assets:

> If you are in charge of a factory, store or other works, organise its defence at once. If you are a worker, make sure that you understand the system of defence that has been organised and know what part you have to play in it. Remember always that parachutists and fifth column men are powerless against any organised resistance. They can only succeed if they can create disorganisation. Make certain that no suspicious strangers enter your premises. You must know in advance who is to take command, who is second in command, and how orders are to be transmitted. This chain of command must be built up and you will probably find that ex-officers or NCO's, who have been in emergencies before, are the best people to undertake such a command.[43]

This was not a general call for the creation of workers' militias, as the very clear differentiation between those 'in charge' and the workers, not to mention the role envisaged for ex-officers and NCOs, made clear. Further, the leaflet threw open the question of how far civilians should take part in active resistance to invasion or attack. Civilians taking part in armed resistance would be in contravention of the rules of war, and there was little doubt that not only would the German military be within its rights to execute any civilians captured bearing arms, but that they would.[44] Indeed, the LDV, which Churchill in a radio broadcast on 14 July referred to as the Home Guard,[45] had already drawn such a threat from the German authorities, and German radio broadcast a threat that captured volunteers would be regarded as *francs-tireurs*, and treated as such:

> 'The British Government is committing the worse crime of all,' said the official spokesman from Bremen. 'Evidently it permits open preparation for the formation of murder bands. The preparations which are being made all over England to arm the civilian population for guerrilla warfare are contrary to the rules of international law. German official quarters warn the misled British public and remind them of the fate of the Polish *francs-tireurs* and gangs of murderers. Civilians who take up arms against German soldiers are, under international law, no better than murderers, whether they are priests or bank clerks. British people, you will do well to heed our warning'.[46]

German threats made no difference to recruitment to the Home Guard, but the military were concerned that the implications of ad hoc defence of factories and other key economic assets by civilians should be understood. A War Cabinet meeting, held on 10 July, heard the Commander-in-Chief, Home Forces, General Sir Edmund Ironside, state that 'actual fighting should be restricted to the military and Local Defence Volunteers and that no civilian who was not a member of these forces, should be authorised to use lethal weapons'.[47] Instead, it was agreed by the War Cabinet that all those organised for the defence of work places should be enrolled in the LDV. Further discussion at the same meeting revolved around the precise role of the force, and it was suggested that there might be two classes of volunteer – 'the first class comprising those who would help in the defence of factories etc, and the second class those who would use arms only in defence of their homes'.[48] In fact, the two functions were integrated into overall plans of local defence, and there were never 'two classes' of LDV or Home Guard. Finally, the question of women and armed defence was raised. Interestingly, given that women never *officially* bore arms in the force, at this early stage, the minutes of the same meeting noted that 'it was urged that those [women] who wished to do so should be provided with uniforms and allowed to use arms'.[49]

The defence of key economic assets was one, then, of the early tasks allocated to the new force, and many volunteers remembered being involved with this task. Prior to serving in the Royal Navy, John Bone served in the Chislehurst Home Guard's machine gun platoon from 1940 until August 1941. One of their key tasks was to deploy their solitary .303 Vickers machine gun, which was towed in a trailer by a Riley saloon, in defence of a key railway junction:

> At Chislehurst, we had a rather complicated rail junction, and one of our jobs was to patrol that in case the Germans decided to send any parachute people down to disrupt the railway junction. Because if they had been able to hit the centre of it, they would have paralysed all the services in the south east of London.[50]

Bone believed that had such an airborne attack been made, then he and his Home Guard colleagues would have made a determined attempt to defend the vital rail junction. He noted, however, that the only 'action' that they in fact saw was following air raids, when the Home Guard were called upon by the police to protect damaged shops against potential looting.

The Home Guard's role in defending key economic assets also extended to destroying those same assets in the event of it being likely that they would fall into the hands of invaders. The commanding officer of the 7th Battalion, Northamptonshire Home Guard, Lieutenant-Colonel Herbert Allsopp, a school master, and officer commanding of the Officer Training Corps (OTC), at Wellingborough School, had, like all battalion commanders, a secret list of local factories that were to be immobilised in the event of imminent German capture. His instructions noted: 'Orders have been issued through the Government Departments concerned for the immobilisation of Power Plants, the removal of essential plans, equipment etc from selected important factories.'[51] The list for the East Central District that encompassed Wellingborough consisted of 414 factories, including, for example, Ultra Electric Ltd, United Steel Co Ltd, and the Wellingborough Iron Co Ltd.

Stop Lines and the 'Coastal Crust'

On 25 June, three days after France's acceptance of German surrender terms, the British War Cabinet met with the Chiefs of Staff, and listened to the Commander-in-Chief, Home Forces, General Ironside, outline the plans for the defence of the UK against the expected invasion. At this stage, the military were still collecting and analysing intelligence about the Battle for France, and the German blitzkrieg in the west, and attempting to incorporate new lessons into planning for what was expected to be the next stage of the German war effort. In consequence, the plan for home defence which was outlined to the War Cabinet was not a definitive plan, and defence thinking changed over time. The defence plan General Ironside put to the War Cabinet had three main components:

(i) A 'crust' on the coast with local reserves to move and fight the enemy on the beach wherever he may attempt a landing.

(ii) A line of anti-tank obstacles running down the centre of England to the Blackwell Tunnel, thence to Maidstone and southward to the sea.

(iii) Mobile reserves in rear of this anti-tank line whose role is to strike at the enemy either on the beach or wherever he may have penetrated.[52]

Within this overall plan, there was a role for the LDV. Not only was the force to be on watch for parachute and airborne attack, as well as being a key element in the fight against the Fifth Column, but it was expected to provide local defence. Behind the coastal defensive crust and the system of stop lines – which were 'in essence anti-tank lines with a continuous anti-tank obstacle formed by a waterway, an artificial ditch, a line of concrete obstacles, or a railway embankment'[53] – the country was to be covered by defended localities, otherwise known as 'nodal points'. This area defence consisted of anti-tank obstacles, road blocks, fortified buildings, and purpose built defences – the great variety of 'pillboxes' that still dot the UK landscape. The concept of area defence was that static defences would hinder and slow down, and perhaps disrupt, the progress of any invading force. This would enable the few available mobile, mechanised and armoured units to respond effectively. The LDV's role in this plan was to provide defenders for road blocks and fortified positions. There was, however, a problem that affected all aspects of the plan in June 1940, and that was a severe shortage of arms, equipment, and troops. For the LDV it meant, as the Chiefs of Staff realised, that, in the short term at least, their main weapon was the petrol bomb, better known at the time as 'the Molotov Cocktail'. At the end of June, the Chiefs of Staffs Committee noted:

> Arming of the Local Defence Volunteers was proceeding, but only a proportion had so far received their weapons. Large numbers of American rifles and ammunition would be available very shortly.

A stock of 'Molotov Cocktails' would be kept at every roadblock, for use by the Local Defence Volunteers or other troops holding it. Mills grenades were at present [in] very short [supply].[54]

Much faith was put in the Molotov Cocktail in the summer of 1940. It was seen as an answer to armour, and it was widely believed that it had been used with great success by the Finns in their Winter War with the USSR, and by the Chinese in their war against Japan. However, in both cases, the defending forces had not been forced to rely on petrol bombs as their sole weapon, which is something that the majority of LDV would have had to do in the summer of 1940.

The LDV's role was, therefore, to consist of the observation and reporting of airborne attack, security against the Fifth Column, and the defence of their own localities. There was a logic in these tasks, insofar as the new force was untrained, ill-equipped, and largely immobile. This did not, however, stop some volunteers clamouring for a more active, offensive role in the defence of the UK. The government itself was aware of the importance of capitalising on the enthusiasm of the volunteers. There was a recognition that, especially given the lack of weapons, uniforms and training available for the LDV, it was vital that the morale of the new force be maintained. The morale question extended beyond the ranks of the LDV, as it was feared that the general public had little faith in the new force's ability to take any meaningful part in the defence of the country.[55] The issue of maintaining morale was made frequently at War Cabinet meetings, and Churchill, in particular, constantly pressed for new ways of supporting the Home Guard. For example, the issue of making full use of LDV enthusiasm was discussed at the War Cabinet meeting held at 10 Downing Street on 1 July 1940.[56] In Parliament, too, there were demands for an extended role for the force, as MPs responded to pressure from their LDV constituents. By early July, 'Eden himself was implicitly accepting the idea pressed on him by critics that the "utmost initiative" should be encouraged in the LDV, and that as well as observing and reporting, volunteers should, when possible, "attack" the enemy'.[57] Further, in his radio broadcast of 14 July, in which Churchill talked of the important role of the Home Guard, 'as they are much better called', he responded very positively to the desire of the volunteers 'to attack and come to close quarters with the enemy, wherever he may appear'.[58] This broadcast was, in the view of the historian, S.P. MacKenzie, a 'huge success, confirming in the public mind that the Prime Minister empathized with the desire for an aggressive role'.[59] The results of such popular and political pressures was that the LDV's 'Training Instruction No. 8, July 1940', stated that 'From the moment the enemy tanks are located

[. . .] they must be harried, hunted, sniped and ambushed without respite until they are destroyed'.[60] What was left unsaid was exactly how even the most aggressive Home Guard was to manage this, bereft of almost any effective weaponry.

The military and political assessments of the likelihood of invasion, and the forms that it would take, were in flux during the summer months of 1940. In consequence, thoughts on the role of the Home Guard changed too. In an important document, Churchill circulated to his War Cabinet colleagues 'a minute by myself dated July 10, together with a note by the First Sea Lord, dated 12 July reviewing the possibilities of large scale raids or invasions'.[61] At a time when Britain was experiencing a gradual increase in air attacks that would develop into the 'Battle of Britain' in August, and the full extent of post-Dunkirk supply shortages for the Army had become apparent, Churchill was sanguine about the Royal Navy's ability to defeat any invasion while it was still at sea:

> The Admiralty have over 1,000 armed patrolling vessels, of which two or three hundred are always at sea, the whole being well manned by competent seafaring men. A surprise crossing [by the enemy] should be impossible, and in the broader parts of the North Sea the invaders should be an easy prey, as part of their voyage would be made by daylight.[62]

In addition, the Royal Navy had forty destroyers between the Humber and Portsmouth, most of which were at sea at night, although it was clear that the destroyer flotillas would need 'strong Air support from our fighter aircraft during the intervention [against enemy craft] from dawn onwards'.[63] It was, as many people noted in the summer of 1940, a case of 'Thank God for the Navy!' This assessment had, in Churchill's view, some important implications for the army and the land defence scheme. He argued that it would be possible: 'to bring an ever larger proportion of [the] formed Divisions back from the coast into offensive warfare and counter attack, and that the coast, as it becomes fortified, will be increasingly confided to troops other than those in the formed Divisions, and also to the Home Guard'.[64] This was a recognition that the army needed to be rebuilt and re-equipped after Dunkirk, and that the task had to be undertaken with, in Churchill's words, 'utmost speed'.[65] The building of a huge range of defence structures continued apace, in the coastal 'crust' (a term that quickly fell out of favour, as it seemed to suggest something akin to a pie crust that was easily broken), the stop lines, and in area defence. By the end of the year over 20,000 pillboxes had been built, and these were just one of the many types of defence structure in use. This was an immediate, and rapid, response to the invasion threat, and as the Home Guard developed it came to have a major role in manning these static defences. However, by the winter of 1940/41, it was realised that the huge effort in constructing these defences might well have been a mistake:

> They were [. . .] considered to have been too vulnerable and waste-ful of resources. From 1941 onwards Britain's anti-invasion policy moved towards a nationwide and intricate system of defended localities: this had formed a minor part of the previous summer's defences in the guise of 'nodal points'. The almost two million men of the Home Guard, gradually armed with relatively modern weapons [. . .] would [. . .] take over the defence of Britain, leaving the regular army to become increasingly involved with overseas campaigns.[66]

The Home Guard, as will be seen, came to have a dominant role in the defence of the country, manning static defences, anti-aircraft and coastal artillery, and thereby enabling the regular army to, as Churchill had argued, fulfil its offensive, war-winning function. Even by the autumn of 1940, the development of the Home Guard was seen to be crucial to the despatch of more divisions to the Middle East, which was, at that time, the only sphere of ground warfare between the UK and its enemies.[67] This increased importance of the Home Guard for the UK's defence meant, of course, that there was, as Churchill and his colleagues appreciated, a need to give 'more regular status to the Home Guard'.[68]

Post-invasion planning and the Home Guard

The perception that Britain was faced by an aggressor who had developed new forms of warfare – the Fifth Column, airborne assault, and the blitzkrieg – led not only to efforts to counter these threats, but to changed views regarding defence. One of these was considered by the War Cabinet on 17 June 1940, which discussed a proposal to add a 'radical and unprecedented'[69] element to the UK's defence. This was the 'selection, recruitment, training and equipping of *civilians* to come directly under General Headquarters with an operational role, but without a military presence or command structure in the field'.[70] This organisation, the GHQ Auxiliary Units, would draw heavily on members of the Home Guard for its personnel. It was, in effect, the first, organised 'stay behind' organisation, described by Colonel Malcolm Hancock, a Great War veteran, and Coldstream Guards officer, who was for a period the Deputy Assistant Quartermaster General responsible for supplying the Auxiliary Units, as:

> A very big organisation [. . .] formed for the purpose of setting up a huge sabotage organisation in the event of invasion. The whole coast of England and Scotland was divided up into areas of roughly county size, the whole way round from Land's End to the north of Scotland [. . .] we would carry out sabotage, the men who would do this would be local Home Guard forces. All these Home Guard units were instructed and trained by us in the use of explosives with which they hoped to cause a considerable amount of damage in the ammunition dumps in the rear of the enemy.[71]

The remit of the Aux Units, as they are more familiarly known, was, in fact, wider than attacks on ammunition dumps in what would be, it was hoped, temporarily occupied areas of an invaded Britain. The Aux Units were to carry out night time sabotage, intelligence gathering, and assassinations behind the front line of any German advance. During the day, the Operational Patrols, seven to ten men strong, would lie up in underground hideouts, known as Operational Bases (OBs), which were frequently constructed by regular army troops brought into an area that they were unfamiliar with simply to build them. The Aux Units were commanded by Lieutenant-Colonel Gubbins of Military Intelligence, a Great War veteran, and a soldier who had experienced irregular, or guerrilla, warfare in northern Russia during the Russian Civil War, and in Ireland during the Anglo-Irish War. In the latter case, Gubbins described his experiences fighting against the Irish Republican Amy (IRA) as 'being shot at from behind hedges by men in trilbies and mackintoshes and not allowed to shoot back!'[72] The IRA might have been surprised to learn that the British security forces were 'not allowed to shoot back', but the example of Irish Republicans, Russian guerrillas, and, indeed, T.E. Lawrence's desert campaign during the First World War were inspirations for the Aux Units in their planned campaign against occupying invaders.

The Aux Units recruited men, and women, who had strong local knowledge, and were often known to one another. Jack French, a farmer who served with an Aux Unit in Bekesbourne, Canterbury, remembered that:

> We were the sort of people who played rugby together, we went shooting together, we sailed together [. . .] of course we had an *intimate* knowledge of the surroundings. They [the recruiters] knew perfectly well that we were people who would get on well together.[73]

French was a member of the seven man 'Swede' patrol, whose OB
had been built by Canadian troops. The clearly middle-class background of
his unit was not, however, entirely typical, as poachers were also recruited,
it being assumed that they possessed the necessary fieldcraft to act in a
guerrilla role. All those recruited were given Home Guard identity cards,
and innocuous Aux Unit badges were issued for uniforms. In certain
operational circumstances, however, such as carrying out assassinations, the
Aux Units might well have worn civilian clothes. That, along with the role
of the force raises, of course, the likelihood of the horrors of irregular
warfare being visited upon any areas where the Aux Units might have made
their presence felt.

The creation of the Aux Units continued apace throughout 1940, and by
the end of the year around 300 OBs had been prepared, and another sixty
were being built, while the total in use by the end of 1941 was 534, with one
estimate being over 1,000 OBs by the end of 1944.[74] The headquarters,
and training centre, for the Aux Units, Coleshill House in Oxfordshire, was
occupied from the autumn of 1940, and recruiting continued apace. Within
four months of the creation of the Aux Units, 'a force including somewhere
in the region of 3,500 "civvies", many recruited directly from the Local
Defence Volunteers and the Home Guard, had grown [. . .] with unbelievable
rapidity'.[75]

Conclusion: The First Year

The LDV experienced a sudden birth at a traumatic time for the United
Kingdom. Facing military defeat on mainland Europe, and the apparent
probability of invasion and occupation, the LDV was a child of its time. As
such, its early days were marked by enthusiasm and a determination on
the part of the people and government to 'do something' to help defend the
country. But they were also characterised by an inability to arm or equip
the force, and difficulties in delineating the exact boundaries of its role. The
government was anxious to support that groundswell of enthusiasm that
marked the creation of the LDV, but had little in the way of resources
to bolster it. Nonetheless, military roles were assigned to the force. It was
seen to be in the forefront of anti-airborne preparations, was a key to guarding against the pronounced fear of Fifth Column activity, and was a way
of assuring people that their homes were to be defended. Further, led by
Churchill's commitment to the volunteers, the government and the military
moved to incorporate the force into the military structures of defence. The
first Inspector General of the LDV, Lieutenant-General Sir Henry Pownall,
was appointed on 20 June 1940, and began work immediately to 'establish
close contacts between the LDV and Army at all levels [with] liaison officers

[. . .] assigned to many Home Guard formations [who] regularised and considerably improved the organization, training and mobilization procedures of local LDV units, all of which up until that time were still primitive and having a detrimental effect on morale.'[76] The force became known, again at Churchill's insistence, as the Home Guard, and saw its status and standing, in both civilian and military eyes, increase. As defence plans changed and developed, reflecting improving military conditions in the UK, and changed assessments of the likelihood of invasion, so the Home Guard took on a greater role in defence plans. By the end of 1940, it was an increasingly well trained and better equipped force, having developed considerably since the days of fear, confusion, but enthusiasm, in May and June 1940.

Chapter 3

The Long Haul; June 1941–December 1944

From Defence to the Offensive

In the summer of 1941, the strategic situation took on a new and potentially war-winning aspect. On 22 June, German forces struck east, invading Soviet occupied Poland, and Soviet territory itself, in Operation Barbarossa. Other Axis allies, led by Romania, whose forces joined the offensive on 2 July, soon entered this new phase of the war. Overnight, the USSR had gone from being a co-conspirator with Nazi Germany, sharing in the division of large parts of Eastern Europe, into being a new and crucial ally for the United Kingdom. Churchill recognised the significance of the changed situation, famously remarking of the UK's new alliance with the Soviet Union that, 'If Hitler invaded Hell; I would at least make a favourable reference to the Devil in the House of Commons'. Although Soviet forces staggered and retreated in the face of the German blitzkrieg, losing hundreds of thousands of men, Churchill appreciated that Hitler had taken Germany into a new phase of war whose outcome was far from certain. In a similar global shift, the Japanese attack on Pearl Harbor on 7 December 1941 brought in the very ally that Churchill had spent so much time attempting to draw into the conflict on the UK's side – President Roosevelt and the United States. Not only did the Japanese strike into the Pacific remove the threat to USSR's eastern flank, but it also gave the Allies an amazingly productive war economy that was beyond the reach of the Axis powers. The USA was eventually able to supply not only its own armed forces, but those of the USSR and the UK. Even though the Axis were able to flood across European Russia, the Pacific and Britain's far eastern empire, bringing all the horrors of total war, the dice were now loaded in favour of the newly expanded Allied camp. In the space of six months, the United Kingdom, its Commonwealth and Empire, had gone from being the sole Allied bloc still in the field, to being a third of a powerful grand alliance – the Big Three.

For the Home Guard, the period from the summer of 1941 until the 'stand down' of the force in December 1944, was one that saw changing roles and changing effectiveness. The force was fully integrated into, and increasingly took on a central role in, the defence of the UK. It lost many of its earlier civilian aspects, men began to be conscripted to the force, and it fulfilled a wider range of functions, including key roles in the coastal and anti-aircraft defence of the UK. As the threat of full-scale invasion diminished, so problems arose in connection with competing civilian and military claims on manpower, and Home Guard morale and absenteeism. Nonetheless, it was an increasingly well-equipped and trained force, and its central role in the defence of the country enabled military planners to task greater numbers of the regular forces for operations overseas, most notably for the invasion of western Europe in June 1944. That period proved to be the swansong of the Home Guard, which stood by to repel any possible German reactions to the invasion of Normandy. By then, the Home Guard was a fighting force that played an important role in enabling the UK to finally take the offensive in western Europe.

This chapter examines the development of the Home Guard during the long haul to victory in Europe. Its role in area defence, the protection of key installations, problems associated with manpower issues, and the development of the Home Guard as a fighting force, are examined using War Cabinet records, veterans' testimony, and Home Guard records.

The Home Guard – a key defence asset

By the spring of 1941, the Home Guard had taken on the form of a permanent force, a key part of the defence of the UK. It was in March that Home Guard officers and non-commissioned officers were permitted to wear normal army rank badges on shoulder straps for officers and chevrons on both arms (as opposed to the left arm only) for NCOs. This was more than a symbolic gesture, as it marked 'the close of the original citizen force and its transition to a branch of the Armed Forces of the Crown'.[1] In addition, much to the satisfaction of Home Guards they were issued with shoulder titles and battalion flashes for their uniforms. It was during the spring of 1941, too, that there was a renewed sense that Britain was still vulnerable to invasion, or large-scale attack. The German airborne attack on Crete, Operation Mercury, which took place between 19 and 30 May, saw 22,000 German air landed troops take the island in the face of fierce British, Commonwealth and Greek opposition. Over 7,000 Germans were killed or wounded, but the operation appeared, nonetheless, to illustrate, once more, the continuing threat posed by airborne assault. The renewed fear of attack from the air was, however, short-lived, as Operation Barbarossa started within a month of the fall of Crete, and German military attention shifted fatally east.

Static Defence – passive

Increasingly better equipped, and with more training opportunities, the Home Guard were constantly reassured that the force had a central role to play in the defence of the country. In terms of the exact tasks to be fulfilled by the Home Guard, the official view was that:

> Home Guards may be allocated a guerrilla and mobile role or a static defence of an area, factory, road block, etc. Static defence implies a series of defences utilizing fire power in combination with obstacles to hold off the enemy infantry and/or tanks. The term static defence must not be misunderstood; defence is both passive, in the sense that a unit is tied to the ground in order to carry out its task, and active. Active defence entails full use of patrols, observers, reconnoitring parties, in order to obtain information of the enemy, and fighting patrols to delay and destroy his infantry and tanks. Provided there are sufficient men to carry out the tasks, every effort must be made to prevent the enemy surprising the defenders and to conceal up to the last moment the position of the defences.[2]

This official memorandum from early in 1941 highlights the tensions that still existed in the Home Guard. Some in the force argued for irregular, guerrilla style action, a view that was particularly notable during the early days of the LDV. However, the dominant view was that the primary, over-riding role of the Home Guard was to provide static, area defence, and, when resources and training made it possible, operate active defence whose aim would be to further safeguard the effectiveness of the core task.

During the early summer of 1940, when the equipment and training shortage issues dominated defence thinking, General Ironside had overseen the creation of the stop-line approach to defence, built around interlinked, fixed field fortifications designed to obstruct and slow any German advance, until the small mobile forces of the Regular Army could counter the enemy attack. Ironside's successor as Commander-in-Chief, Home Forces, General Brooke, was able to benefit from an improving supply and training situation, and brought new thinking to defence planning. It was under General Brooke that the stop line approach was superseded by area defence, which, in many places, was able to incorporate the fixed defences built during the summer of 1940. The Home Guard were then given primary responsibility for manning the defence works that were incorporated into the area defence, or nodal point, scheme. Areas, particularly in coastal regions, that were seen to be in the immediate path of any invasion, were defended by Regular Amy troops, who manned a series of Forward Defended Localities (FDLs) 'on a 24–hour basis, with regular patrolling'.[3] But even in these areas, 'the Home Guard played an important role in supporting the front-line Field Army troops, by occupying defence positions to their rear, by manning roadblocks, and by acting as a mobile force to counter enemy parachutists. The role of the Home Guard was generally written into division, brigade, and area defence schemes'.[4] The Home Guard was, of course, in a position to bring their intimate local knowledge of the local landscape and conditions to their area defence role. An example of the strength, and contribution, made by the Home Guard in this role was provided by William Foot in his account of the defence plan for Littleport in Cambridgeshire. The defences of Littleport, on the banks of the canalised River Great Ouse, were built around the Home Guard, which in 1941 consisted of 100 men from 2nd Battalion Ely Home Guard, equipped with ten spigot mortars, 200 anti-tank grenades, and 200 anti-tank mines.[5] This was the sort of core, defence role that the Home Guard played for the remainder of its existence, and one that they were increasingly better trained, equipped and prepared for.

The archives of the National Army Museum, in Chelsea, contain the wartime Home Guard papers of David Bevan Rutherford Roberts, which give a remarkably thorough picture of the force's training and role.[6] The papers also give us a pen-portrait of a Home Guard and his life. David Roberts was born on 7 November 1908, and at the outbreak of the Second World War was living with his wife, Mary Willa Roberts, at 24a High Street, Ewell, Surrey, and he owned an Austin 10, registration number UJ8914, and a bicycle. Roberts was an electrical engineer working for the London and Home Counties Joint Electricity Authority and was 'responsible for the installation and maintenance of substation plant, viz switchgear, transformers and protective equipment.' This made Roberts an essential war worker, and, much to his frustration, evidenced by his repeated attempts to be released from his civilian job, he was unable to join the Regular Army even though he was classed as medically fit – Grade 1. With the creation of the Royal Electrical and Mechanical Engineers (REME) in October 1942, he hoped that his chances of enlisting would be improved, but, once again, his employers refused to release him. Instead, Roberts' wartime military service was confined to the Home Guard, in which he served from June 1940 until the force's stand down in December 1944. On joining the 55th Surrey Battalion, 'E' Company of the Home Guard, he was made a Section Commander (the equivalent of a sergeant), before being promoted to Platoon Sergeant with 19 Platoon. He was eventually promoted to the rank of lieutenant on 9 August 1943, and by March 1944 was with the HQ Company of the 57th Surrey (Mitcham) Battalion, as an instructor. During his time in the Home Guard, Roberts attended a variety of training courses that provide a good picture of the roles of the Home Guard in defending the UK, and was attached to the 1st Battalion, Royal Norfolk Regiment for seven days during May 1942.

Among the residential courses Roberts attended was one on the organization of defence in built-up areas, and one on demolitions; in addition, he attended a summer camp for NCOs. Typically, the courses were conducted over a weekend, and his local training area was usually at Nonsuch Park, the site of Henry VIII's famous, but long demolished, palace. The training courses on urban defence, demolitions and reconnaissance reflected the core roles of the Home Guard from 1941 onwards. Following his attendance at the defence of built up areas course, Roberts wrote a series of lecture notes, which he used to instruct other Home Guards in this essential task. His lecture watchword was, 'PLAN AND PREPARE NOW', and he opened his instruction with three pointers to successful Home Guard urban defence: '(a) Concentrate your forces; (b) No failure can be conceived; (c) Don't be rushed – morale built on confidence'. The main body of Roberts' lecture concerned the preparation of a fortified house as part of a Home Guard 'Defended Locality' scheme. These instructions make clear that preparing such a defensive position was not something that could be accomplished in a very short time, as they consisted of fifteen separate tasks:

1. Clear fields of fire – have at least 75 yards
2. Prepare weapon positions and conceal them: (a) well back in room, (b) half curtains [to be used], (c) loopholes splayed
3. Render bullet proof – chests of drawers and soap boxes filled with rubble etc
4. Barricade doors (open 12″ only) windows etc
5. Prepare communications between houses and even rooms
6. Block staircases (nail planks on stairs – one removable). Burn the banisters for firewood
7. Prepare alternative positions
8. Remove plaster and glass – two reasons: glass causes casualties and if removed from all windows difficult for enemy to know which are real fire positions
9. Shore up ceiling
10. Provide outside protection [barbed] wire. Wire obstacles must be under fire
11. Remove drain pipes
12. Have observation holes and nail wire over all windows downstairs

13. If your D[efended] L[ocality] is a block of terrace houses gut
    one here and there
14. Remember fire risk – water and sand ready
15. Store food, water etc, and have candles and torch. Cut off all
    gas and electric. Provide latrines.

This type of fortified building would be incorporated into other fixed defences, such as pillboxes, anti-tank ditches, road blocks and weapons pits to create interlocking local defences. In addition, as Roberts learnt on his demolition course, the Home Guard were also responsible for the destruction of material and assets that might be of use to any advancing German forces. Although he noted that bridges, viaducts, tunnels and other large scale works would be destroyed by army engineers, there were still demolition tasks that the Home Guard could perform. These included destroying petrol supplies, smashing electrical and mechanical plant using hammers and crowbars, and destroying railway track. In the latter case, Roberts' lecture notes for his fellow Home Guards stated: 'sleepers saturated with petrol or paraffin and fired will buckle rails. Bent rails can be straightened on site but buckled rails must be re-rolled'.

Static Defence – active
David Roberts' papers not only illustrate the static defence role of the Home Guard, but also shed light on its active defence role. In the summer of 1942, Roberts attended an NCO's course at Nonsuch Park. In his papers there are notes for a night exercise undertaken during the course, which shed light on the perceptions of the threat that the Home Guard faced, the equipment they had at their disposal, and the active defence tasks that they might be expected to carry out. The 'narrative' that accompanied the orders for the 'Reconnaissance Exercise with Troops' gives a flavour of perceived threats and roles:

> An abortive attempt at invasion has been repulsed with heavy loss on both sides, but much confusion and dislocation exists owing to work of Fifth Columnists, use by the enemy of our uniforms and equipment and also the existence of small enemy groups not yet rounded up. Your Platoon is occupying defensive positions in Nonsuch Park with special instructions that for strategical reasons no further mopping up operations are to be carried out until tomorrow.

Interestingly, the Fifth Column is still seen to be potential battlefield threat, long after the government ceased to believe that any organised Fifth

Column did, in fact, exist. The 'use by the enemy of our uniforms and equipment' was much more likely. Indeed the most famous of this type of *ruse de guerre* came later, with extensive German use of US uniforms and equipment during the Germans' penultimate counter-offensive in the west – the Battle of the Bulge, December 1944 – January 1945. The exercise that Roberts took part in at Nonsuch Park involved night reconnaissance at section strength to determine enemy positions. The orders indicated that for the exercise Home Guard section strength was one section leader, a second in command, and ten–twelve other ranks, which formed a slightly larger than normal section for the British Army at this time. Their equipment also suggests that by this time, the summer of 1942, the Home Guard could expect to be well armed; in this case with nine rifles, one light machine gun, one Thompson Sub Machine gun, twelve No. 69 Bakelite grenades (a blast/shock grenade designed for house-clearing), and twelve No. 36M grenades (the famous Mills bomb). Finally, 'transport' for the exercise was 'two cycles'. The exercise that Roberts took part in was focused on battlefield reconnaissance at night, but in addition, the Home Guard was also trained to undertake 'fighting patrols', the aim of which was to attack and destroy the 'small enemy groups not yet rounded up' that Roberts' exercise scheme identified. It was this type of training, allied to greatly improved levels of equipment, that meant that the Home Guard were able, by this time, to play an active part not only in static defence, but also in active defence designed to improve their capacity to fulfil its primary area defence role.

Vulnerable points

A further category of defence was comprised of those military and economic assets that were seen to be key installations. They consisted of communications centres, such as telephone exchanges, bridges, gasworks, power stations, sewage works, reservoirs, and military targets such as airfields, radar stations and searchlight sites. Together, these installations were known as vulnerable points, and the Home Guard had a vital role to play in their protection and defence. Edward Kirby was an NCO in the Field Security Section of the Intelligence Corps, and was, in 1942–43, attached to MI5 as part of a counter sabotage unit, part of whose role was to test Home Guard security at vulnerable points. Kirby explained the rationale behind the defence of economic assets:

> We were told that certain parts of the nation's economy were bound up with essential services, the collapse of which would mean ultimate defeat in the war. A nation without electricity, without

gas, without water, could not possibly win the war. [. . .] We were given lectures on the working of power stations, later on it was reservoirs and gasworks. Power stations – we were told which was the most sensitive part of the building. Now, they could be bombed from the air, but they could be pinpointed and destroyed by hand-picked saboteurs on the ground, and the people in charge of looking after these public utilities had to be alert not to allow intrusion.[7]

Kirby was part of a counter-sabotage team that tested Home Guard protection of these vulnerable points. Kirby and his colleagues were trained by MI5 and Scotland Yard in a range of techniques for entering buildings. They were tasked with bluffing their way into vulnerable points during the day, and breaking in at night. This was a potentially very dangerous task, as the defending Home Guard were not warned beforehand to expect mock saboteur raids, and Kirby and his comrades did everything to give the impression of a real raid. He remembered what he had been asked to do, and how he went about his task: 'We are asking you to assume the role of German saboteurs, and we were told how to get in, the kind of bombs to be used, all dummy bombs, they were all plasticine, very, very much like gelignite, where to place the bombs to secure maximum destruction'.[8] Kirby and his regular associate, a soldier called Freddy, travelled the length and breadth of Britain, attempting to enter power stations. It proved to be an extremely difficult task, fraught with danger, and not just that involving Home Guard protection. In particular, Kirby remembered a botched, attempted attack on Battersea Power Station in February 1943:

At night, approaching the power station, I happened to tread on a big sheet of corrugated iron, which absolutely rent the air with noise, and Freddy turned on me, and said, 'You fool!' [. . .] What happened next was that we climbed up, and there was an electrified fence that you had to get over. But we weren't aware of it, it was like a trip wire, and Freddy [. . .] got caught up on it and set the alarm going. It was then that we got caught.[9]

In this case, it was Home Guards patrolling the perimeter of the power station that captured Kirby and Freddy. Both men were taken inside the power station, and when the police arrived, they gave the name of a senior army officer in London who later arrived to explain who they were. Later on, following the invasion of western Europe, Kirby had the arguably less dangerous task of being responsible for General Montgomery's personal security.

The Home Guard also had a role, and one that expanded as time went on, in providing defence for military vulnerable points. Among these were RAF airfields, which typically possessed fixed defences – pillboxes, fire positions and bunkers – as part of an all-round defence scheme. The RAF itself had provided protection for its stations, and this was formalised in February 1942, with the establishment of the RAF Regiment. However, the increasing demands on the Regiment for airfield protection in the UK and overseas gave the Home Guard an additional role. At a War Cabinet meeting on 27 November 1942, the downgrading of the invasion threat and manpower shortages led the War Cabinet to accept that 'some reduction in the scale of our precautions against risks could therefore be accepted. Thus, consideration might be given to the possibility of diverting some part of the RAF Regiment to other duties', with the Home Guard being given a more significant role in airfield defence.[10] It was in these sorts of roles that Home Guardsmen found themselves being trained and equipped with heavy weapons used by the Regular Army. For example, the withdrawal of the RAF Regiment from airfield defence duties in Northern Ireland towards the end of 1942 meant that some Ulster Home Guardsmen were equipped with 25-pounder field guns and 75mm anti-tank guns for airfield defence.[11]

Strains on manpower

As the war progressed, the Home Guard faced a number of problems that resulted from the downgrading of the invasion threat, the increased tempo of the UK's offensive operations and preparations for the invasion of western Europe, and competing demands on manpower (including, of course, for women war workers and military personnel)[12] from both civil and military quarters. For the Home Guard, these issues led to problems associated with absenteeism, morale, and exhaustion on the part of men who were full-time workers, on civilian rations, but who also had to train and parade with the Home Guard. However, there were also new opportunities and roles for the force which originated with the same pressures on manpower. In particular, the Home Guard found themselves playing an increasingly important role in the anti-aircraft and coastal defence of the UK. By the spring of 1944, some 7,000 Home Guards manned coastal artillery batteries, and 111,917 Home Guards were serving in anti-aircraft units, a figure which rose to 141,676 by late summer 1944.[13]

Concerns about manpower shortages were discussed repeatedly at War Cabinet level from late 1941 onwards, and often in relation to the Home Guard. The general public was as aware as the government that, following the German invasion of the USSR, the likelihood of a full-scale German invasion of the UK was greatly reduced. This, in turn, led some Home

Guards to feel that the extra demands on their time, with weekly parades, weekend and 'holiday' training, were unnecessary. However, given the central role in military planning that the force had in providing a key part of home defence, one that would grow as plans for the invasion of western Europe took shape, it was important that the Home Guard continued to increase its effectiveness. There was clearly a problem, both in terms of manpower in general, and in the Home Guard. The force was constantly losing young men to the regular armed forces as they were called up, and as the Home Guard was a voluntary organisation, members could resign after giving two weeks' notice; in addition, there was the increasing problem of absenteeism. In the last six months of 1941, for example, the Home Guard lost a net total of 150,000 men.[14] Worse, 'in the East and South-East of England [. . .] units were sometimes considerably below strength and unable effectively to carry out the tasks they had been assigned in the event of invasion'.[15] This was in the context of a continuing problem with building the Regular Army in preparation for the invasion of western Europe, maintaining forces in North Africa, and feeding workers into the war industries. By the summer of 1942, it was estimated that there was a shortfall in these areas of at least 1,089,000 people.[16] Part of the solution was to extend conscription, by means of a National Service (No. 2) Act, both into the regular armed forces, but also into civil defence and particular occupations.

The place of the Home Guard in the proposed National Services (No. 2) Act resulted in a good deal of War Cabinet debate on how the matter should be handled. There was concern that conscripting men – known as 'Directed Men' – to what was a successful volunteer force would change the character of the Home Guard. The concern was that reluctant conscriptees would damage morale, and that some volunteers would not wish to serve with the new men. There was an additional complication in that it was proposed to extend the age limits for recruitment to the Home Guard from eighteen years to fifty-six, although boys and men outside these age limits had previously been enrolled. The concern was that conscripting men in their fifties to the force meant that it was highly likely that these men had not already volunteered for the Home Guard and would, therefore, often be reluctant recruits. At first, consideration was given to exempting the Home Guard from the Act, but that raised the problem of making the force the only exception to the Act, with consequences for Home Guard morale if members wondered why they were not being included in an important piece of defence legislation. Finally, after a number of high level discussions, the War Cabinet decided to include the Home Guard in the proposed Act, and to introduce compulsory service in the force in areas where Home Guard numbers were deemed to be too low.[17] Compulsory Home Guard service came into effect on 2 December 1941, and marked another stage away from the enthusiasm of a 'voluntary citizens Army',[18] and, in consequence, the 'volunteers' in the ranks became 'privates' (this came into effect in February 1942), and the Home Guard rank system finally came to match that of the regular army.

Other approaches to the general manpower problem involved extending the Home Guard's role further. The first of these, to provide support for Civil Defence, something that Home Guards had been doing on an ad hoc basis since the blitzes of 1940, was not an overly popular addition for many Home Guards. The second extension, tasking the force to provide anti-aircraft and coastal artillery crews, was more in line with the military function of the Home Guard, although anti-aircraft units in particular would suffer from Home Guard absenteeism. The decision to give the Home Guard civil defence duties was made in February 1942, following a recommendation to the War Cabinet by Home Secretary, Herbert Morrison and the Secretary of State for War, David Margesson, that 'a portion of civil defence workers might join the Home Guard, and members of the Home Guard might perform civil defence duties'.[19] This role was deemed to be yet another contribution that the force could make as the threat of invasion receded. By October 1942, the Home Guard was being reminded by GHQ that 'it is not desirable to lay down any rigid division of time between Home Guard and Civil Defence (CD) duties'.[20] Typically, Home Guard and Civil Defence co-operation involved the Home Guard and Air Raid Precautions (ARP), or the Home Guard and the provision of First-Aid Posts. The meshing together of local military and civil defence planning took time to achieve, and Home Guards sometimes argued that had they wanted to be part of Civil Defence then they would have joined a Civil Defence organisation and not the Home Guard. Charles Graves, in his contemporary account of the force, explained how the linkage was supposed to work by referring to two examples in the West Country, one of which appeared to suggest failings during an air raid:

> The importance of this combined effort was noticeable in the opposite cases of Bath and another West Country town. Bath was a good example of co-operation between the CD and the HG, and the latter was detailed to stand by, having been instructed in what it was to do – and where and when. In other words, if the CD Control Room received a direct hit, the Home Guard Commander could step in and take over. In the other town the ARP authority refused help from the Home Guard, which was the chief reason for unnecessary damage by fire.[21]

In other areas, co-operation between the Home Guard and ARP was good, with the 7th Battalion, Tynemouth Home Guard, providing an example. This Home Guard unit had an observation post on the top of Billy Mill, a vantage post overlooking an extremely wide area. As a result, a special Home Guard observation unit was trained to provide information during air raids to the ARP as well as to Home Guard command and the police. 'The Billy Mill post developed into the "eyes of the borough" and was to provide a significant aid to the ARP organisation'.[22] The overlap between Home Guard service and CD service was eventually great. For example, of the 1,781 officers and men of the 7th Battalion Northamptonshire Home Guard, Wellingborough, 905 were categorised as 'List II' in 1944, indicating that they had a CD role as well as a Home Guard role.[23]

Although the danger of air attack on the UK had diminished since the blitzes of 1940–41, the threat remained, and the Luftwaffe continued to mount nuisance raids, and larger air attacks, such as those carried out in the Baedeker Raids in April, May and June 1942. Later, the Luftwaffe would also attempt another offensive against London with Operation Steinbock (known in Britain as the 'Baby Blitz') in early 1944, and there would also be the unmanned rocket offensive involving V1 and V2 rockets. Nonetheless, it was felt that the overall threat from the air was diminished, and in the search for more men for the field army, Anti-Aircraft Command was an obvious target for the combing out of men in preparation for the invasion of western Europe. By the end of 1941, Anti-Aircraft Command had already lost 50,000 men to other army formations,[24] and the subsequent shortfall was partially made up by women from the Auxiliary Territorial Service (ATS),[25] and, increasingly, men from the Home Guard. Home Guards began to be compulsorily enlisted into heavy anti-aircraft batteries in the summer of 1942, by which time light anti-aircraft batteries manned by the Home Guard were already operational. The need for more Home Guard anti-aircraft crew increased, not only to relieve regular gunners, but also because preparations for the assault on western Europe had created new targets for air attack. The Chiefs of Staff reported to the War Cabinet in the spring of 1943 that:

> We propose to effect a reduction of 26,250 men below the basic allotment of July 1942 and to fix the ceiling for AA Command at 180,000 men and 77,000 ATS. The 1942 ceiling for ATS was 110,480, but 77,000 is the maximum number which can now be provided [...]. It should be possible within this man-power ceiling, by means of certain expedients, such as a greater use of the Home Guard [...] to provide approximately the same degree of Anti-Aircraft defence for this country in 1943 as was provided in

1942, taking into account the growing number of points now to be defended.[26]

At this point, in April 1943, the UK was defended by 2,260 heavy anti-aircraft guns, and 1,450 light anti-aircraft guns, figures that were an increase from 1,888 and 812 heavy and light guns respectively a year earlier.[27] What is of interest here is that the 'manpower' shortage was affecting the numbers of women available for Anti-Aircraft Command. This problem would also become apparent when women were formally, and finally, given an official role in the Home Guard. Despite the fact that perhaps as many as 50,000 women were already serving in an unofficial capacity in the Home Guard, in addition to the support provided by the Women's Voluntary Service (WVS), it was not until April 1943 that an official scheme for 'nominated women', otherwise the Women's Home Guard Auxiliary (WHGA), came into being.[28] Although preference was given to women over the age of forty-five for this role, with the expectation that 100,000 women would volunteer, and a ceiling of 80,000 finally being set, only 28,000 women were serving as WHGA by March 1944.[29] This is a low figure compared with the earlier estimate of 50,000 women acting in an unofficial capacity, and may suggest that either the earlier figure was inaccurate, or that by the spring of 1943 many women were less willing to assist the force.

Extending the Home Guard role to anti-aircraft defence continued apace throughout 1943–1944, with 118,649 Home Guards making up half of all anti-aircraft battery crews by August 1944.[30] This was a vital contribution not only to the defence of the UK, but also released around 100,000 Royal Artillery gunners for service overseas in the country's contribution to the final offensives against Germany. Nonetheless, some of the Home Guard anti-aircraft units suffered with problems of morale, war-weariness and absenteeism, which affected Home Guard service in general. One historian has argued that 'the public believed that as the Army turned its attention away from home defense and toward preparing for combat on the Continent, the Home Guard became less useful, less important, and little more than low-quality garrison troops. As a result, Home Guardsmen took less pride in their service than they had prior to mid-1941'.[31] Nonetheless, the Home Guard had increased the scope of its activities, and was not only a major contributor to area defence, security, civil defence, and anti-aircraft defence, but was also a source of coastal defence.

The UK's coastal defences were, in 1939, much as they had been at the end of the Great War, twenty years earlier. Confidence in the strength of the Home Fleet, and the RAF's arguments that torpedo carrying aircraft would destroy any invading fleet before it reached the coast, was, however, threatened by the events of spring 1940. At that point, it was decided to reinforce the coastal defence artillery with the creation of 'emergency batteries'. Over 150 6-inch naval guns, First World War stock stored in naval arsenals, and some 4.7-inch guns, were mounted in pairs in a crash programme to defend the east coast of Britain, from Sullom Voe in Shetland to Worthing in Sussex. Within a year, the number of these batteries had doubled, with existing batteries reinforced, and the chain of coastal artillery defence extended to Devon and to vulnerable areas on the North-West coastline.[32] Each battery was manned by two officers and sixty men. It is unlikely that all existing batteries were fully manned, except during the summer of 1941,[33] and as with anti-aircraft defences, as the threat of invasion diminished after that summer, so the need for artillerymen in other, offensive, roles grew. The solution was to downgrade the readiness of some batteries, and train the Home Guard to man others. By June 1944, when German E-boats were active off the coast, and Home Guard coastal batteries saw action against them, some 7,000 Home Guards were members of coastal batteries.[34] The effectiveness of Home Guard coastal battery gunners was high, as evidenced by the testimony of William Aikman, a regular Royal Artillery officer who was a staff officer and gunnery instructor with the South-West Sector of Southern Command, 1943–44.[35] It was on this type of Home Guard foundation, as the War Cabinet noted in February 1943, that 'the defence of the country will increasingly depend as our armies take the offensive'.[36]

A fighting force

As the Home Guard evolved, so it benefitted from better equipment and improved training, which increased the capabilities and effectiveness of the Home Guard. The force also coalesced in other ways, with officers and men developing social ties that helped maintain morale during the long haul from 1941 to 1944. Further, the government, ever mindful of the need to support Home Guard morale, and maintain the population's confidence in the need for, and the capabilities of, the Home Guard, made efforts to publicly acknowledge and recognise the achievements of the organisation.

Weapons for the Home Guard were a priority concern from the outset, and the government and the volunteers were only too aware of the fundamental shortage of rifles and small arms in the summer of 1940.[37] The initial situation was characterised by the use of privately held weapons (often shotguns and sporting rifles), and the combing out of any stores of weapons, no matter how old, that might exist. One source of modern rifles was that held by the Officers Training Corps (OTC), whether the Junior Training Corps (JTC) of schools, or the OTCs of universities.[38] An example of the limited provision that this provided can be found in the papers of Herbert Allsopp, who, in May 1940, was the officer commanding the OTC of Wellingborough School in Northamptonshire. Allsopp's position as a Territorial Army officer in the OTC, and a school master at a noted local public school, made him an obvious candidate to lead what became the 7th Battalion, Northamptonshire Home Guard. At its height, in 1944, the battalion consisted of seven companies, a headquarters company, and a battalion headquarters, of eighty-nine officers and 1,692 other ranks, plus seventy-one women in the WHGA.[39] Allsopp's records clearly show the changing fortunes of his battalion in terms of rifle provision from 1940 until 1944. On 5 July 1940, Allsopp listed, on a piece of Wellingborough examination script paper, the rifles he had available for his LDV volunteers, all of which came from the Wellingborough School OTC armoury. In total, it amounted to forty-eight .303 rifles, with a mere ten rounds per weapon. Allsopp noted that 'In Case of Alarm' the first sixteen rifles were to be used by the schoolboy members of the Wellingborough School OTC, rifles number seventeen to twenty were to be issued to section commanders, and the remaining twenty-eight rifles were to be divided among four companies of the unit. In 1941, in contrast, the battalion never possessed less than 863 .300 rifles (these were in all likelihood US M1917 rifles, known to the Home Guard as P17s), and in 1942, 809 of these rifles. A monthly tally for 1943 shows varying stocks, from a minimum of 735 to a maximum of 807 rifles, and the battalion ended its war, in December 1944 with 809 .300 rifles.[40] In addition, the battalion would have also been equipped with revolvers, sub-machine guns, light machine guns, medium machine guns, a range of grenades, and various Home Guard specific equipment such as Spigot Mortars, Northover Projectors, and the Smith Gun. The improvement in weapons provision that Allsopp's battalion experienced reflected the overall picture for the Home Guard. In September 1940 there were 847,000 rifles, 46,629 shotguns and 48,750 automatics for 1,682,303 volunteers.[41] By January 1943, there were 900,000 rifles, 30,145 shotguns, 23,630 Browning Automatic Rifles, 248,234 Sten guns, 12,895 Thompson sub-machine guns and over 20,000 Lewis, Browning and Vickers light and medium machine guns for the force.[42] The Home Guard armoury was also boosted by a wide range of heavier equipment, including improvised armoured vehicles, both locally fabricated and of those of more regular manufacture, like the Bison and the Armadillo series of mobile pillboxes, and the more orthodox light part-armoured Beaverette scout cars.[43]

In addition to improved equipment, the Home Guard saw a steady increase in the training available to it. At first, private initiative marked much of the force's training opportunities. The most notable, and innovative, case was the training school set up by a group of former communists and veterans of the International Brigade, at Osterley Park in the early summer of 1940. The leading lights in this initiative were Tom Wintringham, a one-time commander of the British Battalion of the International Brigades and Hugh Slater, who had been officer commanding of the British anti-tank unit in the Spanish Civil War. Working with other enthusiasts of irregular warfare, and Edward Hutton, the proprietor of *Picture Post*, as well as the owner of Osterley Park, the Earl of Jersey, these men created what would become the model for weekend, residential Home Guard training schools.[44] In the summer of 1940 some 5,000 volunteers passed through Wintringham's training school, taking their new knowledge back to their units, and although the War Office and the Army eventually managed, by May 1941, to wrest control of Osterley Park from the Home Guard socialists, their message continued to be read by the huge audience for their books, pamphlets and newspaper articles. Further, the very success of the Osterley model led to similar schools being set up all over the UK, and it was this type of course, that David Roberts attended at Nonsuch Park, near Epsom, in 1942 and 1943.

The Home Guard eventually developed effective military skills, and it is important to realise that this was achieved by men who, by and large, were working long hours in full time jobs, and benefiting only from limited civilian rations. In addition to parading in the evenings and on Sundays, Home Guards were also subject to the other discomforts and alarms of the rest of the civilian population, and were expected to assist Civil Defence during air raids. The question of long hours, and war-weariness was one that the government, and the Home Guard itself, were well aware of. As part of the reforms introduced under the National Services (No. 2) Act, a recommended maximum number of hours service – forty-eight hours per month – was laid down. Charles Graves' contemporary comment was that 'this was regarded with some amusement by members of the Home Guard Battalions who were doing anything over sixty hours a month already'.[45] Much of this time was taken up by routine duties, and the scope for platoon and company level training was limited. David Roberts, in notes prepared for the Headquarters Company of 57th Battalion Surrey (Mitcham) Home Guard in 1943 calculated that the time available for evening training for each individual Home Guard amount to only fifteen hours per quarter, or sixty hours per year. He commented that for a Home Guard three months' worth of evening training was only equivalent to two days of a regular soldier's training time. To this, he added an additional three days' worth of Sunday parade training per quarter, plus fourteen days per year of possible camp training, to give a grand total of thirty-nine days per year. He further noted that all this training time was expected of a Home Guard at a time when many thought that they would not, in fact, be required.[46] Nonetheless, NCOs and officers like Roberts continued to disseminate the training that they themselves had received. The core of this training, for most Home Guardsmen, focused on battle craft and battle drill. Roberts listed the key elements of Sunday parade Home Guard training in these areas:

Camouflage

Messages, local knowledge, map reading – observation, tactical route march (including march discipline)

Patrolling – recce., standing, fighting & mobile

Selection of fire positions

Crawling

Fire control

Fire Orders

Fire Discipline

Judging Distances

Fighting in Built-up areas

Section and individual stalking, crossing obstacles.[47]

Home Guardsmen were expected to work towards the Home Guard Proficiency Badge, introduced in April 1941, which tested a wide range of knowledge, including proficiency on eight types of weapon, battle craft and signalling, as well as local and unit general knowledge. Some of the weapons training could be dangerous, as a result of a combination of poor training, defects in ammunition and weapons and individual factors. By the end of 1944, seventeen Home Guards had been killed in training, with many more wounded, along with thirty others involved in bomb disposal; with a total of 1,206 Home Guard killed on duty. This contrasted with the dangers faced by regular soldiers in the UK. 'The average on-duty death rate for the Home Guard was about 0.7 per thousand, as against an average rate of about 0.05 per thousand among regular troops in the UK [...] In very approximate terms, the chances of a Home Guard dying on duty from causes that had nothing to do with the enemy were at least four times those of a regular soldier'.[48]

The continued commitment to training, better equipment provision and the established nature of the force meant that it was increasingly able to fulfil its core function of area defence, in both the passive and active roles. Lieutenant-Colonel Allsopp's 'Battalion Defence Scheme', dated January

1942, for his battalion of the Northamptonshire Home Guard gives a clear indication of the type of area defence that the Home Guard was trained, and equipped for. The aim of the battalion defence scheme was, 'To halt any attempted advance of the enemy through this Battalion area'.[49] Allsopp's premise for battalion defence of the area was that there could be a number of types of enemy action that would necessitate the deployment of his battalion. These were: aerial bombing attacks, parachute attacks, airborne assault, actual invasion, or a combination of those events. The battalion defence scheme identified vulnerable points, and important installations and bridges that needed specific defence. In addition, key vulnerable areas and possible tank harbours were noted as requiring special attention. The localities which had been identified as particularly favouring the Home Guard's defence were also indicated; the two main areas being the line of the River Nene and the River Ise. Allsopp's plans also detailed the requirements for the defence of the town of Wellingborough itself. The battalion was to defend the town against tank or armoured car attack, infantry or airborne troops. His instructions were that the Home Guard garrison in Wellingborough would:

(a) observe enemy entering the areas of constituent companies and pass all information to higher command and adjacent units.

(b) deny the enemy road communications through the Town.

(c) keep open those road communications for friendly troops.

(d) destroy such enemy raiders as may try to seize V[ulnerable] P[oints].[50]

This plan for the 7th Northamptonshire Battalion Home Guard from early in 1942 illustrates the core tasking of the Home Guard. Allsopp's force was to defend an area of ground, including vulnerable points, secure the main town in his district, and keep access to their part of the front open to regular army mobile forces which would be expected to arrive to deal with the stalled enemy assault. This is a description of the 'passive' defence outlined in the official statement from early 1941 of the Home Guard's role, which reminded the force that: 'static defence must not be misunderstood; defence is both passive, in the sense that a unit is tied to the ground in order to carry out its task and active. Active defence entails full use of patrols, observers, reconnoitring parties, in order to obtain information of the enemy, and fighting patrols to delay and destroy his infantry and tanks.'[51] As the Home Guard's skills improved, so they were expected to be capable of providing active defence, as well as static defence. From the autumn of 1942, Home Guard training was built around battle-craft and battle drill, which was taken to be 'proof of the tremendous headway made by all ranks in the previous twelve months'.[52] Home Guard units were encouraged to develop the skills necessary for the operation of fighting patrols, designed to find and engage pockets of enemy troops. Training scenarios increasingly used narratives that imagined Home Guards facing air or sea borne raiders, rather than a full scale invasion. However, the capacity of most Home Guard units to react quickly, in an active defence mode was, in reality, limited. In his history of the Leicestershire and Rutland Home Guard, Austin Ruddy argued that, 'despite the Home Guard's desire for mobility, they did not have enough vehicles. It was the Home Guard's local knowledge, planned defences and anti-tank ambush weapons that meant, despite their limitations, they were better suited to manning defended localities and other static defences'.[53] Despite this, the changing focus of training was, in all probability, a good way of maintaining the morale of a force that increasingly feared that it was, in essence, of only secondary usefulness in the war effort.

The government frequently addressed itself to boosting Home Guard morale, while the Home Guards used inter-company and inter-battalion competitions, sporting and social events to maintain morale and improve the cohesion of their part-time members. The yearly anniversaries of the founding of the force were publicly acknowledged, and the third anniversary, in particular, was marked by parades, a message from the King, a radio broadcast by the Prime Minister, Home Guards on duty at Buckingham Palace, and the gazetting of gallantry awards for Home Guards who had distinguished themselves during enemy air action, or in other acts of heroism. Churchill was particularly keen to acknowledge and celebrate the achievements of the Home Guard, and was well aware of the function of ceremony. In the run up to the anniversary in 1943, the Prime Minister outlined his thinking to the War Cabinet:

> The Prime Minister said that the 14th May would be the third anniversary of the formation of the Home Guard. He thought that this should be celebrated by holding ceremonial parades throughout the country, accompanied by special arrangements for publicity. This would have a heartening effect on the morale of the Home Guard; and, from the strategical point of view, there would be advantage in demonstrating to the enemy that, even when we had sent substantial forces overseas, we could still rely for the defence of this country on a strong and efficient body of volunteers in addition to the regular troops retained for home defence.[54]

The parades were held on the nearest Sunday, 16 May 1943, but Churchill was insistent that the parades would not be Church Parades (ie, without weapons), but would be 'armed parades held throughout the country'.[55] The day was designated 'Home Guard Sunday', and, where possible, parades were followed by 'displays of skill at arms, field-craft and battle drill, and the Home Guard [was] assisted by the Regular Army in matters such as the loan of bands and the participation of tanks and carriers'.[56] The immediate impact of Home Guard Sunday was good, with the Home Intelligence Division of the Ministry of Information (which compiled weekly reports on domestic morale) reporting that the public was generally impressed with the Home Guards.[57] However, as the historian David Yelton has noted, for many Home Guards the boost to morale provided by Home Guard Sunday was temporary, and 'during late 1943 and in 1944, Home Guardsmen's complaints of war weariness became endemic and demands for a reduction in the frequency and intensity of training were widespread'.[58]

The Home Guard themselves developed social networks that, in many cases, long outlasted the force. Given that Home Guard units were built around localities, work places, and schools, this is, perhaps, not so surprising. But Home Guard service added in an additional layer of shared experience, and an additional opportunity for socialising. Without doubt, local pubs quickly became associated with individual companies and platoons, and there is much photographic evidence of Home Guards rounding off duty in their local public house. In addition, officers and NCOs also developed their own social networks, with dining in nights, for example. It was following such an event that Lieutenant-Colonel Allsopp received an amusing letter from East Central District headquarters, which, appropriately enough, was quartered at Brewery House, Dunstable. The letter read:

> My dear Allsopp,
>
> Owing to a technical and tactical error no charge was made for port on guest night at Howbury Hall, and there is as well a debit of £4.5.9d for guests and WVS emoluments. The port consumed cost £11.5.0d so that we have a deficit of £15.10.9d. I propose therefore to charge the Reg[ular] Offrs [officers] on the course 10/– per head and HG offrs 4/–, both additional to the 2/6d already subscribed. Will you therefore kindly forward a cheque for 8/– at your convenience.[59]

The consumption of over £11 of port seems to suggest that a good time was had by all in this example of morale building. Of interest, too, is that the Home Guard guest night saw them dining with regular officers, while it appears that the WVS volunteers (presumably involved with preparing the meal) were paid for their efforts. The social links that the Home Guard made during the war were frequently maintained afterwards, with reunion dinners being a more formal example of this. There was also the unfortunate fact that the British Legion refused permission for men with Home Guard service to join the Legion or use its clubs. The Legion's argument was that the force had not seen active service, which was a moot point given the part it played in the anti-aircraft and coastal defence of the country, not to mention the role the Home Guard played during air attack. As a result, former Home Guards went on to found their own old comrades clubs, such as the still extant Home Guards Club of Royal Leamington Spa, founded by some of the 3,500 men who served in the 1st Battalion Royal Warwickshire Home Guard, drawn mostly from the Warwickshire constituency of Anthony Eden.[60]

Stand Down

By June 1944, the Home Guard provided the core of the United Kingdom's home defence, and was, in essence, the force that guarded the jumping off point for the western Allies' assault on German occupied France. The Home Guard and Civil Defence organisations in southern England were put on full alert on D-Day and on the days and nights following in case the Germans made an attempt at spoiling raids. After much bloody fighting in Normandy, the British, Canadian and US armies broke out, and the retreat of German forces to the Rhine had begun. The war was far from over, and millions more would die before, and after, Victory in Europe, but the threat of invasion for the UK had finally disappeared. On 6 September 1944, Sir James Grigg made a War Office announcement on the radio that Home Guard operational duties were suspended, and that attendance at parades was now voluntary. As the historian S P MacKenzie noted, 'most members of the Home Guard, particularly the directed men, were heartily relieved. The more keen volunteers, however, were rather upset by the suddenness of it all'.[61] In fact, a poll in the *News of the World* indicated that a majority, some 55 per cent, of the Home Guard hoped the force would become a regular feature of the UK's defences, even after the war was over.[62] But in October came the news that far from becoming a permanent part of the United Kingdom's military forces, the Home Guard was to be stood down prior to disbandment. In November, Home Guard units received their stand down order from General Sir Harold E Franklyn, Commander-in-Chief, Home Forces, which included a laudatory assessment of the Home Guard's contribution:

> The Home Guard came into being at a time of acute crisis in our history, and for over four years has stood prepared to repel any

invader of our shores. The reliance that has been placed on you during these years has been abundantly justified and it has enabled our Regular troops to go overseas in sufficient numbers to give battle to the enemy with the magnificent results we have seen.[63]

Stand down parades were held, the King broadcast the nation's thanks on 3 December, and the Home Guard held their valedictory dinners. David Roberts and the other officers of the 57th Surrey (Mitcham) Battalion Home Guard held their dinner at The White Hart Hotel in Mitcham on Wednesday 6 December 1944. The White Hart was the symbol of Richard II, and is a common pub name throughout England. It was fitting therefore that the Mitcham Home Guard officers sat down to a traditional English dinner of, 'Soup; Roast Beef; Roast and Boiled Potatoes; Brussels Sprouts; and Trifle.'[64] Roberts' commanding officer Lieutenant–Colonel S W Mills MC, DCM (whose decorations indicate that he had risen through the ranks, presumably in the Great War) and brother officers signed the menu card and said farewell to their wartime service in the Home Guard.

Conclusion: The Home Guard's contribution

The wartime Home Guard had a short history, yet it was one marked by a number of stages in terms of enthusiasm, equipment, training and significance to the defence of the United Kingdom. In the early days of the LDV, the force was characterised by enthusiasm and the unbounded desire on the part of its volunteers to help protect their country from invasion and occupation. Yet that enthusiasm was not matched by the country's ability to arm, equip or train the new force. That task was, however, increasingly achieved over the following year, and the Home Guard became an integral and reasonably capable part of the UK's defence plans. The core role that the Home Guard was configured for was the area defence of their own localities. The volunteers were there to do their utmost to slow down any invaders in order to give the field army time to bring its mobile assets into play. In effect, this meant that the Home Guard were, literally, to lay down their lives for their homes, factories, workplaces and localities. In addition to its area defence role, the Home Guard also had a security and guard function, protecting Vulnerable Points, and guarding against the supposed Fifth Column. With the German invasion of the Soviet Union, in June 1941, the threat to the United Kingdom greatly decreased, and continued to decline thereafter. However, the Home Guard was now firmly part of the planning that envisaged the force taking on as much home defence as possible, so that regular troops could be released for offensive operations overseas. The irony was that just as the principle reason for the creation of the Home Guard – the threat of invasion – receded, so the importance of the Home Guard in strategic terms increased. But for many Home Guards, that bigger picture was obscure, and war weariness, long working hours, limited civilian rations, and the need to parade and train with the Home Guard, affected morale. Counter-balancing this, the Home Guard found itself increasingly better equipped, better trained, and called upon to provide significant numbers of men for anti-aircraft and coastal artillery duties. The government and the army had no doubt that the force was of importance, and much effort went into maintaining morale, and, indeed the force itself, when Home Guard service became compulsory. Indeed, it was not until it was quite clear that Germany was no longer able to mount even raids on Britain, did Home Guard service become optional.

December 1944 saw Home Guard stand down parades around the country, farewell dinners, and the gazetting of honours to deserving Home Guard commanders. The Wellingborough schoolmaster, OTC officer, and commanding officer of the 7th (Wellingborough) Northamptonshire Battalion, Home Guard, Lieutenant-Colonel Herbert Allsopp, was awarded the OBE,[65] which he collected in October 1946. He returned to his civilian life at Wellingborough School, and continued to command the Wellingborough cadets, but at the less exalted rank of Captain. Home Guards across the United Kingdom did the same. All those Home Guard who had completed three years service could receive the Defence Medal, with its green, black and orange ribbon, symbolising the green of the land, the darkness of the black-out and the fires of bombing raids. In addition, a certificate of thanks was issued to Home Guards, and to women Home Guard Auxiliaries. The Home Guard certificate stated: 'In the years when our Country was in mortal danger [name of Home Guard] gave generously of his time and powers to make himself ready for her defence by force of arms and with his life if need be.' For 1,206 Home Guards, their service had cost them their lives, and many other Home Guards risked their lives in training and under enemy air attack. This had been acknowledged by the award of gallantry medals and commendations throughout the war. For example, Lieutenant W Foster, 7th Wiltshire Battalion, who had already been awarded the Military Cross and the Distinguished Conduct Medal in the Great War was, according to *The Times* of 27 November 1942:

> instructing a class in throwing live grenades [when] a Mills bomb rebounded to the firing position. Without hesitation Lieutenant Foster threw himself on the bomb one second before it exploded, thus saving the lives of his comrades nearby. This officer's gallant

action was not carried out in the heat of battle, but deliberately in cold blood, and with full knowledge of the consequences. As a result of this action Lieutenant Foster lost his life.[66]

Home Guard Lieutenant Foster was posthumously awarded the George Cross, which his widow received at an investiture on 2 March 1943.

Part III

Old Men, Young Men, and Women – the People in Arms

Chapter 4

Playing Fields and Factory Yards

Defending the Workplace

Throughout the Home Guard's history, the force was not only organised on a geographic basis, but also on the basis of factories, industries, and schools. Although the broader vision for the Home Guard changed, from an early warning force designed to spot enemy paratroop landings, to the area defence view and the provision of anti-aircraft and coastal artillery crew, the defence of individual workplaces remained a Home Guard task. In this respect, the Home Guard were defending not only their homes, but also their working lives. This aspect of the Home Guard is examined in this chapter in relation to three key types of unit: schools, factories and national communications. Using the personal testimonies of eight volunteers, the particular contribution of these institution-based Home Guard units will be examined. Each of these unit types had unique, and important, contributions to make to the local defence of Britain, and their personnel were able to bring particular, work-place based knowledge and skills.

Playing fields at war

When, on 14 May 1940, Sir Anthony Eden broadcast the appeal for volunteers to come forward for the LDV, there was one source for the new force that was fully equipped to take up arms. Contrary to the picture of the early volunteers being grey-haired veterans of the First World War drilling with broomsticks, patrolling with shotguns and old service revolvers, the group that was ready in 1940 were schoolboys in public schools. These youngsters were members of school Officer Training Corps (OTC), and had already received initial infantry training, and, furthermore, were equipped with .303 Lee Enfield rifles.[1] The OTCs had emerged as part of the reforms of Lord Haldane in the period leading up to the Great War. Haldane's reforms of the military in the years following the great Liberal Party victory of 1905 transformed Britain's Regular and Territorial forces. His success was such that he has been seen as the saviour of Britain in 1914. As one historian, Geoffrey Cousins, noted: 'In the face of considerable opposition from public, Press and critics inside and outside Parliament, Haldane had carried through a reform that was to save Britain from disaster in the World War to come'.[2] Part of Haldane's reforms saw the creation of OTC units at public schools and universities. The intention was to build a cadre of educated young men with basic military training who would, in wartime, provide an important source of officer material. When the LDV was formed, therefore, public schools already had in being the basis for fully equipped units. In fact, the school OTC units were more important than the university OTCs, as the numbers of male students at all universities began to fall rapidly as eligible students volunteered or were conscripted for the regular armed forces.[3]

Harold 'Jimmy' Taylor, James Lowther and Michael Bendix were senior boys at Eton College during the early war years, and were all members both of Eton's OTC and its Home Guard. All three Etonians also went on to serve in the regular armed forces after leaving school. Their reminiscences of their time with the school's LDV and Home Guard unit provide an insight into what were, in the summer of 1940 at least, probably the best equipped of LDV units. In addition, the testimony of the three throws a fascinating light on the attitude of one section of the British social and political elite in the run up to the outbreak of war with Germany. Further, as Etonians, they enjoyed long holidays from school, and during those weeks and months they were members of Home Guard units in their home villages, and were able to compare the two different varieties of unit – school and village.

Like most public school boys, James Lowther was at home when war was declared on 3 September 1939. Unlike most British schoolboys, he was staying at his family's country house in the Highlands of Scotland, and his family was well connected in the political and social world. As a result, the teenage Lowther already had an insight into the attitudes of his family circle to war, and, in particular, war with Germany.

> I was nearly 17 at the time, in September 1939, so it wasn't unexpected. In fact, in 1938, Munich time, when I was 15, there was quite an involvement. My father, who had been in the First War, and was involved with the British Legion, volunteered, an abortive scheme, for the British Legion to raise a force to go off to Czechoslovakia to administer the partition. And there was a great deal of talk about Germany and the forthcoming war in those days [...] So, when the 1939 war broke out, it was not unexpected for me, or in my family. At the time, I was up in Scotland, in a remote part of the Highlands, near Mallaig, staying with cousins for fishing, and most of the men staying in the

house disappeared to join their regiments. [...] In the 'thirties, particularly the mid 'thirties, from about 1935 onwards, there was always a lot of people staying in this house [...] mostly well-established members of society, many of them involved in politics – for instance, one of our father's closest friends was the local MP, Oliver Stanley, who later became [secretary] for war during the war. And, of course, another member of parliament was Rob Hudson, who was Minister of Agriculture during the war, early part of the war. And they were always in and out of the house, and were always talking about what was going to happen. What was astonishing, I was a boy about 15 or 16, or depressing, was that there was considerable sympathy amongst them for the German approach to the, what you might call the isolation of, or the prevention of, Bolshevism or Communism in the Western world. So they were not unsympathetic towards Germany [...] Winston Churchill was quite well known to this family, and they'd been involved with him for quite a long time, and they used to talk about him in the 'thirties as being somewhat of a traitor to the Conservative cause, and a warmonger, and so forth. He wasn't popular.[4]

This is an interesting account of what might be seen as the mainstream view of Conservative Party supporters in what transpired to be the long run up to the Second World War. The ingredients of the view that Lowther attributed to the adults in his extended family, and their influential friends, combined the experiences of the First World War, the fear of Bolshevism, class and party interests, and a hope that war would not be necessary. But when it came, Lowther describes his family as fulfilling their patriotic duty:

As soon as war broke out, the average people who used to come to the house all turned completely round, and said, 'Well, here we are, we've got a war to fight'. Most of them, so many of them, had been involved in the First World War, my father's generation. And after all, he was born in 1898, so come 1939 he was only 41 or 42. He had been a regular soldier in the First World War, so he was on the reserve officer list, so he immediately embraced the war with enthusiasm, and rushed off to the War Office, and said, 'Here I am' [...] and he was very disappointed when he was sent [...] in the winter of 1939–40 [to be] in charge of a Pioneer Corps in a Butlin's Holiday Camp.[5]

James Lowther returned to Eton, and in that school year began his LDV service. But Eton was already marked by preparations for war. During the Munich Crisis of 1938, the whole country had seen preparations for war, with gas masks issued to the population, public buildings sandbagged, and the peacetime silver finishes of RAF aircraft covered with wartime camouflage. At Eton, the famous playing fields, which stretch from the school almost to neighbouring Slough, had also been affected by the crisis:

> I remember at the time of Munich, in 1938, a large excavator appeared and dug trenches all over the playing fields of Eton [. . .] to prevent German gliders landing in the event of war. And they were still there when war broke out, and they were enlarged and increased. So [. . .] imagine the famous playing fields of Eton being interlaced with a rectangular grid of deep trenches to prevent gliders.[6]

Harold Taylor was a contemporary of Lowther's at Eton, and he, too, remembered the preparations for war that accompanied the Munich Crisis: 'My house at Eton in 1938 – we sandbagged the dining room as an air raid shelter, and we did it again in 1939. We had concrete shelters put in the garden of each house at Eton – and we spent a lot of time in those shelters.'[7] With the creation of the LDV, both boys immediately found themselves in the school's LDV unit, created from the older boys and masters in the OTC. Both Lowther and Taylor described this experience as being an exciting one for teenagers like themselves. Eton's closeness to London also meant that the enemy threat was real, with German bombers frequently passing over the town and school. In addition, there were two railway lines that ran close, the Thames was navigable past the school, and there were key local assets to protect both in Eton and nearby Slough. The extent of the school site, and its closeness to lines of communication and the light industry of Slough, meant that for the Eton College Home Guard there was a clear local defence role from the outset. James Lowther recalled:

> We were all mobilised, those of us who were over 16, into what was initially called the Local Defence Volunteers [. . .] So the Eton College contingent of the LDV all had armbands saying 'LDV' which we wore over our OTC uniform. We all volunteered for all sorts of activities. At the time when invasion was threatened, for instance, we used to mount guard over strategic points in the district, which were considered strategic targets, at night time. And I remember sitting up in the astronomic observatory at Eton, night after night, four hours on, two hours off, with a fully loaded

.303 rifle, Lee Enfield .303 rifle, gazing at the stars, supposed to be looking out for paratroopers. In the summer of 1940, I gave up a fortnight's holiday to guard the artesian pumping station, which is outside the playing fields of Eton, which supplied the water for Windsor, Datchet, Slough and so forth. It is still there, somewhat bigger now, but the same old flat roofed buildings where we used to stand all night on guard.[8]

Harold Taylor's memories were also of night patrols, excitement, and the defence of key local assets.

When the war came, I think it was, for me, an excitement. I joined the Home Guard, I patrolled the playing fields, the railway lines, the gas works at Slough, with masters, with loaded rifles. And, for a young boy of 17 or 18, this was much more adventurous than school would normally be.[9]

In good schoolboy fashion, Taylor remembered how boys would find excuses to leave their houses when German aircraft were flying overhead, and anti-aircraft fire meant that there were war souvenirs to be had:

I remember when there were air raids going over Windsor towards London, the anti-aircraft guns would fire and bits of shrapnel would fall around us. If we found an excuse to go out of our house, to go and see a tutor on some academic business, we would take the opportunity if we could in order to enjoy the shrapnel falling and so on, even though we had strict instructions to stay indoors under these conditions.[10]

On one occasion Eton was bombed, by, in all probability, a returning German bomber jettisoning its payload over the town and school (which run into each other). Another Etonian, Michael Bendix, who was a couple of years younger than Lowther and Taylor, remembered the night that the school was bombed during the winter of 1940: 'I was doing my prep, because the bombs came at about six o'clock on a winter's eve [...] I can remember being blown off my feet and all the windows coming in'.[11] Being an older boy, James Lowther was involved in tackling one of the incendiary bombs that fell into his house during the same incident, and he gave an account of both the bomb load mix dropped on Eton, and the effect of a delayed action high explosive bomb:

A bomber [...] obviously made a mistake, and unloaded its cargo all over Eton – about 600 incendiary bombs and half a dozen high explosive bombs. Three of the high explosive bombs were delayed action and three exploded on contact. Sadly, one of the delayed action bombs fell through the Elizabethan part of the school – Upper School as it is called. It didn't go off. The bomb disposal people came and inspected it the next day, but they found it was too dangerous and they couldn't move it. So it went off the following night, in other words twenty-four hours delayed action, and demolished a large chunk of the Elizabethan part of the school [...] An incendiary bomb came through the roof of our house. A four storey house, and it finally came to rest on the second floor, and we did all the classic stuff that you are supposed to do, with a bucket of water, the stirrup pump, spray the incendiary bomb [...] and it all went quite well![12]

The raid destroyed the homes of two masters, as well as Upper School, but there were no casualties.

Etonians not only served in the Home Guard, undertook ARP duties, and trained local Home Guard in rifle drill and musketry,[13] but they also volunteered for war work. Michael Bendix served in the Eton Home Guard, but he also worked in an aluminium casting works in Slough on Sundays. His account is interesting in that it highlights class differences in Britain, but is also an example of how they could be bridged in a war for national survival:

At the weekends in school, we used to have to go and work in factories instead of playing games, and I worked in an alloy factory, a foundry, in Slough – and they were absolutely marvellous. They were a bit suspicious of an Etonian, as you may well imagine, but when you are stripped to the waist and shovelling black sand, it's a great binder, and they accepted one as a friend [...] it was one of the best lessons in getting on with people. Because I knew I would be very unpopular to begin with, and then, without being vulgar, I realised that we all had to go to the loo in the morning.[14]

This experience of finding common ground with other English people from classes that the Etonians would normally have little contact with, was one that was also raised by Taylor. Both these boys also served, during school holidays, in the Home Guard units of their home villages. In these units they mixed with villagers, and came to admire their knowledge and patriotism. 'Jimmy' Taylor was, in his school holidays, a member of the Home Guard unit in Headley, Hampshire, which was commanded by his father, the head master of a prep school and a clergyman. 'Jimmy' Taylor's role in his village Home Guard was as a bicycle mounted despatch rider. This role, both for the Home Guard and for Civil Defence organisations, was often carried out by Boy Scouts, particularly in 1940.[15] Taylor, though, was an armed member of his village unit, and felt that the village men would have put up a strong resistance had the country been invaded:

> I had a profound respect for local people [. . .] I think the Germans would never have had such resistance as they would have had in England from every single village and hamlet, every corner, every ditch, every river would have been defended, even with obsolete guns. They would never have had an inch that they wouldn't have to fight over. The scenes that we knew in France and Belgium during the blitzkrieg would not have been repeated in Britain, in my estimation. And, in fact, the attitude that we had when France fell, I remember, was one of relief. A feeling of 'Thank God we don't have to depend on anyone else, now we can stand on our own feet. Now let them come and we will give them a bloody nose'. I can distinctly remember that the morale was much higher in 1940 than in 1939, even after Dunkirk. [. . .] And the old villagers that we had, forty of them, they knew the lie of the land, better than any military person would be able to do [. . .] For the first time I got to know the villagers.[16]

Taylor's and Bendix's accounts of village Home Guards add confirmation to the well-known account contained in *When Village Bells Were Silent*, by the prolific rural writer, Fred Archer. In Archer's account of the force in Ashton-under-Hill, the local agricultural workers, led by, and including, First World War veterans, possessed some natural advantages over towns-men, especially in the early, LDV days:

> When the first Local Defence Volunteers were formed to keep watch and stem a possible invasion, countrymen in the main had certain advantages over the townsmen. A villager who has been used to stalking rabbits and pigeons with his shotgun uses the natural lie of the land to hide from animals and birds, he cowers down, bent low beside the high hedge or stone wall, his dress is less showy than that of his friends in the town.[17]

Being members of both Eton's Home Guard and their village Home Guards, enabled Taylor and Bendix to make comparisons between the two types of unit. Whereas the Eton Home Guard were equipped with the standard British army rifle, Taylor's village Home Guard were equipped, in 1940–41, with non-standard rifles and improvised equipment:

> We had very ancient American rifles, .300 calibre, very long things, but they were usable. We had a mortar which was made out of a drainpipe. And my brother set up a signals section using signal lamps and Morse code, so that we could have a detachment sleeping in a shepherd's hut up on the Hampshire Downs [...] We spent a lot of time making Molotov cocktails.[18]

Michael Bendix noted, in addition, that in the early days of the LDV, OTC training gave the Eton unit an advantage over his Sussex village unit: 'I think because of the [...] OTC, I think the Eton Home Guard was in a better position to handle weapons, certificate A and all that, which the Billingshurst Home Guard, of course, hadn't got that advantage, but morale was tremendous'.[19] All of these Etonians were clear on this latter point, that morale in their units in the summer of 1940 was high.

After service with the Home Guard, James Lowther first served with the Royal Corps of Signals, then with the Royal Armoured Corps, and fought in Normandy, landing on Sword Beach with his troop of Sherman tanks at mid-day on 6 June 1944. Harold 'Jimmy' Taylor became a photo-reconnaissance pilot with the RAF, and flew Spitfires over Europe, crashing in the Netherlands in November 1944, and being taken prisoner after five days on the run. Michael Bendix left Eton in 1943 and joined the Coldstream Guards, landing in Normandy as a nineteen-year-old junior officer, and fighting through North-West Europe until VE Day.

Factory defence

Factories were regarded as being integral elements in the defence of localities, but it was also the case that there was a need to provide security for individual factories. At the same time, factories provided a source of Home Guards who were known to each other, and had common interests in defending their livelihoods. The image of factory-based defence also received a boost once the Soviet Union switched from being a friend of Nazi Germany to being its victim. Soviet factory militias were called upon to both maintain production and defend their factories, and this soon became part of the British perception of the Soviet war effort. In Britain, factory Home Guards were encouraged to guard against the threat of sabotage and the Fifth Column as well as providing defence in the wider, geographic sense. An example was to be found in Hugh Slater's best-selling book, *Home Guard for Victory*, published by the left-wing publisher Victor Gollancz in 1941.

The book had been snapped up by Home Guard readers, and within a few months of being published had gone through six printings. It was 'mostly technical in nature, but had definite political overtones'.[20] This was not surprising, as Slater, who had been educated privately and at the University of London, was a former member of the Communist Party of Great Britain (CPGB). Further, Slater had been the officer in charge of the anti-tank company of the British battalion of the International Brigades in the Spanish Civil War, and had served as a staff officer in the Republican Army. It was, therefore, a combined political and military motivation that led Slater to stress the importance of factory defence by factory workers.[21]

The organisation of factory defence by the workers in the factories was seen to have beneficial effects in terms of morale and the even closer identification of the work force with the war effort. Members of factory Home Guard units were often highly skilled manufacturing workers producing vital war materials. One example was Maurice 'Peter' Bradshaw, a skilled lathe and milling craftsman working for Supermarine, producing Spitfires. Although Bradshaw was eighteen in September 1940, he was in a reserved occupation, and it was not until the war in Europe was over that he was able to join the RAF. Nonetheless, like many British civilians, he had been caught in air raids, and had joined the LDV at its inception.

'Peter' Bradshaw had started his apprenticeship at the Supermarine works in Southampton, but such a vital factory was deemed to be too vulnerable to air attack there, and was relocated to Newbury, Berkshire. Bradshaw went with the works and, as soon as the LDV was formed, joined up and told a familiar tale of improvisation and hastily collected firearms:

> I joined the LDV, it was before my father joined up, and he was concerned with the starting of the Local Defence Volunteers. Our weapons were bayonets tied onto broomsticks, and old rifles and odd 12 bores [shotguns]. And I myself had managed to get hold of a .455 Easy Colt revolver, but I only had five rounds of ammunition.[22]

Bradshaw's initial LDV role consisted primarily of checking vehicles and drivers, looking for saboteurs, Fifth Columnists, and downed German air crew. But the re-siting of the factory had clearly not gone unnoticed, as a lone German raider attacked Newbury, bombing and destroying houses, a church and school, killing fifteen people in the process. The general belief was that the raider, which was subsequently shot down, was after the factory, and had targeted buildings with large rooves, only to hit the church and school.

Bradshaw's overall assessment of his Home Guard unit was that, once the early days of equipment shortages were over, the Home Guard was an effective force. Many of the men in his unit would have been, like him, young, fit, and skilled, and like many other veterans of the Home Guard, he thought that the BBC TV comedy series, *Dad's Army* had, unfortunately, helped sustain a myth about the force:

> The Home Guard, a lot of people I think have got the wrong impression from a certain television programme. Because it was *never* like that. They became quite a professional unit. I remember at least a year before the European war finished, that one of the training exercises we went on was in the same manner as the regular forces – battlefield inoculation. We had live bombs thrown at us and live ammunition shot over our heads, and we had aircraft dropping bags of flour on us.[23]

Hawtin Leonard Mundy was an LDV and Home Guard in Wolverton Works unit in Oxfordshire. He was born in 1894, and had seen extensive active service in the Oxfordshire and Buckinghamshire Light Infantry (Ox and Bucks), and had been wounded on three separate occasions, finally being wounded and made prisoner at Arras on 3 May 1917. Mundy's account of his works Home Guard unit is interesting in that he made an extended comparison between his Ox and Bucks' training, equipment and preparation for the Western Front in 1914–15, and that of his works Home Guard. Like 'Peter' Bradshaw, the veteran Mundy was keen to argue that the popular, post-*Dad's Army* perception of the force was inaccurate. Speaking with the benefit of his military experience in the First World War, Mundy said:

> I'll make a statement now that you'll hardly believe, when I tell you that [in] the last year of the Home Guard [...] the Home Guard was better trained, more intelligent, better equipped, and I could almost say, equal physically with, I think, the men who went in 1915 with the 'Bucks in the First World War.[24]

There were a number of strands to Mundy's argument. A key strand was that the men of his works unit were all highly skilled and trained men, and that this gave them an edge over his contemporaries from the First World War:

> You had the young men, who was in reserved occupations in Wolverton Works [...] they were young chaps round about 20

and 30. And they were no mugs, because those young men were skilled technicians, engineering, woodworking, drawing office [. . .] foremen, well educated, and knew the job well, so you couldn't say they were a lot of mugs.[25]

Of the 5,000 people employed in the works, there were 250 in the works unit, and the young, skilled workers in reserved occupations were buttressed by men like Mundy who, as he pointed out, were not only veterans of the First World War, but were still active men in their forties:

> There were old soldiers, and when I say old soldiers, they were men what was in the Regular Army in the First War that was only past 18 years of age when the war finished. And they were between the ages of 30 and 40, and a man between the ages of 30 and 40, or more, is as physically fit as when he was a young man [. . .] and the old hands, like me, they had military training, and knew every trick, how to train them [the younger men] in musketry, armaments, and all that sort of thing. So they learnt all the tricks![26]

Mundy was promoted to platoon commander of No. 4 Platoon, D Company, Wolverton Works Company, which was led by Colonel Hagley, who was also the managing director of the factory. The company not only defended and protected the works, but also guarded the railway, and extended its role to the wider defence of Wolverton. This combined role emerged from the widespread early tactical view that factory defence sections should merely safeguard their factories from sabotage, and, when invasion came, defend the factory precincts. But it became clear that the defence of factories, many of which employed thousands of workers and were spread over many acres, had to be integrated with wider geographic defence if both factories and towns were to be defended effectively. As Charles Graves explained in his wartime history of the Home Guard:

> The system was therefore adopted by which a portion of factory detachments was made mobile and ready to move out in accordance with the general plan of defence of the area. These detachments usually consisted of the younger men, whilst the older men were to remain in the factory as a kind of 'obligatory garrison' to guard against sabotage or minor enterprises which might be undertaken by Fifth Columnists in collaboration with the enemy's main operations.[27]

For Hawtin Mundy the combination of skills and experience in his works Home Guard unit gave it an edge that was enhanced, by 1943–44, with good weapons, enabling it to fulfil its dual role:

> We had modern Lee Enfield rifles, the same as they were using at the front, the latest Lee Enfield. Each one had a rifle. And, at the finish, the officers had a Sten gun. I had a machine gun in my platoon – fifty-eight men I'd got in my platoon – a water cooled machine gun that was used in the First World War, and all the ammunition, as much as I wanted. I had two Spigot Mortars [...] with a 20lb bomb, grenade, anti-tank, and it also fired a 16lb bomb up to 3–400 yards. I had all those in one platoon, which equalled more than the whole battalion had when we went to France [in 1915]. Now that's not laughable, you know'.[28]

Mundy's proud comparison of his platoon's firepower with that of early 1915 is instructive, because while true, it was, perhaps, a flawed comparison, as the Wolverton Works Company would have had to fight on a 1940s battlefield, not one from over a quarter of a century earlier. Nonetheless, his account presents a picture of a workforce drawing upon the variety of skills, education and military experienced of its workforce to defend manufacturing against attack – all under the command of their managing director. For Mundy himself, service with the wartime Home Guard was not the end of his military career, for, in 1952 when the Home Guard was re-activated, Mundy was again called upon to defend his country – this time from the Soviet threat.

The defence of national communications

Certain assets were believed to be particularly vulnerable to attack, either by saboteurs or in the event of invasion. These included railway lines, telegraph lines and telephone exchanges (both run by the Post Office), docks and waterways. In these cases, it was natural that defence would be largely in the hands of the employees. In the case of the railway companies, these vital services were spread over large areas of the country, and their management had to decide, as soon as the LDV was formed, what policy would be taken in respect of their workforce and the defence of such vital communications. The Southern Railway Company largely operated in the area of England that was most likely to be in the path of any invasion force. The Southern Railway quickly decided, in May 1940, that 'the interests of defence and the preservation of essential communications could be best secured by forming local defence volunteer units from the staff of the Company'.[29] Within a month of the formation of the LDV, over 16,000 of the Southern Railway

Company's staff had volunteered, and the resulting units of the LDV were brought together to form the companies and battalions of the Southern Railway Group. The Company also seconded eighty full time workers to organize its LDV force.[30] These steps made the company the first of the railway companies to organise its staff in this way, and the others soon followed the example.

The main tasks, especially in 1940–41, for all the railway companies were to defend key elements of the railway system – bridges, viaducts, tunnels, signal boxes, depots, and control offices. Guard rooms were established at stations, and in old coach bodies, the Railway Rifle Clubs formed the basis of rifle training, and weekend training camps were provided by the railway companies for their units. In addition to forming the core of railway defence, the railway units, like all works units, also formed part of their local area defence. The exact role of railway workers who were also volunteers in the LDV was spelt out by a War Office circular in the summer of 1940, which stated that railway 'members of the LDV have a dual function, i.e. to keep the railways running, to defend themselves, the communication system, and to assist in defeating the enemy'.[31] The War Office advice gave instructions on how railway LDVs should respond in certain likely events should invasion take place:

> If railway operations cease, then for the time being, broadly speaking, all members of the LDV are available for defence. If on the other hand, the railway is still running, or attempting to run, but the particular place concerned is being attacked by the enemy, then the first thing to do is to defeat the enemy, and to protect communications, because unless this is done it is clear that the men will be lost and railway operations will cease. It follows, therefore, that in the latter event the course of action to be pursued must depend on the circumstances at the place and the time, and calls for energy and initiative on the part of the Company, Platoon, and Section Officers who must endeavour in every way to:
> (i) defeat the enemy; (ii) carry on the operation of the Railway.[32]

The defence of the railway system was seen to be vital to the prosecution of the war, not least if invasion took place.

Three Home Guard volunteers who served with communications industry units were Stanley Brand, Frederick Cardy and Robert Nosworthy. Stanley Brand was an underaged volunteer in a railway LDV unit in Middlesbrough, which also covered the marshalling yards at Middlesbrough. Brand himself was an apprentice at the ICI works in Middlesbrough, but had been able to join the railway unit because his friend's father was a signalman and a sergeant in the unit. The railway unit had a very clear idea of their role, especially in 1940 and 1941, when invasion seemed to be a strong possibility. Middlesbrough was a key industrial centre in North East England, with a combination of heavy industry, docks and ship building that was vital to the war effort and a notable prize for any invader. The railway Home Guard saw their task as defending the railway and marshalling yards, but also preparing to sabotage them in the event of invasion:

> We had to get to know every signal and every point, so that we could sabotage them if Jerry came in. And we were going to sabotage the swing bridge at the entrance to Middlesbrough docks. So we had to learn how to run a locomotive and trucks against the points that we would set against them, to derail them in the appropriate places. It was a very interesting experience, I learnt so much about railway operations.[33]

The railway Home Guard also made use of their access to rolling stock, and the steel and shipbuilding works of the area, fabricating an improvised armoured train to defend the railway and docks:

> We got steel plates, rejects, from South Docks. If they punched holes in a plate for the rivets and had them in the wrong place, it was a reject [...] and there were many plates they rejected, and we scrounged some of these, and we lined a truck with the steel plates, so we had armoured trucks. [...] The trucks we used were just ordinary, four wheeled general goods trucks. Inside, they were probably about three feet deep, because we would have found it difficult to take a Lewis gun over the top [of a bigger truck]. We lined the two long sides with plates, as thick as we could scrounge. And the two ends, we wanted them armoured in case we were the rear one, because we felt that a lot of the shooting would come at us against the end. [...] It was just a case of lining them with whatever we could get, which would cover us if we were lying down in the bottom.[34]

After his service with the Home Guard, plotting to destroy the communications infrastructure of Middlesbrough and riding in the armoured train – which, as Brand said, was, 'to a boy, like reading the *The Hotspur*, *The Rover* and *The Wizard*' – he joined the Fleet Air Arm (FAA). He served as a naval airman in the FAA in Britain and the North Atlantic from 1944–45, and returned to the North East to study at Durham University.

The importance of specific railway knowledge was also stressed by another member of a railway Home Guard unit, Frederick Cardy. He was a railway clerk with the Southern Railway Company who served with the railway Home Guard in the garrison town of Colchester in Essex, then with a railway unit in Northamptonshire. Cardy was in charge of the ambulance section of his unit, having already received training with the St John's Ambulance Brigade. During one joint Home Guard and Army exercise in Colchester, soldiers seized the railway station, and made their headquarters in the main waiting room:

> An [engine] driver by the name of Jack Hayden, and his mate, Butcher, they'd been on duty in the Home Guard headquarters, which were in Colchester Laundry [...] and Jack Hayden said to his mate, 'Come on, we can have a bit of sport'. And they went down to the loco [sheds] and said to the foreman, 'You got an engine in steam? Yes? Get permission from the signalman, I want to go down into the siding'. So they got the engine, and they got permission from the signalman, nothing coming on the down road, so they went with this tank engine, and stopped outside the general waiting room on the down side, dashed across the platform to the door, which was open – 'Come on you lot, hands up!' Captured them all![35]

Robert Nosworthy was born on 23 June 1900, started working with the Post Office in London at the age of fourteen, and enlisted in the 3rd Battalion the London Regiment – the Post Office Rifles – as soon as he was of age. But his first deployment was to Newport in South Wales to help break a miners' strike in August 1918. He was preparing for embarkation at Southampton for the Western Front on 10 November 1918. The next day, the Armistice came into force. Nonetheless, he served with his regiment until November 1919, undertaking occupation duties in Bonn, and, in another sign of the economic and social stresses exacerbated by the First World War, a further experience of strike breaking, this time in Coventry. After demobilisation, he returned to work with the Post Office in London, and when war came again joined the Post Office Home Guard. Like the railway system, the Post Office was seen to be of central importance in the operation of wartime Britain, but also in the event of invasion. Within days of the appeal to form the LDV, over 50,000 post office workers like Robert Nosworthy had volunteered for the new force. They were organised by the Post Office into zones that matched the regional structure of the Post Office. Like railway LDV volunteers, the Post Office volunteers had specific job-related tasks. The importance of these communication and defence roles was acknowledged with the issue of a Post Office LDV armlet: 'it was agreed by the War Office that a broken circle with the letters GPO in red should be stamped on each side of the block lettering of the LDV armlet worn by the PO volunteers as an indication to Area Commanders, whose districts they might be moving through during an invasion, that they were engaged on the specific task of covering key communication points and maintaining essential defence circuits'.[36]

The unit that Nosworthy was part of – B Company the City of London Post Office Home Guard – was dominated by veterans of the Post Office Rifles from the First World War. Robert Nosworthy remembered: 'The unit was formed by nearly all Post Office riflemen. The commanding officer was an ex-sergeant who was with the Post Office Rifles, [they were] nearly all Post Office Rifles'.[37] The predominance of the veterans in his unit, and the sense that they were a trained, disciplined body, made Nosworthy, like Hawtin Mundy of the Wolverton Works, indignant about the picture of the Home Guard painted in people's minds by the *Dad's Army* television series. Mundy explained:

> As a matter of fact, I rather resented the programme *Dad's Army*, because it ridiculed the Home Guard. I know I had a chuckle myself, occasionally, at it, but we were a very, very smart unit. We were trained and drilled at Wellington Barracks at everything, weapons, machine guns, everything they had. [...] All our unit were all ex-army men, all about the 45–50 mark, and we used to fall in before we marched down to Wellington Barracks, outside the Army and Navy Stores, and the main door men there, they were all ex-army men, and one said to me that we were as smart a unit as any he had seen.[38]

There is a clear sense here of a pride in sharing standards with regular army regiments, perhaps strengthened by the fact that these Post Office Home Guard were from the City of London, the very heart of the capital. Nosworthy's account indicates that what was important for him, and, one might expect, for his comrades, was that as a Home Guard unit, they were aiming to be efficient infantryman. In addition to duties shared by other Home Guard units in London, the Post Office units were also tasked with guarding and defending Post Office assets and property. In the aftermath of air raids, the unit secured and guarded damaged post offices, and tele-communications assets, such as telephone exchanges. In part, this was to prevent sabotage, but, also, to prevent looting and theft.

Robert Nosworthy was promoted to lieutenant, and took charge of grenade training, first for the Post Office Home Guard, and then for all Home Guard units in London. Working with two sergeants that he knew, and trusted, Nosworthy ran the bombing school at the Surrey Docks. Grenade practice could be dangerous, and many of the awards for bravery to Home Guard personnel were associated with grenade accidents.[39] In some cases, the Home Guards attending Nosworthy's live grenade practice had no knowledge of grenades at all, and, in addition, there was always the problem of potential indiscipline:

> To tell you the truth, I think it was one of the most dangerous things I could have ever thought about doing, because of these squads that were sent down to me from various places, parts of London, had never even handled a dummy bomb [grenade]. And a lot of them were larking about, and you had to come down on them pretty stiff. And we didn't have any actual accidents, but we had very near misses [...] In a lot of cases, the idiots would pull the pin out beforehand, and all that sort of business, and I'd have to chuck the bomb over quick, and all dive down. They hadn't the slightest idea. But some were very good.[40]

Nosworthy ran the London Home Guard bombing course for nearly two years, until the force was stood down in December 1944, and some of the stress that he was under in his dangerous training role comes through here.

Conclusion: all round defence

The school boys, young men in reserved occupations, and Great War veterans who joined the LDV in the summer of 1940 not only sought to protect their homes, but also their daily lives – at school and work. Interestingly, the best armed and prepared LDV units were, at first, to be found in the public school and university OTC units. But, as the LDV developed, becoming the Home Guard and receiving better equipment and training, so other works and company units developed greater potential as a defensive force. Not only did these units contribute to the overall defence of the United Kingdom, but they also provided knowledgeable, skilled Home Guard for the defence of wartime production and vital communications.

Chapter 5
Celtic Defenders

A United Kingdom

The wartime propaganda slogan, 'We're All In It!' applied to the entire population of the United Kingdom, not least to the Home Guard. From the English counties facing occupied Europe across the English Channel to the northern shores of Sutherland in Scotland, and from the long East Coast of Britain to the Atlantic edge of Northern Ireland, the Home Guard was increasingly important to the defence of the UK. Although the Home Guard fulfilled the same basic roles throughout the UK, there were, nonetheless, some differences between the constituent parts of the Kingdom. For example, the particular landscape and geography, combined with a scattered population, in the Scottish Highlands and Islands presented different challenges to the Home Guard than those faced, for example, by their comrades on Clydeside, Tyneside, or Birmingham. But there were more than geographic differences in Northern Ireland, where the UK possessed its only land border, with neutral Eire. Further, the complex political and religious divisions in the province also added a unique dimension to the history of the Home Guard there. Finally, there was the case of the Isle of Man, a small island in the Irish Sea, with its own Parliament, and the site of internment camps holding thousands of enemy aliens, fascists, Irish Republicans, and friendly 'aliens' being processed by the security services. Further, the island was the site of airfields and important radar bases. Yet, despite these differences, the standard histories of the Home Guard have paid little attention to the force in these countries of the UK. For example, S P MacKenzie's, *The Home Guard; a Military and Political History*,[1] devotes only two pages to Northern Ireland. Nonetheless, there have been two notable recent works that have begun to address this deficiency. David Orr's *Duty without Glory; the story of Ulster's Home Guard in the Second World War and the Cold War*[2] is an excellent account, and stands as the definitive history of the force in Northern Ireland. Similarly, Brian Osborne's history of the Home Guard in Scotland, *The People's Army; Home Guard in Scotland, 1940–1944*,[3] has provided an account of the force there. The differences between the Home Guard in Scotland and England, or, indeed, Wales, were not as great as those between Northern Ireland and the rest of the UK, but a

Scottish history was needed. However, there is still no dedicated history of the Home Guard in Wales, and the force on the Isle of Man has no historical voice. The intention in this chapter is to examine the Home Guard in what is loosely known as the Celtic areas of the UK, with a particular focus on Northern Ireland and the Isle of Man. These Celtic defenders were vital in the defence of key areas of the UK, and faced different challenges and tasks from their comrades on mainland Britain.

'Wake Up, Ulster!'[4]

Charles Graves, in his contemporary account of the Home Guard, summed up the strategic importance of Northern Ireland:

> The province of Ulster is, of course, an integral part of the United Kingdom and it has been rightly described by eminent people as the flanking bastion of the United Kingdom. It has sea and air bases which play a vital part in guarding the western approaches to these islands. Added to this is the fact that its long land border separates a neutral state from a state that is at war. When these factors are considered it is realized that its position is vital to the successful prosecution of the war.[5]

The importance of Northern Ireland was further enhanced by its industrial capacity, particularly the shipyards that had built such ships as the *Titanic*, its textile industry, including the flax industry, and the productive small farms of the province. The latter, for example, exported enough eggs to Britain 'to supply the whole of Greater London throughout each year' of the war.[6]

Northern Ireland faced particular security issues that were unknown in the rest of the UK. The history of Irish Nationalism, Republicanism, and Unionism provided a unique context in Northern Ireland that fundamentally affected the formation, organisation and development of what, eventually, became the Ulster Home Guard.[7] Further, the differences between Northern Ireland and the rest of the UK meant that, for a time, the Ulster Home Guard was uniformed quite differently from their comrades throughout the rest of the UK.

The Irish context, the seeds of territorial defence

Northern Ireland was not unused to the concept of a citizens' defence force. The political struggle in the United Kingdom around the 1911 Liberal government's plans for Home Rule for the island of Ireland, led to the creation of opposing forces – Nationalist and Unionist – in the years immediately before the Great War. Although Dublin was, prior to 1922, a majority Protestant and Unionist city, the greatest concentration of Unionists and Protestants[8] were to be found in the northern counties of Londonderry, Antrim, Down, Armagh, Tyrone, and Fermanagh, being two thirds the Province of Ulster. Most Unionists strongly objected to the British government's plans to establish an all-island parliament in Dublin, and formed the Ulster Volunteers in 1912 to resist by force such an eventuality. In response, Irish Nationalists formed the Irish Volunteers, and both forces received weapons from Germany. However, it was war with Germany in 1914 that postponed violence in Ireland, with the Ulster Volunteers forming the 36th (Ulster) Division, and the majority of the Irish Volunteers also fighting in the British Army as the 10th and 16th (Irish) Divisions. But the minority of Irish Volunteers who did not join the war against Germany and the Central Powers went on to form the basis of the Irish Republican Army (IRA) and the Irish Citizens' Army (ICA) who ignited the Irish War of Independence, or the Anglo-Irish War, following the failed rebellion in Dublin at Easter 1916. That war led to the creation of the Irish Free State (Eire), and Northern Ireland, each with its own Parliament, in Dublin and Stormont, under the Anglo-Irish Treaty of December 1921. The Anglo-Irish War also saw the creation of the Ulster Special Constabulary, as the Royal Irish Constabulary (RIC) and the British Army, struggled to contain terrorism and guerrilla war in the North, and local, Protestant and Unionist militias were formed. To gain official control over the Unionist militias, the British government created the Ulster Special Constabulary (USC) in December 1920. The USC continued in being during the Irish Civil War, 1922–23, when the new Irish Free State government fought their erstwhile comrades from the IRA, while Republicans attempted to continue fighting in Northern Ireland as well.

The USC is important to the Home Guard story, as in Northern Ireland the Home Guard was built around the USC. That force had, from the outset, a number of categories of service, and, which, to a degree, foreshadowed the structure of the Home Guard:

> The USC was organised on a county basis and was divided into several different categories. A first for Irish militias, there was a full-time, uniformed 'A' category; then part-timers, the uniformed 'B' category, who served in their home districts at evenings and weekends; and the 'C' category, who served only occasionally, if required, and in static guard duties near their homes, and who wore police caps and USC brassards.[9]

The 'A' and 'C' categories were disbanded in December 1925, as the security situation in both the Irish Free State and in Northern Ireland stabilised. However, the 'B' specials were retained, 'they were cheap and had proven their effectiveness. In 1924 they had an establishment of 19,950, including a tiny full-time component to provide essential command and instructional classes'.[10] The 'B' specials were, however, viewed with hostility by most of the Catholic population of Northern Ireland, who saw the force, with justification, as being dedicated to the maintenance of the Protestant supremacy in Northern Ireland. On the Unionist side, the 'B' specials were seen as a guarantee against Republican terrorism, either from across the new border, or from within Northern Ireland. Whether famous or infamous, the force would, nevertheless, be crucial to the formation of what would become the Ulster Home Guard.

War in Europe

With the invasion of Poland by Nazi Germany, then Soviet Russia, in September 1939, the authorities in Northern Ireland moved quickly to put the 'B' specials on a wartime footing. The Royal Ulster Constabulary (RUC) sent a warning order to all County Commandants on the 1 September, saying that if the UK declared war then the 'B' specials would be placed in patrol mode, 'purely as a precautionary and temporary measure'.[11] The USC began road checkpoints, which they continued to mount throughout the war. The precaution that the RUC was taking was as much to pre-empt any increase in Republican activity, as to prevent any invasion, which, at that stage, was not envisaged. As if to confirm this fear, the IRA shot and wounded a British soldier in Belfast the day that the UK declared war on Germany. But it was not until the events of spring and early summer 1940, when the German *blitzkrieg* engulfed western and northern Europe that the invasion threat became a reality. Anthony Eden's broadcast of 14 May, calling for volunteers for a Local Defence Volunteer (LDV) force was greeted with as much enthusiasm in Northern Ireland as it was in the rest of the UK. However, the British government had not considered including the Province in the formation of the LDV, and Ulstermen who went to police stations were turned away, after the British government belatedly told the Stormont government of its decision. The British government's argument was that Northern Ireland was a low risk target in terms of the threat of a German invasion. However, it is likely that the complexities of conflicting Westminster and Stormont legal responsibilities and the unique nature of Northern Ireland in the UK had more to do with the decision. In addition, the Northern Ireland Prime Minister, Lord Craigavon, was unwilling to see the creation of an LDV on the same basis as in the rest of the UK as it would mean arming elements of the population who might be less than loyal to the Stormont government.

Despite the problems, pressure for a Northern Irish LDV grew rapidly, as it was clear that the Province now faced the same external threat as the rest of the UK. Indeed, the heightened sense of urgency was also felt in the south, where the Fianna Fáil government of Eamon de Valera interned hundreds of IRA men, declared an Emergency, and began the process of building up the Irish defence forces. In Northern Ireland, the government announced on 28 May that the USC would form a new section, to be called the Ulster Defence Volunteers (UDV). This force, which was, therefore, part of the RUC, was to be Northern Ireland's version of the LDV formed a fortnight earlier in Britain.

Mobilising the Ulster Defence Volunteers

The creation of the UDV proceeded with much greater speed and effectiveness than the LDV. Recruitment to the UDV began on 29 May, and within four weeks, Northern Ireland possessed the basic structure of a fully armed and uniformed defence force. It would take the rest of the UK until the end of 1940 before that was the case. RUC stations held large quantities of rifles which were available for the new UDV; also referred to as the National Defence Volunteers. There was ammunition for these rifles, with, for example, one eighteen-year-old volunteer, Bruce Douglas, remembering that on joining the UDV in July 1940, he was 'given rifle number N3226 and 100 rounds of SAA [small arms ammunition]'.[12] It was not until August that a temporary halt was called to recruiting because of a shortage of weapons. The UDV also benefited from the outset from access to Great War period Lancia armoured personnel carriers, inherited from the RIC and the army at the end of the Anglo-Irish War. The question of uniforms for the new force was solved remarkably quickly in Northern Ireland. David Orr described how 20,000 new uniforms were made and issued within a month. Interestingly, the rapidly supplied uniforms were black, and made the Ulstermen unique in appearance in their black denim blouses, trousers and side caps.[13] Buttons on the uniforms came from a variety of sources, and included Army general service, RUC, and even old RIC buttons. The side caps sported the harp and crown badge of the RUC.

A number of important questions arose concerning the legal status of the UDV, the relationship between police and the army, and between Stormont and Westminster. The UDV was part of the RUC, an extension of the 'B' specials of the USC. This meant that, in legal terms, they were a species of armed police. The problem here was that, under international law, if they took part in fighting against an invading force they would not have the protection of international law, and could be shot out of hand if captured. But the structural means to organise an army based local defence force did not exist in Northern Ireland, as although there were a small number of coastal defence Territorial Army units, there was no Territorial Army Association structure as there was in the rest of the UK.[14] There was, therefore, no alternative but to establish the force as part of the USC. The eventual solution to the problem came in the decision that the UDV would be under police command until the moment that Northern Ireland was invaded. At that point, the Army would take command of the force. This solution also addressed the issue of political control. As a police organisation it was within the remit of the Stormont government, which it would not have been as an Army organisation, when it would have fallen within the powers pertaining to the British government.

The UDV continued to grow and develop, with the new Northern Irish Ministry of Public Security having political control. By October 1940, there were 26,115 volunteers in the force, with a small number of British Army staff officers attached at RUC headquarters and in each county area. Although most of the volunteers were Protestants, there were a small number of Roman Catholics in the ranks, and this characterised the force throughout its history.[15] In July 1940, the British LDV changed its name to the Home Guard, a change formally confirmed on 24 August. But there was no similar name change in Northern Ireland at the time, and it was not until April 1941 that the Ulster Defence Volunteers took the title 'Home Guard'. But even then there was a difference, as the Stormont government wanted to maintain its influence, something that was signalled in the formal title of the Ulster Home Guard (UHG).

Before the spring of 1941, however, the UHG had begun to meta-morphisize into a force that looked more like its British counterpart. In December 1940, for example, during the bitter winter of that year, the War Office issued 30,000 khaki great coats to the volunteers. This, unfortunately, meant that the force was then uniformed in black and khaki – a reminder of the 'Black and Tans' of the Anglo–Irish War. However, the great coat issue was the first move to completely uniforming the UHG in army khaki battle-dress, the first issue being in April 1941. Army boots and leather, Home Guard pattern, anklets were also issued at the same time as the greatcoats. New weapons and training were also introduced, as the UHG began to develop beyond the emergency force it had been in the early summer of 1940.

Threats to Northern Ireland
Alone of all the Home Guard in the UK, the UHG faced a genuine internal security threat, in the form of the IRA. The Germans had hopes that the IRA would act, effectively, as a Fifth Column in Northern Ireland,

and the IRA was active. During the 1930s, the IRA had made tentative approaches to both Nazi Germany and Fascist Italy, and German agents from the *Abwehr* were in contact with the IRA in Eire. The IRA carried out a bombing campaign on mainland Britain during 1939, and it was feared that the organisation would act as a Fifth Column should the UK be invaded. Indeed, what might be regarded as Fifth Column tactics were used by the IRA in Northern Ireland in the spring of 1940. Although the IRA numbered around 300–400 men in Northern Ireland, they were short of weapons, and de Valera's clampdown on the organisation in Eire meant that the Ulster IRA had to rely on its own efforts. A number of IRA men joined the British Army, and five of them who were stationed at Ballykinler Camp were able to ensure the success of an IRA raid for weapons, capturing 200 rifles for the organisation.[16] This use of planted agents to attack from within was just the sort of tactics that were ascribed to the Fifth Column. For their part, the Germans rather ineffectively attempted to infiltrate their agents into both Eire and Northern Ireland. But the authorities on both sides of the border kept a close eye on these attempts, although the German spy, Hans Marchner, escaped, with IRA help, from internment in Eire.[17]

Attempts were also made to use two key IRA men to act as liaison officers between Germany, the IRA and the Dublin government. The men were the IRA's Chief of Staff, Sean Russell, and Captain Frank Ryan. Ryan had fought with the International Brigades in Spain, and had been captured by the Spanish Nationalists in March 1938. They, in turn, handed him over to Germany, where he was kept under house arrest. By August 1940 Ryan and Russell were on board the German U-boat, U65. They were to be landed in Eire, and Russell was to contact de Valera with a German offer regarding the use of Eire as a launch pad for an attack on the UK. But Russell died on the submarine, possibly of a perforated ulcer,[18] and Ryan (who did not know of the details of the plan) was taken back to Germany, where he died of natural causes in June 1944.

If grandiose plans involving agents dropped by parachute or landed from submarines made little headway, the IRA in Northern Ireland still made military efforts. At Easter 1942, RUC constable Patrick Murphy was killed in an IRA ambush. Similarly, the IRA killed Constable Patrick Forbes in Dungannon in 1942, and Constable James Laird and Special Constable Samuel Hamilton were both fatally wounded by the IRA at Clady near Strabane. IRA gunmen also killed Special Constable James Lyons in October 1942 and Constable Patrick McCarthy a year later. In addition, the IRA carried out bank raids for funds, arms raids, intelligence gathering, and bomb and gun attacks on RUC and army barracks. This was a real threat, and, in consequence, the UHG had to be particularly vigilant concerning the securing of weapons, and the possibility of IRA attacks also necessitated the carrying of sufficient ammunition during training to defend Home Guard units against surprise attack:

> The Belfast County Commandant issued a directive to all battalions to counter IRA activity. All ranks were reminded about the steps to be taken to safeguard personal weapons and ammunition. During training all Section Commanders were to carry a fully loaded Thompson SMG and a bandolier of 80 rounds of .303 ammunition for distribution to riflemen. All ranks entitled to carry revolvers were to do so during training, fully loaded, with six extra rounds of .455 ammunition. Armed guards were to be posted at the training halls during training periods, and personnel were also advised to proceed to and from their training parades, especially during darkness, in twos or threes, but not bunched together.[19]

For the volunteers of the UHG, the threat of a Fifth Column attack was not, unlike in the rest of the UK, an imaginary threat.

If the British authorities believed that Northern Ireland was, in 1940, a low risk as far as a German invasion was concerned, they might have been concerned that the Germans did, in fact, plan for just such an invasion. At least five plans for the invasion of Northern Ireland were developed, to one degree or another, by the IRA and the Germans, or by the Germans alone, but with their expecting support from the IRA. The two most developed plans were the western prong of the general plan to invade the UK in 1940 – 'Operation Sealion' – and a 1941 plan – the 'Viking Raid' – for an airborne assault on Northern Ireland.

Although the victory of the RAF in the Battle of Britain, allied to its successes in bombing German invasion barge concentrations in Channel ports, and the continued strength of the Royal Navy, meant that Operation Sealion was never to be tested, it still remains the nearest that any foreign power came to invading the UK in the twentieth century. Part of that plan envisaged a western thrust at the UK, through Eire. This was known as 'Operation Green', and involved an initial landing of some 39,000 German troops on an eighty-five mile front on the south-west coast of Eire, between Wexford and Dungarvan. A bridgehead would have then been established to threaten Britain's western flank, and Northern Ireland. Had this assault taken place on Eire in the late summer of 1940, the Germans would, of course, have faced opposition not only from Britain, but also from Eire's rapidly expanding wartime defence forces. Although the Irish Army had only mustered 20,000 men in September 1939, the response of Dublin to war in Europe, especially after the German onslaught in the west, had been to put its military onto a wartime footing. A year later, 30,000 new recruits had been enlisted, new branches of the army had been formed, and Eire's version of the Home Guard, two classes of men in the Local Security Force (LSF) and the Local Defence Force (LDF), had added a new reserve that would eventually total 100,000 men.[20] With every month that the Germans delayed an assault on Eire, as on the UK, the defences they would have faced grew stronger.

Operation Sealion was postponed in October 1940, but planning for an airborne assault on Northern Ireland, as part of a revived invasion plan of the UK, began in January 1941. General Kurt Student, officer commanding of the 11th Airborne Corps, presented Hitler and Goering (German paratroops were part of the Luftwaffe) with a plan that would avoid war with neutral Eire, involve the seizure of the military and industrial assets of Northern Ireland, and act as a major diversion to an assault on the southeast of England that would draw off British resources to assist in Northern Ireland. German airborne troops were the elite of the German military, and Student's plan – the Viking Raid – envisaged 20,000 paratroopers capturing, in a surprise assault, the airfields at Aldergrove, Langford Lodge, Nutts Corner, and Long Kesh. Luftwaffe transport aircraft would then land 12,000 more men at the captured airfields. The force would then move out from its bridgehead, seizing communications, and securing a defensible area, 'a triangle between the northern half of Lough Neagh and Divis Mountain [...] from this position the parachute forces would have dominated the richest and most vital part of Northern Ireland – the Lagan and Upper Bann valleys'.[21]

As the UHG developed, so it trained for all these eventualities. Well aware of the IRA Fifth Column threat, the UHG also trained for anti-parachute warfare, and were integrated into the defence of RAF airfields. In 1942, the North Derry battalion of the UHG received eight 25pdr field guns which they deployed for the defence of airfields in the area. In addition, the RAF Regiment was withdrawn from airfield defence towards the end of 1942, and the UHG took over their role of airfield defence, including the manning of 75mm antitank guns, which were distributed at the ratio of two per airfield.[22] By this time, the UHG lay at the heart of the defence of what Charles Graves had termed 'the flanking bastion of the United Kingdom'.

Defending Ellan Vannin, the Manx response
If the Ulster Home Guard has found a worthy chronicler in David Orr, the same cannot be said for the Manxmen and women who formed the Manx Home Guard.[23] From a population of 50,000, the Isle of Man provided the

15th Light Anti Aircraft Regiment (The Manx Territorial Regiment) which saw active service in the Western Desert, Crete, and in North-West Europe. Manxmen also served with the Royal Navy, the RAF, and the merchant marine. In addition, some 5,000 Manx men, and around seventy Manx women served in the Home Guard on the island, while others served with the police and the various elements of Civil Defence. Their task was to defend their small island, thirty-two miles in length and between seven and ten miles in width, situated in the Irish Sea, some 128 miles from Glasgow, eighty miles from Liverpool, and sixty miles from Belfast – all key ports in the UK's strategic lifeline to both the Empire and the USA. Not only was the Isle of Man in an important, central position in the Irish Sea, it also was the site of internment camps, which, by 1941 held between upwards of 15,000 enemy aliens, British fascists, IRA men, and refugees from Europe awaiting clearance by the security services. The war also brought important radio and radar installations to the island, in addition to the RAF stations at Jurby in the north-west and Andreas in the north, and the Royal Naval Air Station (RNAS) at Ronaldsway in the south-east.

The Manx have long made a contribution to the defence of the British Isles. The earliest corps was raised by the Duke of Atholl in 1779, with the French Wars of the late eighteenth and early nineteenth century heightening invasion fears, and leading to the three more corps of 'The Royal Manx Fencibles' in 1793, 1795, and 1803.[24] The Fencibles were not on continuous duty, but were only raised when the regular army was serving overseas. The Fencibles, like their successors, the Loyal Manx Volunteer Corps,[25] first raised in 1860, could serve outside the island, but there was a sense that the Isle of Man therefore had the capacity to make a notable contribution to the defence of their shores. The Loyal Manx Volunteer Corps became part of the territorial movement in the 1880s, and began a long association between the Manx volunteers and the King's (Liverpool) Regiment, an association that was renewed by the Manx Home Guard. The Great War absorbed most of the volunteers from the Volunteer Corps, and by the early 1930s, the island had no Manx defence force. This fact caused some unease on the island,[26] and the raising of a light anti-aircraft regiment of two batteries in 1938 was seen by some to be an overdue move.[27] However, the 15th LAA Regiment was a territorial regiment that was likely to be called upon to serve outside the island if war came. The sense that Europe was drifting to war meant that across the UK new civil defence organisations were created, and existing ones were put on a heightened state of readiness. On the Isle of Man, in addition to the raising of 15th LAA Regiment, the Loyal Manx Association was raised, following a government announcement of December 1938. A Manx government circular announced that, 'the establishment (of the Loyal Manx Association) has been fixed for the time at 150, of whom 50 shall be persons willing to parade with their own motor cars to be known as the mobile section'.[28] This was not a new form of volunteer corps, however, but merely an extension of the Special Constabulary, as the uniform of the Loyal Manx Association – blue serge tunic and trousers, blue overcoat and cap – attested. It would not be until Sir Anthony Eden's broadcast that a new, armed defence force for the island would be raised.

The Beginning

Immediately following the national call for volunteers for the LDV, an official Manx call went out for volunteers. Interestingly, it was realised that men who had volunteered for the Loyal Manx Association might well want to join the new LDV:

> His Excellency the Lieut. Governor will be glad if men wishing to serve as LDVs (unpaid) within the Isle of Man would give in their names to their local Police Stations. Members of the Loyal Manx Association will be allowed to transfer from the Association to the Defence Volunteers [...] The need for volunteers is greatest in the rural parts.[29]

The reference to 'rural parts' is a reminder that although some 50,000 people lived on the island in 1940, the largest concentrations of population were in and around Douglas, and in the small towns in the south and west – around Castletown, Port St Mary, Port Erin, and Peel. The rest of the island is, with the exception of the broad northern plain, hilly, indeed mountainous, with the 2,034 foot peak of Snaefell, cut through with deep glens running down to a varied coastline. That landscape meant that the island had long been a favoured training ground for Army and Territorial units from England. It therefore offered opportunities for defence, but also presented difficulties in terms of the possibility of parachute assault or the landing of agents from submarines.

It was believed that the island would be able to raise 1,000 LDVs, but, in the event, 2,000 came forward within a few weeks. The recruiting process was, as in the rest of Britain, a reflection of the class-based nature of society, allied to the role of ex-servicemen in the British Legion. The first two recruits enrolled in Douglas were the Clerk of the Rolls (*Cleragh ny Lioaryn*), Deemster Reginald D Farrant, and Deemster William P Cowley.[30] These two men were the senior judges on the island, and had, at that time, a key place in the island's Legislative Council. The British Legion created a special District Council to manage recruitment to the LDV, and special enrolment booths were set up across the island to handle the process. Over 1,000 men came forward within a week, and by the end of a fortnight, 1,500 men had enrolled.[31] These men were formed into six 'groups', based on Douglas, Ramsey, Castletown, Peel, Kirk Michael and Ballaugh, and Laxey. On 6 June, less than a month after recruiting started, 500 LDV paraded in Douglas, and recruiting was temporarily suspended in July, by which time 2,500 men had joined the LDV.

Although khaki denim uniforms began to be issued early in June, weapons were in short supply. As elsewhere in Britain, sporting rifles and shotguns were used, and the Isle of Man Rifle Association put its nine small bore ranges at the disposal of the LDV for weapons training. One source of weapons was the pre-Great War rifles of the defunct Manx Volunteers. This was also the source of 90,000 rounds of .303 ammunition which had been manufactured in 1909. After testing, it was discovered that the ammunition was in good condition, and all of it was eventually used in training, apparently without a misfire.[32] The arms situation in the early summer of 1940 was, then, much as it was in the rest of Britain:

> Very few rifles were received until towards the end of July and arms training was carried out largely with ancient rifles of various patterns which were recovered from the dungeons of the Police Station. Most of these dated from before the Boer War [...] In addition, as in England, the men were armed with rubber truncheons and bayonet standards known as 'Croft's Pikes'. Shotguns and locally obtained weapons were pressed into service, and were used by men taking up guard duty.[33]

Given the long coastline that the LDV had to watch, and the fear of airborne assault, a series of observation posts were set up throughout the island. Fifty-two of these were quickly established. Some of these were permanent fixtures, and a few concrete Observation Posts still survive on the island, which had, unlike the rest of the UK, little in the way of pillboxes, except those built to guard the airfields. Other Observation Posts were mobile, and here the island's Highways Board, and the Eddison Rolling Company, provided caravans to provide sleeping accommodation for LDV on observation duty. This watch on the Manx coast and sky has a parallel in the same type of role created in Eire, where a Coastwatching Service, known colloquially as the 'Saygulls' was established. This service manned eighty-three Look-Out Posts around Eire's 2,800 miles of coastline and provided accurate and constant reporting on sea and air movements.[34] Given that the Manx LDV manned fifty-two similar posts on a much smaller coast watch, it is likely that they offered an even more effective first line of defence.

Within a relatively short space of time, the Manx LDV had recruited 2,500 men, established an infrastructure for the new force, begun the acquisition of weapons, started weapons training, and established an all-island watch. As Home Guard Major, S W Corlett MBE, remembered, 'by the middle of July 1940 the Isle of Man Zone was thoroughly organised as an irregular fighting force, and by this time more modern rifles and ammunition were to hand'.[35] From this base, the Manx LDV would grow in sophistication and military worth.

Organisation and re-organisation
The first reorganisation of the Manx LDV replaced the six town-based 'groups' with a 1st Manx Battalion, based on Douglas with around 1,200 volunteers, and a 2nd Manx Battalion, consisting of five independent detachments – Ramsey Company, Castletown Company, Peel Company, Laxey Platoon, and Ballaugh–Michael Platoon – under Zone Headquarters in Douglas. Each company had approximately 357 men, while platoon numbers were around eighty-nine, and sections were approximately twenty-two men. The Manx Battalions were, in turn, under the command of Western Command, included in the West Lancashire Area.

In addition to the LDV battalions, the junior section of the Officers Training Corps (OTC) at King William's College, at Ronaldsway, which had been established in 1911, also provided fifty-one cadets, who were integrated into the Castletown Company. These were not the only boys to serve with the Manx battalions, as an 'appeal in the island's newspapers during May 1942, was made to boys under the age of seventeen to become affiliated to the 1st M[anx] B[attalion] as messengers, orderlies and guides. By 23 May, twenty-four boys had joined'.[36]

The Manx LDV was tasked with routine manning of the Observation Posts, the protection of vulnerable points, assisting with civil defence, and reporting to police suspicious incidents or the presence of suspicious persons in the neighbourhood.[37] This latter role had a particular significance on the island, as it not only included the usual watch for Fifth Columnists or enemy agents, but also for escapees from the island's internment camps. On the night of 22 September 1941, for example, five IRA men and a member of the British Union of Fascists, Arthur Mason, broke out from Peveril Camp at Peel. Mason and two IRA men, including a noted IRA commander, Joe Walker, headed for Castletown via Glen Maye. Their progress was greatly hindered by Home Guard patrols, although the three men did escape from the island in a stolen boat, only to be recaptured by the Royal Navy.[38]

The tasking of the Home Guard was, of course, different if the island was invaded. In that situation the volunteers would have been mustered by the sounding of alarms, and the force had five key tasks:

- Rounding up parachutists within a limited radius
- To give battle in towns and villages so as to deny to the enemy the use of roads essential to his advance
- Observation and the prompt and accurate reporting of information to the nearest military commander
- Providing guides for troops of the regular army
- Co-operation in measures for the immobilisation of petrol.[39]

The Manxmen received new battledress in February 1941, to replace their LDV denim overalls; boots, anklets and other equipment was also issued. The change in appearance was also matched, in April 1941, by a change in title, from LDV to Home Guard. However, on the Isle of Man this threw up a legal problem. As the Local Defence Volunteers, the force had been established under an 1886 Act of Parliament that allowed the Manx government to raise a volunteer force. However, the Home Guard had the status of a British Army Corps, and its officers held commissions. This was not covered by the 1886 Act, and it took an Order in Council in May 1942 to regularise the position of the Manx Home Guard.

The change from LDV to Home Guard also renewed the old Manx Volunteers' connection with the King's (Liverpool) Regiment, as the Manxmen sported the King's 'White Horse of Hanover' cap badge on their headgear, with 'Isle of Man' on their shoulder flashes. Despite a call from at least one officer of the 1st Manx Battalion that the Home Guard should be allowed to wear the famous 'Triskelion', the 'Three Legs of Man', all the photographic evidence suggests that the wartime Home Guard only wore the King's Regiment cap badge.[40] The connection with the King's Regiment saw officers from that regiment appointed as adjutants to each Manx Battalion, and in February 1942, the independent detachments of the 2nd Battalion were re-organised along the same lines as the 1st Battalion, as a fully integrated command, under Lieutenant-Colonel G W Howie who in civil life was the Agricultural Organiser for the Isle of Man.[41] By the winter of 1941/42, the Manx Home Guard was a more tightly organised, better trained and equipped force than it had been the year before. Changes in doctrine concerning the use of Home Guard units, in addition to the improved capabilities of the Home Guard brought changed roles and new training.

An established force

The Manx Home Guard began to develop an offensive capacity in the winter of 1941/42, with a new emphasis on 'fighting patrols'. As Major Corlett remembered, 'fighting patrol work had now become a very important part of Home Guard training, and every company had been required to form as many patrols as possible'.[42] To add impetus to this training, a number of inter-company competitions were established, and the Manxmen competed fiercely against each other at camps and weekends. During the autumn of 1942 fighting patrol work was superseded by Battle Platoon training, and Major Corlett believed that as a result of intensive training during the winter of 1942/43 'the Force was fully armed and very efficient'.[43] A surviving 1st Battalion exercise brief held at the Manx National Heritage Library, dated 17 June 1944, gives a clear picture of high tactical expectations of the Home Guard, which was able to draw on motor transport, and deploy mobile wireless communication. The task for the fighting platoons in the exercise was to find and engage 'German paratroops (which have been) dropped in several parts of the island [. . .] their object, in all cases, seems to be to disrupt communications [. . .] there is an important Wireless Station in KIRK MICHAEL, and an important Radio Location Station near GOB Y DEIGAN 760 100'.[44] By 17 June 1944, it was highly unlikely that the Germans could, in fact, deploy paratroops in this fashion, but there was a fear that commando style operations might be mounted to distract the western allies from the invasion of Normandy.

The Manx Home Guard also gained extra firepower in March 1942, when an anti-tank unit was created – 'Manx Troop Artillery, Home Guard' – under Captain H S Cain. This unit consisted of fifty-seven men with Hotchkiss 6pdr guns, configured for the anti-tank role. The following year, in October 1943, women were enrolled in the Manx Home Guard, first as 'nominated women', then as Women Home Guard Auxiliaries, who took on driving, clerk, cooking and telephonists' roles. In all, seventy women served in the Manx Home Guard.[45]

By September 1944, when it was generally realised that there was no longer the possibility of an invasion of the UK, the Manx Home Guard was an established force. Some idea of its military capability was given by Major P D Kissack MBE, in his record of the Southern Company of the 2nd Battalion Manx Home Guard. On the 30 September 1944, the Southern Company's weapons inventory stood at: 172, .300 P17 rifles; ten, .303 rifles; eight, EY Cup Dischargers [a rifle attachment designed for lobbing grenades]; seven, Enfield .303 long rifles; 5, .22 target rifles; twelve, Lewis light machine guns; thirteen Browning machine guns; and sixty Sten sub machine guns. For these weapons, the Southern Company held 147,292 rounds of

.300 ammunition, 7,955 rounds of .303, 18,614 rounds of Sten ammunition, 1,627 No. 36 Mills grenades, 154 No. 74 Sticky bombs (anti-tank), and 168, No. 75 land mines.[46] The force had come a long way from Boer War rifles and shotguns.

Scots in Arms

As Brian Osborne's history of the Home Guard in Scotland, *The People's Army*, shows, in most respects the history of the Home Guard in Scotland was much the same as that in the rest of Britain. That should come as no surprise, in that the majority of Scots lived the same type of urban, industrial life as the majority of the English or Welsh population. Neither was there the same political and national background that made Northern Ireland different in many respects, although the religious divide was strong, particularly on the west coast, and in Edinburgh and Glasgow where political Protestantism was still a force to be reckoned with, and the Roman Catholic Church held sway among Scots of Irish origin. However, there were aspects of the experience of the Home Guard in Scotland that reflected geographic and social differences to conditions in the rest of the UK, particularly in relation to remote and difficult terrain, and areas with sparse populations.

Charles Graves' contemporary account of the Home Guard contains a range of reports from Scottish Home Guard units. These include graphic accounts of Home Guard heroism during the intense Clydebank Blitz of the nights of Thursday 13, and Friday 14 March 1941, when this important shipbuilding and repair area was heavily attacked by the Luftwaffe. Over 400 bombers destroyed the town, killing 528 people, and seriously wounding 617 others, while over 35,000 people were made homeless. During this sustained attack A Company, 2 Battalion Dumbartonshire Home Guard, Clydebank, was on duty throughout, and two volunteers were killed, along with seventeen seriously wounded. The second in command of the 2nd Battalion Dumbartonshire Home Guard took up the story of the Home Guard during the Clydebank Blitz, an account that can be taken as representative of Home Guard actions throughout the UK during air attack:

> When the sirens sounded on March 13, 1941, [. . .] A Company were all training at their various centres. On making an early reconnaissance from my headquarters I could tell that with the number of enemy aircraft overhead the town was likely to be subject to heavy bombing. I immediately, as second-in-command of the Battalion, ordered the stand-to of all ranks to assist in whatsoever capacity they could, i.e. fire-fighting, rescue work,

demolition, controlling traffic, and generally assisting Civil Defence, police, etc.

As the Works Companies were concentrated within their own works endeavouring to deal with fire-fighting, it was left to A Company to give all the necessary assistance possible in Clydebank. [...] The same thing happened on Friday night, March 14, 1941, when the enemy came over the town again and subjected the town to an even more intense bombardment. [...] All ranks of the Company will always remember two members of the Company who were killed in assisting to clear people from houses where there were large unexploded bombs, viz., Pte. C. Campbell and Pte. S. Dennis, and seventeen others who were badly injured and taken to hospital. [...] Undoubtedly very many acts of heroism were performed by members of the Company during both nights, but it is pleasing to note that the Company had the great honour to receive several awards, viz., Cpl. James Stewart, who was awarded the BEM, Military Division, for his great example and heroism. He stood by the telephone under intense bombardment until the telephone cables were severed. He then took charge of a party on rescue work, when he was instrumental in saving the lives of several civilians by getting them evacuated from the debris. Sgt. McKenzie, RM, was commended in the *London Gazette* for his bravery. CSM Duncan was also commended in the *London Gazette* for bravery and leadership. CQMS Bales, a disabled soldier from the last war, and Sgt. Paton, a young Home Guard soldier of this war, have latterly been commended through the Scottish Command for their work during the enemy action in March, 1941, and also their keenness in Home Guard duties and training since.[47]

These experiences were repeated throughout the United Kingdom, and the deliberate linking of 'CQMS Bales, a disabled soldier from the last war, and Sgt. Paton, a young Home Guard soldier of this war' neatly encapsulates the combination of youth and age that came to typify the composition of the force. The heroism displayed by the men of the Dumbartonshire Home Guard during the Clydebank blitz in fact gained more recognition. Platoon Commander A R Ballantyne was awarded the George Medal for his 'conspicuous courage, energy and determination' during the raids; while Duncan and Latimer received the King's Commendation for Brave Conduct, as did Sergeant McKenzie.[48]

If the Home Guard of Scotland's industrial belt had to face the full effects of the Luftwaffe's bombing capacity, in other areas of Scotland the difficulties arose out of remoteness and a sparse population, itself the result of the Clearances that had forcibly depopulated the Highlands and Islands. Captain McCormack reported that, for the 1st Sutherland Home Guard, 'the great difficulty we have to contend with in this scattered Battalion Area is the long distances to be travelled by the Battalion Commander in visiting his Platoons and Companies, in some cases 160 miles there and back'.[49] A fascinating account of the Home Guard in this remote area was given by William Scroggie, who served with the LDV in Dundee, then as an officer with the Cameronians.[50] Before seeing active service with the 1st Battalion, Lovat Scouts in Italy from 1943–45, Scroggie was responsible for training the Home Guard in Sutherland in anti-parachute tactics, and later gave a fascinating insight into society and life in the Sutherland Home Guard.

William Scroggie was born, to Scots parents, in British Columbia in 1919, but returned to Scotland with his parents at the age of three. He received a middle-class Scots' education at John Watson's, took his Higher Leaving Certificate, and went to work at the famous Scottish publishers, D C Thomson in Dundee. When war was declared, he said that, as a nineteen-year-old he was 'absolutely thrilled', for, as he said:

> One of the snags is that the young don't realise what a rotten thing war is, so they are always spoiling for a fight. And all of us being young, and being in jobs, which you half liked and half didn't, it seemed a dramatic way of getting away from the humdrum everyday affairs of life [. . .]. We were delighted when war broke out![51]

Not surprisingly, Scroggie immediately volunteered for officer training, as he 'had a leaving certificate and a half decent education'. While waiting for call-up, he joined the Dundee LDV as soon as it was formed:

> We manned strategic points in Dundee – railway junctions, telephone exchanges, at night and so forth. We were armed with rather antiquated P14 rifles coming from the United States, Ross rifles. And it was rather good fun because there was a mixture of young laddies like myself and the old grey beards from the First World War who could tell us stories.[52]

Scroggie was a marvellous story-teller himself, and provided a small insight into Scottish social mores:

> I was a LDV man, not a Home Guard man, it hadn't come to be called that. There were two companies in Dundee, and I belonged

to the West End Company [...] The ancient division of Dundee into the East End and the West End. The West End, the posh area, the East End, the not so posh area.[53]

His commanding officer was a Dundee solicitor, and he remembered others in his company as including a stockbroker, another solicitor and a grocer, all of whom were Great War veterans. And, in middle-class style, his LDV 'uniform' consisted of 'a sports jacket and a pair of flannel trousers, with a distinctive forage cap'.[54]

From the LDV, Scroggie joined the 7 Battalion, The Cameronians, and trained in mountain warfare in Speyside, where Scots trained alongside Indian mountain troops. While at Bridge of Allen, in September 1941, his commanding officer asked for a volunteer to train the Sutherland Home Guard in anti-parachute tactics. The concern was that the Germans would attempt to attack the vital Royal Navy base at Scapa Flow in the Orkney Islands, and that as part of such an assault, airborne troops would be landed on the mainland, in Caithness and Sutherland, to act as a flank guard to the main assault on the Orkneys. The Germans had, in fact, at the very outset of the war attacked the navy in Scapa Flow, when the famous U-boat ace, Günther Prien, took U47 into the base and sank HMS *Royal Oak*, with substantial loss of life. This fear of airborne assault meant that the Home Guard in the area were tasked with anti-parachute roles, and Scroggie was despatched to train these men.

Scroggie's account of his training role in the far north of Scotland provides a fascinating insight to the Home Guard of Sutherland:

I got to Brora, which is on the east coast of Sutherland, to the Links Hotel, manager, D.L. MacCrae [...] and he was the adjutant of the local Home Guard. The commanding officer was the Duke of Sutherland. Now, the Duke of Sutherland did not know much about warfare. He knew quite a lot about getting off with the girls, him and the Prince of Wales were notorious in their younger days.[55]

If the Duke of Sutherland did not possess the necessary qualities to be commanding officer of the Home Guard, Scroggie soon met an ex-soldier whom he thought did, and should have been the commanding officer:

I met a prowling, white-haired leonine character called Colonel Forbes-Robertson. If ever anybody looked like a soldier, and an exceedingly belligerent and dangerous one, it was him, even though he was in late middle age by this time. And he got from the First

World War, the VC, DSO and bar, MC and bar, but he didn't get on with the Duke of Sutherland, so he had been relegated to the job of patrol leader.[56]

Scroggie felt that there was an aristocratic elite at the top of the Sutherland Home Guard, and one that was insulated from some of the rigours of a country under rationing:

> The beautiful thing about this was that rationing was in full swing in the British Isles at the time. But all the platoon commanders of the Home Guard in Sutherland were lairds and landowners, and it was as if the war did not exist there! These chaps still had oysters coming up from London, they'd got champagne, vats of white wine. There was a rumour that one of them when he had heard that the war was coming on, emptied his private petrol pump, cleaned it out, and filled it with malt whisky![57]

The petrol pump filled with whisky might well have been a marvellous apocryphal story, a sort of aristocratic *Whisky Galore*,[58] but it puts into relief the impact of rationing on the Home Guard. As civilians, they received the civilian scale of rations, yet often had to take part in exercises and training, in addition to the civilian jobs. Brian Osborne made the point with reference to a report of the Fife Home Guard, made by its adviser, the Earl of Elgin: 'On occasion it could be noticed that the strain of working hard all day and doing strenuous duties at night told its tale [...] at one parade of over 500 men, mostly country men at that, a look of under-nourishment was plainly to be seen, which seems to indicate that (for Home Guards at least) should have been of equal quantity to that given to the serving man, as those then serving in the County had a "well-fed" look as compared to the Home Guard on parade'.[59] It was the ordinary 'country men' that William Scroggie had most admiration for: 'there were the grizzled veterans from the First World War, some of them were just splendid blokes, still speaking the Gaelic'.[60] It was with these men that Scroggie spent much of September 1941, in 'glorious weather' helping them bring in the harvest.

Following his training duties with the Sutherland Home Guard, Scroggie undertook further mountain warfare training in the Canadian Rockies. He then saw active service in the Apennines with the Lovat Scouts. A few days before the end of the war in Italy, one of his men, a carpenter in civilian life, had an arm blown off by a mine. In going to his aid, Scroggie stepped on another mine, which blew his leg off, and blinded him. After convalescence, he went on to study at Dundee University, and, years later, Scroggie commented:

And the funny thing is, people say, "what a terrible thing, you were blinded and lost a leg in the war, and all the rest of it". Not a bit of it! Once you've adapted yourself to the situation, you just carry on living, without any sense of deprivation whatsoever! I have lived as full, and as interesting, and as an adventurous a life as anybody who survived the war, and I would not change the life I've had since the war – as I am, blind and with a tin leg. I would not change that with anybody. It is interesting.[61]

That, perhaps, could stand as a testament to the bravery of Scots in arms.

Welsh Dragon

On the night of 12/13 July 1940, an eighteen-year-old volunteer in the 3rd Monmouthshire (Newport) Battalion, LDV, Gwyn Jones, was a member of a guard posted in defence of a vital point:

> The post was bombed, one man being killed and another seriously wounded. Volunteer Jones, who was himself in a place of safety, heard the groans of the wounded man and at once left shelter and carried him on his back under cover. During this time, bombs, debris, large pieces of steel work and heavy glass were still falling and Volunteer Jones carried out his task with complete disregard for his own safety. His courageous behaviour set a fine example to all those present.[62]

This young Welshman was the first member of the LDV to win a military decoration – the Military Medal – and the casualties sustained that night were the first LDV casualties caused by enemy action during the war.

The Home Guard in Wales, as in the rest of the UK, varied between the scattered companies of thinly populated rural areas, like that of the North Wales district, and the Glamorgan area. The 4th Glamorgan (Neath) Battalion, for example, was one of the largest in the UK, yet the battalion's report for the Graves' account noted that by July 1940 when a 'mass Battalion Parade was held at Neath. The majority of these men wore uniform and many carried rifles [. . .] quite a creditable achievement [. . .] in those early days'.[63] One of the Neath men was John Stuart Mill, who had served with the 1st Battalion, the Rifle Brigade, on the Western Front from 1916–1918. He joined the LDV at his sheet steel factory – the Neath Steel Sheet and Galvanising Company – in 1940, and was promoted eventually to the rank of Major in charge of a Home Guard Company composed of his works' platoon and two other local works' platoons. The combination of important industrial manufacturing work allied to local defence was typical of industrial workers throughout South Wales, and, indeed, throughout the UK. The 7th Glamorgan Battalion also provided an example of the willingness of vital industrial workers to defend the country, and the additional sacrifices these men routinely made:

> One incident was the rumour that enemy paratroops had landed in the area of B Company. Without orders, every available man of the Company reported at his Headquarters fully armed and ready for action. As most of these men were miners, the local colliery did not work that shift. Needless to say, compensation was not asked for, neither did the men claim subsistence allowance. As some of the guard-posts are situated right on the tops of the high mountains the trials and discomforts of the guards in all sorts of weather can be imagined. Even in summer-time it is cold and damp at these heights, but these volunteers cheerfully carry out their task.[64]

Remembering his time as officer commanding the three works' platoons, and with the knowledge of two years' service on the Western Front in the Great War, Major Mill believed that his Neath volunteers would have performed well: 'I think the Home Guard would have given a good account of themselves if they had been called on. They weren't like "*Dad's Army*", they were well trained, I can tell you that now. Very well'.[65]

Conclusion: All the British Isles

There were interesting differences in the development of the Home Guard in parts of the UK, particularly in Northern Ireland, where historical and political conditions had a profound influence on the formation and organisation of the force. But in all the constituent parts of the UK, volunteers flocked to join, as is evidenced by the case of the Isle of Man, where it was thought that its small population could only support a force of around 1,000, but which actually fielded 2,500 volunteers. From rural Sutherland to industrial South Wales, and from the Isle of Man to Northern Ireland, the response to the threat of invasion, and the need to contribute to national defence throughout the war, was the same throughout the United Kingdom.

Chapter 6

Home Guard Lives

All the People

The Home Guard drew into its ranks a true cross section of the British population – in all its variety. The popular contemporary perception of the force as being filled with ageing men, often veterans of the First World War, represents only a partial truth. In addition to these men, Home Guard units also contained young men waiting call up into the regular forces, women, and non-British subjects. In this chapter, the personal histories of ten individuals who served in the Home Guard will be used to illustrate the way in which the organisation encompassed all sections of the British population – specifically, 'enemy aliens', First World War veterans, women, boys, and young men. Home Guards' accounts of their wartime lives also show how for many people service with the Home Guard was a central part of their wartime life on the Home Front. Finally, personal histories present us with insights into the impact on individuals of government policy.

'Enemy Aliens'

Joseph Otto Flatter served in the trenches for two and a half years with the Austro-Hungarian Army in the First World War fighting both the Italian and British armies. In the Second World War he served with the British Home Guard. Peter Hariolf Plesch was born in Frankfurt in 1918, the son of a German Army frontline doctor who had seen extensive active service during the First World War. A research chemist, he served with the Maidenhead Home Guard, and witnessed the first V1 flying bomb attacks on England. The stories of Joseph Flatter and Peter Plesch reflect the confused reality of life for many people across Europe faced with a total war.

Peter Plesch's father had been Albert Einstein's doctor in Berlin. That alone made the prospect of living under the new Nazi regime difficult, but when added to the fact that the Plesch family were Jewish, made it impossible for them to stay in Germany. Peter Plesch was fourteen when he arrived in England, and already fluent in French, German and English (having had a Scots nanny in Berlin), he was educated at Harrow, before going up to Cambridge University to read natural sciences. His father, who had actively helped other German Jewish refugees escape from Germany, had the foresight to have the entire Plesch family naturalised as British subjects in January 1939. This, unfortunately, was not the case for Joseph Flatter, an Anglophile Austrian artist who came to England in 1934, a year after Peter Plesch and his family fled Germany. Flatter had made no attempt to exchange his Austrian citizenship for British citizenship, even after Hitler's incorporation of Flatter's homeland into the Nazi Third Reich in 1938. In 1918, Flatter was on the Italian front when he was nearly killed by a shell fired by British troops supporting the Italians:

> A British shell nearly killed me. It landed so close to me, my impression was of glass splitting, so many plates of glass splitting. I thought it was the last moment of my life. But when I recovered found that I was still alive [...] I mention this because I am now a Britisher and live, peacefully, in Britain.[1]

Flatter, and his pianist wife, Hilda Lorwa, visited London in the early 1930s, and they both decided that England was a better place to live than their homeland: 'There was poverty and unemployment in London too, but there was not the class hatred we had experienced at home. Life in England, we felt, had dignity and grace. We decided to stay in England'.[2] Flatter's Anglophile stance was strengthened after the Nazi occupation of Austria. He began to produce anti-Nazi cartoons. Later, while in the Home Guard, he would produce a cartoon for the Ministry of Information that contrasted what he saw as a typically British attitude to victory, with the German attitude. In the cartoon, 'How They Celebrate Their Victories' one panel shows an ARP warden giving the thumbs up to a Home Guard. The Home Guard says, 'Hullo, chum, heard Paris is ours?', and the warden replies, 'Grand, isn't it'. This was contrasted with a scene of Nazi mass hysteria, with 'Sieg Heil' blaring from tannoys and wild singing of the German national anthem.

Despite his anti-Nazi views, Flatter was caught up in the British government's programme of the mass internment of all 'enemy aliens' in the spring and early summer of 1940. The fear of Fifth Column activity by people of German or Italian origin, led to the internment of 27,000 people between May and July 1940.[3] Many of those interned were Jewish refugees from Germany, long-term residents of the UK of Italian or German origin, or, like Flatter, Anglophile anti-Nazis. No effort was, at first, made to discriminate between those who were refugees from Axis countries, and those who were pro-Nazi or pro-Fascist. As well as these internees, over 1,000 British fascists, IRA activists, and pro-Nazis were also interned.[4] For internees like Flatter, it was a shock:

I was called to a tribunal [...] and I was called an 'enemy alien'. One day two policemen arrived in my studio [...] they declared that they had never arrested an artist before. They asked my wife to prepare a small suitcase for a weekend, and told her that it was only for a short time that I would be held.[5]

Flatter was held on the Isle of Man, where holiday boarding houses were converted to internment camps[6] holding the whole range of internees. Flatter explained that in the camp he acted as cook:

I cooked for eighty people, with the help of two assistants. One was a bank clerk from Vienna, one was a Scotsman who had been born in Germany, but had been taken to Scotland when he was one year old, and he had never bothered to apply for British nationality [...] His Scottish was quite unintelligible to me![7]

There was another Scot with Flatter, a man with two sons in the British Army, but who was being held because he had expressed anti-Churchill views. Those 'enemy aliens' who were anti-Nazi quickly identified their pro-Nazi peers to the authorities. As a result, men like Flatter were often released relatively quickly. In his case, after two months.

While the refugees from the Nazis were surprised to be interned, Peter Plesch explained that his friends who were Jewish refugees, but, unlike him, had not been able to take British citizenship, understood the policy. Plesch explained his view of the government's internment policy:

I thought that it was very understandable, but mishandled in a very unfortunate way. And we [Jewish refugees] excused it, among ourselves, in the following terms – that all the really bright people who could have worked it out much more methodically were busy with other things. And the rules that did not distinguish between a German Jewish refugee and a German sailor whose ship happened to be in a British harbour, were not [efficient]. This was simply due to the general dimness of the people doing it, and they were in no way malevolent. This was something that we liked to believe, it was a comforting thought. We were not aware of any malevolence, animosity, against refugees. It may have happened, but I never came across it.[8]

In fact, the background to the decision to intern all 'enemy aliens' was characterised by political rivalries, and the competing interests of different government departments, not least between the security services and the Home Office. Further, there was the all-pervading and generalised fear of the Fifth Column, which overshadowed much policy making, especially in the summer of 1940. As the ex-internee, and later British Army officer, Roland Stent commented in his history of internment: 'It is a tale full of muddle, misunderstanding and maladroitness'.[9] There is, nonetheless, a sense in Peter Plesch's account that the government made a mistake in rounding up so many people who were the natural allies of Britain in its war with Nazi Germany. Indeed, many internees subsequently went on to have notable military careers in the British armed forces, and some 10,000 of Britain's 'enemy aliens' fought with Britain.[10] In the case of Joseph Flatter, he was too old to serve in the regular forces, but on release from interment, he took British citizenship and joined the Home Guard in London: 'I started with the Home Guard when I took British citizenship, and I was allowed to have a rifle, and join the company of [other] London people'.[11] Flatter was employed by the Ministry of Information, the Free French and the Free Belgian governments in exile to produce anti-Nazi cartoons which were used in leaflets and newspapers dropped into occupied Europe. After the war, he also discovered that his cartoons had been used in Soviet propaganda too. Many of Flatter's cartoons are today held at the Imperial War Museum, testament to one 'enemy alien's' love of England, and hatred of Nazism. Joseph Flatter also had the distinction of being, along with David Low, one of the two official British cartoonists at the Nuremburg trials.

Peter Plesch, too, made a contribution to British war effort, with his work as a research chemist, working on substitutes for strategic materials like balsawood. During two years in a research unit near Maidenhead, Plesch served with the Home Guard, where, as he put it, he rose to the dizzy heights of 'temporary, acting, unpaid lance-corporal'. It was while enjoying this rank, in charge of a night time guard on Maidenhead's Thames bridges, that some of the first V1 'Doodlebug' missiles were launched at Britain:

> In Maidenhead I was a member of the Home Guard, and one night I happened to be in charge of the section which mounted guard on the big road and rail bridges over the Thames at Maidenhead [. . .] My company had charge of mounting guard on these bridges, and one night I was in charge, and the alert went. And we couldn't hear the aircraft, and the 'all clear' didn't go, and it was bright daylight before we got the 'all clear'. So, we had to keep the platoon stood to all night, and every now and then we heard a strange noise, described as a two stroke engine in rather bad repair, which would suddenly cut out and then there was a loud bang. And we didn't know what it was, and I phoned through to headquarters, and they didn't know. Nobody knew what it was, we were

just told to keep on alert throughout the night. And that was the first V1 attack.[12]

Later, Plesch was caught in a V2 attack in London, but survived both that, and the war, to go on to be one of the founding academics of Keele University, and professor of chemistry.

Service in the Home Guard was not the only contribution that thousands of 'enemy aliens' made during the Second World War, but both Flatter and Plesch can be taken as representative of the thousands of émigrés and refugees who gave such valuable service on the British Home Front.

Old Soldiers, Sailors and Airmen

For two veterans of the First World War, Cyril Punt and Edward Hillson, service in the Home Guard represented just one element in their military careers over two world wars. Edward Hillson was born in 1896, and served with the Cheshire Regiment in Britain from 1916–1917, then with the East Lancashire Regiment and the Welch Regiment on the Western Front during 1917 and early 1918. He was a sergeant when he transferred to the newly formed Royal Air Force in 1918, and was trained as an observer. He joined the Local Defence Volunteers (LDV) at the outset, and went on to be the Company Commander of Cosham Home Guard in Hampshire.

Cyril Punt was also in his early forties when he joined the LDV in Tyneside. He had served as an officer in the merchant marine from 1912–1915, had then transferred to the Royal Navy, serving as a leading seaman at Gallipoli and on HMS *Courageous* in the North Sea. He joined the LDV as soon as it was established, and spent six months in it before returning to sea as a lieutenant in the Royal Navy Volunteer Reserve (RNVR). He spent five years, during and after the war, on the hazardous task of mine sweeping on the north east coast, off Scapa Flow, and off Norway in 1945.

Both these veterans of the First World War provided interesting insights into the LDV and Home Guard. Cyril Punt's account of his long and varied naval and military service included a fascinating account of the early days of the LDV, while Edward Hillson's experiences as a company commander in the Home Guard informed his account of local defence in Hampshire. One similarity in their accounts of the LDV and Home Guard at opposite ends of England, one in a rural area close to Portsmouth, and one in a mining and industrial area, is the role of class both in the creation of the LDV, and the day to day operation of the Home Guard. In the north east, Cyril Punt described the key organising role of a local landowner, while Edward Hillson's account of his Home Guard unit stressed the middle-class nature of his officers.

Cyril Punt was a forty-three-year-old married man, with two young children, employed in the then new industrial estate of Team Valley, Gateshead, when the call came for volunteers for the LDV:

> Then one night I came home, listening to the nine o'clock news, and Sir Anthony Eden came on the radio and told us of the fall of France [...] and we'd have to form a citizen's home guard. So, would anybody with experience who could help in any way report to the nearest police station. And after it was broadcast, I said to the wife, 'Well, what do you think of that?' She said, 'I think you ought to go to the police station'.[13]

Following that marital conference, Punt then went to volunteer. His account illustrates the key role class had in the formation of the LDV in his area:

> I went to the police station and saw an inspector, and they ushered us all into a big hall there and sat us down, and a local man, Colonel Scott-Owen, he had no roof in his mouth, so they say, well, he stuttered a lot, he addressed us. He apparently was a land agent for Lord Lampton from around here, apparently a big noise in the coal industry [...] He asked us to attend the next day at one o'clock. We met Scott-Owen, he said they'd picked out certain people that they were going to nominate to take charge and try and organise their little districts. And my name was down to take charge of Leamside. Don't know why they got me, because I'd never had any officer qualifications in the [Royal] navy. I had officer qualifications in the merchant service, of course. I got nominated. Before I knew where I was I was in charge of a crowd of people, old and young.[14]

In Cyril Punt's account of the foundation of his local LDV unit, and his appointment, in all probability a result, despite his modesty, of his merchant marine officer qualifications, the local landowner and industrialist, and his agent, played a pivotal part in command appointments to the LDV. Class also played a part in Edward Hillson's account of the Home Guard in Cosham, Hampshire. Having been an NCO in both the army and the RAF in the First World War, Hillson joined the LDV at the outset, and was eventually promoted to lieutenant, then captain, and officer-in-charge of the Cosham Company. A salesman himself in civilian life, he described the officers of his platoons: 'My second-in-command was a director of a motor company in Portsmouth. I had a couple of solicitors, and a good cross-section of various other jobs'.[15] Cyril Punt spent six months in the LDV following its formation, prior to his return to the sea as a lieutenant in the RNVR. He gave a detailed picture of the force in the early days, characterised by no uniforms, little in the way of weapons, and a brief to watch for paratroops. Women were immediately involved in supporting the LDV volunteers, as Punt explained: 'All the women were making black armbands with white tape "LDV" on them. You had to wear them every time you come on duty. [...] Just the black band, with LDV on it'.[16]

As the volunteer in charge of the Leamside platoon, Punt only had eighteen men. That compared to the figure of thirty-four men a platoon commander would have in the army. Punt was armed with his own revolver, which had an interesting history, and his platoon had three shotguns, which they carried while patrolling for enemy paratroops:

> There was eighteen of us altogether. We had to divide it up so that so many turned out for each air raid warning. In those days all we were looking for was airmen being landed. [The only weapons were] local shotguns. I had my revolver I had at sea. Most merchant navy officers those days carried a revolver because you used to have Chinese and coolie crews. We had three shotguns we had got from local farmers.[17]

In addition to patrolling for enemy paratroops, or airmen, Punt and his men decided that they needed a base, or a bunker. Most of his men were coal miners, and they used their skills to create a bunker. From Punt's description, that particular defence works had all the characteristics of a club house for the LDV:

> We had a meeting hall in the Londonderry Hall which was loaned to us [but] we also built a dug out in the side of a hill, where we had a fire and a heating apparatus, and we had a little fortress. We dug into this old pit heap and shored it up, the men that were in this knew what they were doing and made a good job of it, and we had quite a little cave in there, ten foot by ten foot. And we could go there and make coffee. Outside there was a little bit of a rampart, sand bagged up, so it looked like an army post.[18]

Another appeal broadcast over the radio brought Punt's LDV career to an end, and saw him return to naval service. The impetus behind the general appeal for retired naval officers was the magnetic mine threat of 1940/1.

Cyril Punt's accounts of a hastily organised, undermanned force of men with few weapons and a very limited idea of their role in the early days of the LDV, contrasts with Edward Hillson's account of the Home Guard in Cosham. As Hillson himself noted, being in Portsmouth's hinterland, the

Home Guard 'had to keep on our toes' throughout the war. Hillson explained how his three platoons were divided between three local areas, while he had his headquarters in Cosham itself:

> My company, the Cosham Company, was responsible for Portsdown Hill, that's the hill behind. In theory, we knew every blade of grass on there – I didn't – fields of fire, and all kinds of things. I had a company with four platoons. We had one platoon called Christchurch platoon, we had a platoon, or part of a platoon, up in the church tower on top of the hill. Another platoon in Drayton, another platoon in Farlington. My HQ was at the drill hall [...] then in the Masonic Hall, at the end of Albert Road in Cosham [...] I had an office there, a quartermaster's store, and so forth.[19]

The service of Edward Hillson and Cyril Punt illustrates the role played by the veterans of the First World War in the foundation and the continued operation of the Home Guard. Further, Cyril Punt's return to naval service, in his mid-forties, shows that experienced veterans still had a vital part to play on active, frontline service.

Women and guns

The issue of women and the Home Guard was a significant one from the outset. Sir Anthony Eden's appeal for volunteers for the LDV attracted some women as well as men. There were examples of women turning up at police stations throughout the country, only to be met with rebuffs, or uncertainty about their role.[20] It had not been the government's intention that women should join the LDV, but it is clear that local LDV commanders accepted women. Typically, these 'unofficial' women acted in auxiliary capacities, as secretaries, drivers, and in catering roles. Some women did, however, receive weapons training from LDV units. All this unofficial involvement by women led, in June 1940, to an official announcement that 'women cannot be enrolled in the LDV'.[21] As the government newspaper announcement put it the following year:

> The War Office has sent an order to all Home Guard units that the training of women as unofficial Home Guard units has not been authorised. Weapons and ammunition in the charge of the Army or of Home Guard units must not be used for the instruction of women and the name Home Guard is not permitted.[22]

But, for a number of reasons, the issue did not go away. Firstly, Home Guard units continued to co-opt 'unofficial' women, even after the Women's Voluntary Services (WVS), a civilian organisation, was given the role of providing support services for the Home Guard. Indeed, by late 1942, the government itself believed that as many as 50,000 women were serving, entirely unofficially, with the Home Guard.[23] Secondly, some women continued to press vigorously for their full incorporation in the Home Guard, on an equal basis with men. The key issue here was weapons training, the carrying of firearms, and the wearing of Home Guard uniform by women. Some prominent women maintained constant pressure on the government to permit the full participation in the Home Guard, while others took more direct action and set up rifle training for women.

The leading parliamentary advocate of women in the Home Guard was Dr Edith Summerskill, the Labour MP for Fulham West since 1938. She led a relentless campaign to have women accepted in a full combatant role within the Home Guard. She was only partially successful when, as part of a wider government debate late in 1942 about maintaining the Home Guard, it was finally accepted that women could be accepted, officially, in the organisation. They were to be termed 'nominated women', issued only with a small, plastic brooch badge, and not permitted to train with, or carry weapons. But, from the outset, women had trained with weapons. In the summer of 1940, the 'Amazon Defence Corps' was formed by Mrs Venetia Foster in London.[24] A more successful, and widespread, organisation was the Women's Home Defence Corps (WHD), led by Miss Watson–Williams, aided by Mavis Tate, the Conservative MP for Frome. The women of the WHD, which Dr Summerskill claimed had 30,000 members in April 1943,[25] undertook rifle training, often aided by their local Home Guard units.

Eventually, women were permitted to enrol as Home Guard Auxiliaries, but in a non-combatant role, with no uniform except the plastic brooch badge (although most women wore military style clothing, often using the brooch as a cap badge on berets, for example). The government set a ceiling of 80,000 women in the Home Guard in early 1943. However, 'by March 1944 only 28,000 women, most of whom had already been working unofficially with the Home Guard, were enrolled'.[26] As an example of the comparative numbers of women auxiliaries can be found in a surviving note of the total battalion strength of 7th Battalion, Northamptonshire Home Guard in late 1944. This indicates that there were seventy-one women auxiliaries spread around the seven companies of the battalion, which consisted of eighty-nine officers and 1,692 other ranks. Most of these women joined the battalion in the summer of 1944, although the earliest recruit, Miss Jean Baker, joined in August 1943. Of the seventy-five women, six resigned before the Home Guard was stood down, and one joined the regular armed forces.[27]

Despite the government ban on women in the Home Guard on equal terms with men, there is plenty of evidence that women were, in fact, incorporated into some units on equal terms. Ironically, the clearest evidence relates to government ministries' own Home Guard units. Penny Summerfield and Corinna Peniston-Bird's book on women and home defence identifies one such unit:

> Women working in the offices of government ministries: 130 women at the Ministry of Food, which had been evacuated to Colwyn Bay in North Wales, formed a unit affiliated to the WHD in September 1942. They were accepted as a 'women's section', wearing the WHD badge, by the Ministry of Food's Home Guard. The women were organised in six sections (administration, catering, communications, guides, intelligence and transport) and took part in night exercises.[28]

As members of the WHD, these women would have already had weapons training, but Ministry of Food Home Guard weapons training was also carried out.

Mary Warschauer was a twenty-year-old code and cipher clerk at the Air Ministry in London in 1940, and was part of the Air Ministry's own Home Guard. Their role was, in the event of invasion, to provide a defence for their offices. The Air Ministry Home Guard was made up of civilian men and women employees at the ministry. Mary Warschauer was part of a uniformed, armed, and active Home Guard unit, being involved in all the activities that the government declared that women could not be involved in. She remembered:

> We had a Home Guard there. There were men, civilian men, and women as well. There were about ten to twelve women, and about twenty men. And we went to practice rifle shooting [...] We wore air force blue, navy blue, dungarees, and little Glengarry type hats, both the men and women wore the same thing [...] The Captain used to train us, we did more than the Home Guard people would do [...] The Sten guns had just come into being then. They weren't issued to soldiers at that time, but we were allowed, we just had the one that we were allowed to practice on. We didn't fire it, but we did practice rifle shooting at the aerodrome.[29]

In addition, the Air Ministry Home Guard had grenade practice, with inert grenades, and took part in defence exercises:

> We used to go into St James' Park, and practice lobbing the hand grenades, not live ones. There was one girl, dear soul, she was rather podgy and looked like a baby elephant in this thing

[the uniform], and whenever she was throwing a grenade, she would duck before she threw it. [...] We had a mock raid on London, which a lot of people took part in, and we were up on the roof, and I tell you, my heart was in my mouth going up those iron rungs onto the Air Ministry roof, where we had a field telephone. It was a bitterly cold night [...] You could see all London as far as you could in the pitch black.[30]

Mary Warschauer had an eventful wartime life in London, with her cipher work at the Air Ministry, and her Home Guard service. In addition, she survived air raids, and a violent street assault by a Free French sailor. At the end of the war, she was a secretary with the British delegation to one of the first general assembly meeting of the United Nations, and later married a Holocaust survivor.

Women were also part of the secret, Home Guard dominated, Auxiliary Units. That 'stay behind' organisation, designed to be a fully prepared resistance, sabotage and assassination force behind the enemy lines in the event that Britain was invaded, was built around the Home Guard. The leading historian of the Auxiliary Units, John Warwicker, explained the link with the Home Guard: 'With very few exceptions, the men taken into the Auxiliary Units were selected from the Home Guard. The link is undeniable'.[31] But it was not just men who served, for, as Warwicker noted, from the very outset of the LDV and the Auxiliary Units, women were involved too:

By the autumn of 1940, a force including somewhere in the region of 3,500 'civvies', many recruited directly from the Local Defence Volunteers and the Home Guard, had grown from [...] small nuclei with unbelievable rapidity. Women had been absorbed too. All were volunteers for a suicide mission.[32]

These women, serving alongside the LDV and Home Guard recruits to the Auxiliary Units, came from a variety of sources. One of them was the twenty-three-year-old Maria Bloxam, who was a driver with the Women's Transport Service (FANY). The WTS was the new title given to the First Aid Nursing Yeomanry in 1936. The FANY had provided mounted, then motorised nursing auxiliaries for the armed services since 1907. Its role in providing strike-breaking drivers during the General Strike of 1926 led to its appearance on the official Army List.[33] In September 1938, at the time of the Munich Crisis, the driving section of the WTS was transferred to the women's Auxiliary Territorial Service (ATS) driver companies. However, the WTS continued in existence, providing support to the war effort, and, in the case of women like Maria Bloxam, service with the Auxiliary Units.

Early days: a mounted LDV patrol in the summer of 1940. Their only uniform item is an LDV armlet. The men are, however, all armed. (*Author's collection*)

Schools at war: Captain H L Allsopp (left) of Wellingborough School's OTC, standing next to Major General Sir Hereward Wake. Both men were significant officers in the Northamptonshire Home Guard; Sir Hereward Wake was the Commander of the Northants Home Guard from 1940–43, and Allsopp the officer commanding of the 7th Battalion, Northants Home Guard. The photograph, taken on the school's playing fields in the late summer of 1940, shows Allsopp wearing his OTC uniform; the only item of Home Guard uniform is a locally produced armlet. The school's Head Master, T S Nevill, is on the right. (*Wellingborough School*)

Ulster at war: men of the Ulster Local Defence Volunteers present arms at a parade in 1940. (*David Orr*)

Ulsterman: James Millar of the Belfast LDV, wearing the unique black denim uniform of the force in Northern Ireland. Later, they would, by stages, receive British Army khaki, but at first, they wore locally produced uniforms. Note, too, the cloth bandoliers for rifle ammunition. (*David Orr*)

Ulster Home Guard: Corporal T C Courtney of the Ulster Home Guard in his black uniform. The cap badge on his forage cap is that of the Royal Ulster Constabulary, which was the parent organisation of the force in Northern Ireland. Uniform buttons came from a variety of sources, including the old Royal Irish Constabulary. (*David Orr*)

Roadblock: throughout the force's life, one of its duties was the manning of roadblocks and checkpoints. Here LDV men guard a substantial, anti-tank, road block during the summer of 1940. (*Imperial War Museum*)

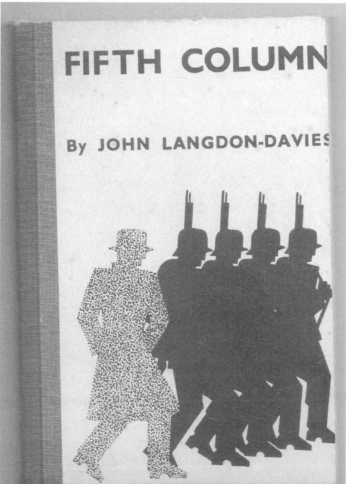

The enemy within: fear of the Fifth Column became almost a national panic during 1940, and provided one impetus behind the creation of the LDV. John Langdon-Davies was a well-known writer who had reported from the Spanish Civil War and the Russo-Finnish War of 1939–40. Langdon-Davies' book correctly identified fear of a Fifth Column as being more dangerous than any likelihood of a real, organised enemy within.
(*Author's collection*)

1,700 years of defence: the massive programme of defence works undertaken in 1940 and 1941 included the refortifying of Pevensey Castle, on the East Sussex coast. First fortified in AD 290, the extensive walls and towers of the castle were refortified with machine gun, anti-tank, and command bunkers. These were defended, in the summer of 1940, by men of the 4th Battalion Duke of Cornwall's Light Infantry, and the 21st (Eastbourne) Battalion, Sussex Home Guard. This preserved machine gun bunker shows how the new fortifications were integrated into the existing fabric of the castle.
(Author's photograph)

Women's armed defence: the issue of women carrying arms was a contested one. It is clear that some 'unofficial' women members of the Home Guard did train with, and bear arms. There were others, like these members of 'Women's Home Defence', probably in Watford, who regularly undertook weapons' training in addition to other wartime service.
(Mrs Harvey)

To the point: an LDV recruiting poster for the Manx force. It was hoped that the Isle of Man would be able to raise a force of 1,000 LDV volunteers. In fact, 2,000 came forward within a couple of weeks.
(Manx Aviation and Military Museum)

MANXMEN OF 17 TO 65

JOIN YOUR
DEFENCE VOLUNTEERS

TO DEFEND YOUR ISLAND IN YOUR ISLAND.

That's All!

ENROL AT ANY POLICE STATION OR BRANCH OF LEGION.

Manxmen: well-armed Manx Home Guard, fully equipped with rifles, Sten guns, and two aircraft pattern Lewis light machine guns. All the men and boys are wearing the cap badge of the King's Regiment (Liverpool). Volunteers on the island had a long association with the Liverpool regiment. (*Manx Aviation and Military Museum*)

(*Left*) Home Guard artefacts: surviving examples of the official, second pattern, LDV armlet, and the 'Home Guard' version which superseded it, along with the enamel lapel badge for wear in mufti. (*Author's collection*)

(*Right*) Self-improvement: publishers, in this case the famous left-wing publisher, Victor Gollancz, quickly produced self-help books for the Home Guard. The author of *Home Guard for Victory!* was Hugh Slater, who had been the successful officer in charge of the International Brigades' British battalion's anti-tank unit, prior to taking a staff command with the Brigades. (*Author's collection*)

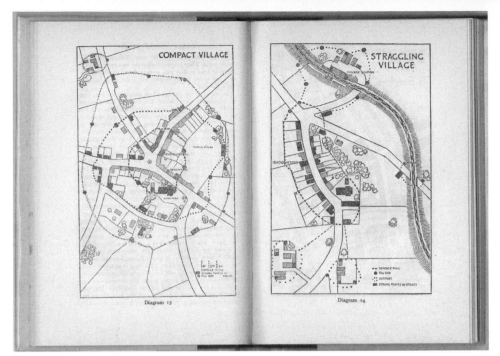

Local defence: Hugh Slater's book provided Home Guard readers with training notes on a wide variety of topics, including a chapter on the local defence organisations needed for different areas; here for two types of village – the 'compact village', and the 'straggling village'. (*Author's collection*)

(*Left*) More advice for the Home Guard: another 'how to' book that sold well, also by an ex-International Brigader, was *New Ways of War*, by the one-time commander of the British battalion, Tom Wintringham. Published in 1940, this Penguin Special paperback was full of practical advice for the new force. Wintringham, Slater, and other veterans of the Spanish Civil War did much to popularise extempore solutions to training and equipment shortages in 1940. (*Author's collection*)

(*Right*) Make it yourself: from Wintringham's *New Ways of War* – how to make a homemade grenade. Much easier to make was the Molotov Cocktail, manufactured by the hundred thousands in the summer of 1940, and believed by many to be some sort of solution to armoured warfare. (*Author's collection*)

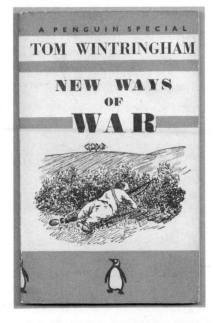

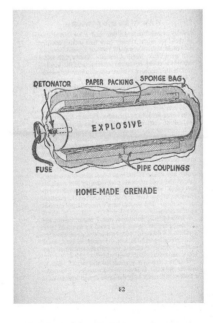

Pocket notes: 'Hints and Tips', this pocket-sized booklet was full of advice concerned with sabotage, silent killing, and setting booby traps. Although recommended by the publishers 'for Home Guard and service use', much of the advice was irrelevant for the Home Guard, given its tactical role. (*Author's collection*)

Advice in pictures: Home Guards received formal training in house to house fighting, where advance preparation was seen to be the key. This commercially published guide also included an illustration of the widely held view that a tank could be stopped by jamming a crowbar in the drive sprocket, or idler, of a tank. Even in this diagram, such an approach to anti-tank warfare seems suicidal and ineffective. (*Author's collection*)

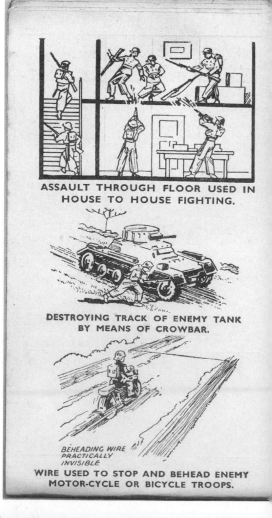

Scouts as guides: Boy Scouts were attached to Home Guard units, and acted in the role of guides and messengers. Here a Boy Scout, in the famous 'Wide-awake' hat, points the way to a Home Guard. (*The Scout Association*)

War service: Boy Scouts receiving rifle instruction from a Home Guard. The Boy Scout on the right is wearing the special armlet, bearing the legend, 'War Service Scout'.
(*The Scout Association*)

Home Guard heavy weapons: Home Guard receive training in the use of the Northover Projector, one of a number of weapons designed specifically for the force. The basic design task was to make cheap, easily manufactured weapons; something that was not always compatible with effectiveness or operator safety. (*Imperial War Museum*)

Anti-aircraft Home Guard: the force eventually provided considerable numbers of men for Anti-Aircraft Command, releasing over 100,000 regular gunners for the invasion of western Europe. Here two Home Guard operate a 'Z battery' anti-aircraft rocket system, this one located in Bootle, on Merseyside. (*Imperial War Museum*)

Home Guard armour: two Home Guard manned Beaverette Mk II light scout cars on patrol in the Scottish Highlands. Some 2,800 Beaverettes were built, using the Standard Motor Company, or Humber Super Snipe, car chassis. Designed in the post-Dunkirk period as a stop-gap vehicle for airfield defence, the Beaverette equipped regular army, then Home Guard units as well. For the Home Guard, this light armoured vehicle was the most useful armour it received in any numbers. (*Imperial War Museum*)

Badge of service: when women were finally admitted, in an official capacity, into the Home Guard, in 1943, they were only issued with this plastic brooch to show membership of the force. (*Bernard Lowry*)

Women in uniform: despite only being issued with the plastic brooch, members of the Women's Home Guard Auxiliary frequently contrived to wear some sort of uniform. Here, two of the women radio operators with the 5th Battalion (Ross-on-Wye) Herefordshire Home Guard are wearing dark, belted raincoats, dark slacks, the brooch, and 'Home Guard' armlets. The HGWA in the check jacket is Xyra J Lincoln. *(Bernard Lowry)*

Everyman: a souvenir photograph of the officers and NCOs of an unknown Home Guard unit in late 1944 or early 1945, possibly taken to mark the stand down of the force. The only clue to the unit or place is a faded note on the reverse of the photograph, 'Capt. Hobbs'. *(Author's collection)*

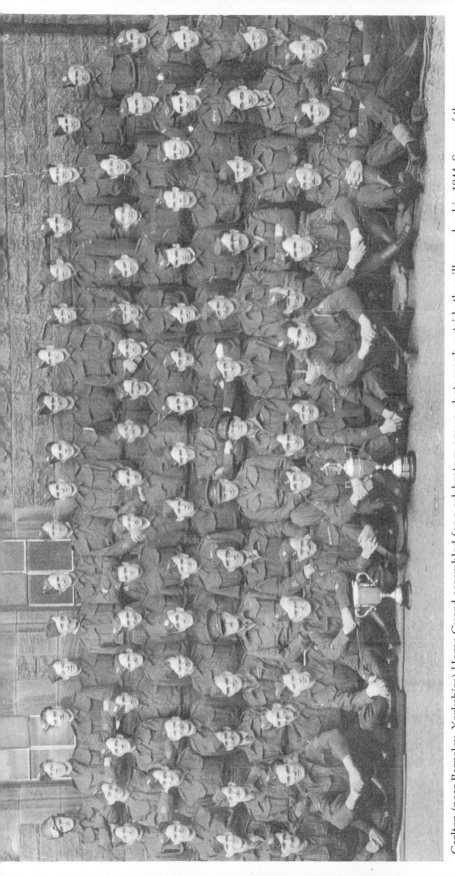

Carlton (near Barnsley, Yorkshire) Home Guard assembled for a celebratory group photograph outside the village school in 1944. Some of them were young coal miners but a smattering of Great War veterans included 'Jack' Skelton (6th right, 2nd row from front) who composed a poem for the 'stand down' farewell dinner which the men attended a year later. Ninth from the left on the back row is Thomas Proctor, who recalled (in 2000) that 'plane spotters used to congregate on Woolley Edge (a prominent escarpment nearby) and we used to gather up there with guns to protect them'. The man wearing the helmet, back row, 1st left, is Eric Simmons, a motor-cycle dispatch rider. (*Brian Elliott*)

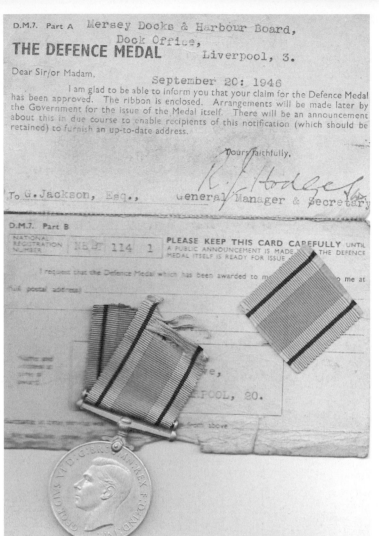

The Defence Medal: much to the annoyance of some Home Guard, the force's members were not given a unique medal for their service. Instead, they were entitled, as were many other military and civilian organisations, to the Defence Medal. This is the notification received by the author's grandfather, George Jackson, that he had been awarded the medal. He was already the recipient of the Great War pair – the Victory Medal and the Great War Medal. The Defence Medal ribbon's colours represented the green of the land, the black of the black out, and the orange of the fires caused by bombing.
(Author's collection)

Home Guard remains: the landscape is still littered with reminders of the Home Guard's role in the defence of Britain. This is a rather battered spigot mortar base, with its characteristic stainless steel mount for that heavy Home Guard weapon. This example now sits at the edge of the car park of the eighteenth-century 'Peacock Inn' in the village of Redmile in Leicestershire. When manned by the Home Guard, this spigot mortar would have been in a weapons pit, protected by sand bags, and camouflaged.
(Author's photograph)

Remembering the Home Guard: the force is remembered in a number of ways, not least by Living History enthusiasts. Here re-created LDV volunteers, from the 'Men of Britain' group, re-enact an LDV tea break in the summer of 1940. (*Bryan Webb and 'Men of Britain'*)

Home Guard again: 'Men of Britain' members in Home Guard uniform check a wartime Austin and its driver – countering the Fifth Column threat. (*Bryan Webb and 'Men of Britain'*)

Gone but not forgotten: how the Home Guard are remembered by many today; a Home Guard re-enactor fixes his bayonet. (*Bryan Webb and 'Men of Britain'*)

Maria Bloxam's testimony gives a very clear picture of the quiet recruitment of women for the irregular warfare of the Auxiliary Units:

> It must have been late '40, or early '41. I was a driver in the First Aid Nursing Yeomanry, which is a FANY. Somebody, I can't remember the name of the good lady who came around, came around to try and find recruits for this Auxiliary Unit [...] She was a fairly senior FANY. My unit released me, they didn't want to, but had to, if you volunteered, they had to.[34]

But, as part of the recruitment process, Maria Bloxam had to be interviewed to see if she was the right sort of woman for the Auxiliary Unit job. Bloxam and another FANY were told to go to Harrods' restaurant, where 'somebody in a tartan skirt would come to meet us'.[35] They went, and 'a reddish haired woman in a tartan skirt' duly arrived. The woman was Emma Myfanwy Williams, who duly passed the women to their new role.

Maria Bloxam recalled her new role, and also explained how vital 'amateurs' (i.e., civilians) would have been in case of an invasion, but, by extension, the risks it would have exposed the civilian population to at the hands of a German army which would have freely applied international law to *franc tireurs* in the form of summary execution. Bloxam explained:

> At the time, a German invasion was not an impossibility; it was thought it could happen. And, therefore, there had to be a means of communication kept up between inner England and, say, national headquarters, and the coast. And the way they did this, and I suppose it was clever really, they recruited amateurs on the coast [...] to take part in this, because if there was an invasion, the Germans might not think of going to the milkman and tapping him on the head, saying, 'You're finished'. It would give him time to go to a house with a telephone and phone on, and the next link would be ourselves.[36]

This 'next link' took the form of hidden radio huts, surrounded by barbed wire, staffed twenty-fours a day by women Auxiliary Unit members, and guarded by the Home Guard. Maria Bloxam remembered:

> We were always in strange places. We were always hidden. We were always in a wood or copse. Difficult to get to, beastly to get to, usually involving tramping over muddy fields. No cars, no bicycles allowed because of the terrain. And we had a hut there, enclosed by barbed wire, guarded by the Home Guard. And we sat in this hut from one o'clock to nine o'clock the next morning.

And during that time, in this hut, there were two or three wireless sets, and code, which we knew the key to. We had it in our heads, and we talked in this code to XYZ. We were never silent. We were keeping the air open. We had never more than two hours sleep at a time. That was difficult, but you got accustomed to it, and at the end of four years, you didn't know how to sleep for more than two hours.[37]

This account sounds as if Bloxam was serving with a Royal Corps of Signals 'Zero' station, but there was clearly a Home Guard role here, in the defence of the sites. Long hours constantly on duty in hidden radio huts was not all there was to the women's role. It was realised that the secrecy of the hidden huts would be short-lived once invading troops had seized the areas they were located in. As a result, secondary hides were constructed for the women radio operators. These were tiny underground bunkers designed for two women at a time: 'They were just big enough to hold a six foot camp bed, iron rations, and you lived there for forty-eight hours. It was unpleasant, cold and uncomfortable'.[38]

Twice a year, on exercise, Maria Bloxam and her fellow radio operators spent their forty-eight hours underground.

Although the government never gave permission for women to be uniformed members of the Home Guard, trained to use weapons, that did not stop many women. Mary Warschauer wore a uniform, and trained with rifles, Sten guns, and grenades, and served alongside men in her Air Ministry Home Guard unit. Similarly, women like Maria Bloxam made a vital contribution to the Home Guard dominated Auxiliary Units, a role that would have been hazardous in the extreme if invasion had come, and, was, in any event, arduous and unsung.

Boys and girls

Apart from schoolboy OTC cadets, the Home Guard had many young volunteers from the outset. The initial call for LDV volunteers had asked for men between the ages of seventeen and sixty-five to come forward. However, many much younger and much older men joined the force, especially in the early days when the LDV was almost completely characterised by the volunteer spirit. However, use was also made of the Boy Scouts in the roles of messengers and guides for Home Guard units. Girl Guides also undertook the messenger role for Civil Defence organisations, particularly the ARP, and Janie Hampton's book, *How the Girl Guides Won the War* provides numerous examples of Girl Guides' bravery and resourcefulness during the war – both in the UK and abroad.[39] Boy Scouts were, however, formally attached to Home Guard units, especially in their role of guides, tasked with leading Home Guards around local areas, where the youngsters were expected to possess the sort of local knowledge that only schoolboys might have. Boy Scouts were also given even more dangerous tasks, such as searching for unexploded bombs after air raids. All this is, perhaps, an interesting reflection on attitudes to youth at the time. In part, this reflects the fact that the majority of youngsters left school at fourteen, if not earlier, and were, therefore, regarded as being much more part of adult society than they are today. In addition, the Scouting movement was founded, in part, on the principles of preparing young people for service in the general, and national, interest. Finally, there was, of course, the natural desire of youngsters to play their own part in the war effort.

Bob 'Ping' Shrimpton was fourteen when war was declared and a member of a Scout troop in Fleet, in Lancashire. He worked at a factory in the town, and when the LDV was formed, he became a Boy Scout guide for his factory unit. He explained his role as a Boy Scout:

> As I was in the Scout movement and knew the area, I was appointed guide to the Home Guard. The factory itself had a Home Guard unit. My main job, if they were going to do an exercise somewhere in Elvetham or Congle Wood, was that I would have to go and guide them there, across country, in the dark to show them where to go.[40]

Shrimpton also explained that Boy Scouts had other duties: 'they helped Air Raid wardens out, they helped with fire watch duties during the day, and fire watch duties on Forestry Commission land, up on the towers'.[41] 'Ping' Shrimpton went on to join the Royal Navy in 1942, and served in the Atlantic, the Arctic, Normandy, and the Far East.

Bob Shrimpton's involvement with the Home Guard appears to have been relatively uneventful, but this cannot be said of another Boy Scout's Home Front service. John 'Chick' Fowles was born in Dalston, East London, in 1924, and did Boy Scout war service (Scouts wore a special armband bearing the designation 'War Service Scouts' when on duty, or a red and gold badge bearing the title 'National Service') throughout the blitz. He remembered that he and his fellow Boy Scouts had a number of Home Guard roles, and explained how closely integrated they were with the force:

> The Scouts provided an intelligence and guide section in the local LDV, before it became the Home Guard, and we literally did do drill with poles and broomsticks, until we got a lot of, they shipped a lot of these long Lee-Enfields over from the United States;

I think they called them P17s. The Scouts were supposed to know
the district, that's why they became guides.[42]

But Fowles, and his fellow Boy Scouts, were also involved in ARP
activities, including the search for unexploded bombs:

One of our little duties was to report to the police station in
Clapton. And one of our jobs there, we would be sent out, this
was at the tender age of sixteen or seventeen, to locate reported
unexploded bombs, and a lot of these were on Hackney marshes.
When I look back, it was pretty fraught, and, really, they shouldn't
have been doing that with young people. But it was quite
exciting.[43]

It was in the aftermath of an air raid in the Spring of 1941 that Fowles
came across the reality of war. A bomb had fallen on a church in Dalston at
four o'clock one sunny Saturday afternoon, and Fowles went there as part of
the post-raid clear up:

I was a bit taken aback when I found that the bundle that was a
bit away from the church, still in the grounds, and obviously not
noticed by anyone else, was the curate. The headless curate. That
rather shook me actually, and I started to realise just what this war
business was about.[44]

'Chick' Fowles' war had only just begun, however, as he later joined the
RAF as a pilot, serving with 253 Squadron. While on occupation duties in
Austria in 1946–47 he met, and later married, an Austrian woman – which
was a more positive result of Fowles' war.

Men preparing for active service

One of the important functions that the Home Guard fulfilled was as
the provider of basic military training for men waiting to be called up to the
regular forces. In the Axis countries this function had been carried out by
the paramilitary arms of the Nazi Party in Germany, and the National
Fascist Party in Italy. But the UK had no equivalent of the brown shirted
Sturmabteilung (SA), or the Italian Voluntary Militia for National Security
(MVSN). But as the Home Guard's early days of improvisation gave way
to better organisation, equipment and training, so the force took on the role
of providing young men with, what was, for many of them, their first
introduction to military matters. Two of these men were Henry McArdle
and Frank Kellaway. They saw extensive active service, with Kellaway
serving with the RAF Regiment, then RAF signals in Britain and during the

campaign in North West Europe, while McArdle served with the Durham Light Infantry in North Africa, and was captured in Tunisia in 1943, and spent the rest of the war as a PoW in Italy and Germany. But before this service in the RAF and the army, both men had served with the Home Guard. Their accounts of the force are of interest as they give quite different views of the effectiveness of the Home Guard.

Henry McArdle was a twenty-one-year-old from Blackhill, County Durham, when Sir Anthony Eden made his appeal for volunteers for the LDV. McArdle immediately volunteered, but he was not impressed:

> I joined up [with the LDV] when I was about twenty-one. And it was laughable. Drill, you know, and all I had was a broom shank [handle]. You know: 'Drill with that!' Then we had shooting practice. 'Oh, great!' So, we goes up the road, and we had one shot each [laughs]. [...] They gave us a uniform, and I was about nine stone, and it was made for someone about eleven stone, or something like that [...] trousers and a tunic. No boots, no boots. The Home Guard? It was laughable'.[45]

Nonetheless, Henry McArdle remained in the Home Guard until 1941, when he was called up for service with the Durham Light Infantry. He was never issued with a weapon in the Home Guard, and most of his duties with the force consisted of fire watching and night patrols.

In contrast, Frank Kellaway, who also joined the LDV at the outset, gave a different account of the force. Kellaway was born in 1906, and is a reminder that active service was not just the realm of very young men as he was nearly thirty-five when he was called up for service in the RAF Regiment in 1941. While waiting for that call up, Kellaway served with the 8th Battalion Devonshire Home Guard in the very small market town of Holsworthy in north Devon. His description of the creation of the LDV in the town is a familiar one, with local middle class professionals taking a lead, along with First World War veterans. The key founding members of the Holsworthy LDV had also belonged to the local rifle club, which met at the drill hall. Frank Kellaway remembered:

> I was waiting to be called up for the air force [...] when the call came for Local Defence Volunteers. Being pretty handy with a rifle, I thought, well, this is something I might be able to do. So, I was one of about eight who reported to the police station on the first day in Holsworthy. Well, in about a few days, I suppose there were twelve or fourteen. So we had a meeting, and amongst the people there was Dr Evans, who was a great friend of mine, and a

bank manager who had been a captain in the First World War. Anyway, Dr Evans, and this chap, Baker, Norman Baker, bank manager at Lloyds Bank – it was decided that he should be assisting him, and the rest of us were just ordinary volunteers.[46]

Kellaway himself ran a small business, and owned a removal van, which quickly became a key asset for the Holsworthy LDV, as they attempted to create some form of defence for the area:

And I'd got a removal lorry, and I used to go out in the evenings, take the lorry out and collect a lot of old scrap cars, and helped to take them round to make road blocks. And other people filled sandbags, so that we could make roadblocks all around.[47]

As the Holsworthy men were integrated into a wider Home Guard structure, and they began to receive arms and ammunition, so Kellaway's lorry was in further demand:

Then there was Colonel Spread, from the First World War, a retired sort of chap. He took over the area, and, of course, it was very convenient for him to ring me up, and say, 'Kellaway, old chap, there's a train coming in at Holtby station in the morning, and it will have so many hundred grenades, so many this and that. Would you get one of your lorries to go down and collect it, and take it down to your store, and I will phone the different platoon commanders to pick up their share'.[48]

Frank Kellaway remembered that the force grew rapidly within six to eight months, so that by the end of 1940 they were in a much stronger position than they had been in May. Kellaway was promoted quickly, and, with his lorries, was also made battalion quartermaster:

The thing grew so rapidly, you couldn't believe it. It was more or less out of control. This old Colonel Spread took over the area from Bradworthy through South Canterbridge, Ashwater, Blackpoint [...] somewhere like two hundred square miles. And the thing grew so fast, they just couldn't believe it [...] At first I became section leader, then I became a platoon commander. By this time we'd got little black bars to put on our epaulettes to show that we had some sort of rank. And within about six to eight months, the thing grew, and Colonel Spread was made battalion commander, and I was made company commander, Number 1 Company, which was in Holsworthy, and quartermaster to the whole battalion, which took in all this area [...] with about three hundred and fifty men, and in my company about sixty, maybe eighty.[49]

Kellaway also received a good deal of training, some of it in the types of unorthodox warfare that was popular among the force in 1940 in particular: 'I was sent off to some secret place in Kent to go on a weekend's course on how to make bombs and booby traps, and things like that, and then I had to come back and teach other people how to do it'.[50] This sounds similar to the weekend courses run at the famous Home Guard training school set up at Osterley Park by ex-Spanish Civil War veterans, under the former International Brigades British commander, Tom Wintringham. That school of irregular warfare became the model for similar schools throughout the country, even after the army had ousted Wintringham and his Spanish War comrades.

Unlike Henry McArdle in the North-East, Kellaway and his men soon received adequate quantities of weapons. In this, they were fortunate, as even by the autumn of 1940 at least 740,000 out of nearly 1,700,000 Home Guards were without personal weapons of any sort, and ammunition was in short supply, with some units only having ten rounds per rifle as late as 1941.[51] But Kellaway and his Devonians were among the fortunate ones, receiving 350 sets of denim blouses and trousers, along with side caps, which were issued through a local tailor's. As for weapons, the usual motley collection of civilian weapons was soon replaced by rifles from the First War:

> In the beginning, it was local shot guns, and the little bank manager [...] he had his revolver that he had left over from the First World War. But then one day, I think it was 350 rifles, left over from the 1914–18 war, they were delivered to me. At least, I went to the station to collect them, in big cases the size of a coffin, ten rifles in a case, all packed away in grease [...]. Fortunately, we'd got a sergeant-major instructor who had been attached to the old drill hall in Holsworthy, and he came to help with these things. And we organised it in the yard at the back of the shop [...] a lot of volunteers. There must have been twenty-five, thirty volunteers, women, and all sorts, and Sergeant Towzer would take all these rifles out and swab them down with paraffin, take them all to pieces and pass the parts on. And they went round the yard in a horseshoe shape, and came out at the top end all clean and ready to use.[52]

Within a comparatively short time, the dozen or so men who had, along with Frank Kellaway, gathered in Holsworthy as the nascent LDV, had been transformed into number 1 company of the 8th Battalion of the Devonshire Home Guard – 350 men under Colonel Spread, uniformed, equipped with rifles, and with access to training.

Although Henry McArdle regarded the Home Guard as 'laughable', Frank Kellaway was more confident about the effectiveness of the force. He made no great claims, but argued that they would have had some impact in a static defence role, saying that the Home Guard:

> would certainly have made things difficult. You see, around here we put up road blocks in sunken roads, wherever the road was going down in a bit of a valley at a corner, we put a roadblock there, and the Home Guard people would [have] been at the top of the hedge, each side [. . .] They [the Germans] would have to slow, and, probably, [we would] inflict a lot of casualties, bound to! And because we were up to all sorts of tricks, most probably, the first person to come along would be a despatch rider, and we would have taught wires across the road, so when the bloke came along on a motorbike, he would probably get his head knocked off. [. . .] It would have made it awkward.[53]

Kellaway's final assessment that 'it would have made it awkward' for any invading Germans might well be near the truth.

Frank Kellaway's Home Guard career came to an end in July 1941, when he was called up for service in the RAF Regiment. Injured during commando training with the Regiment, Kellaway saw active service in North-West Europe in 1944–45 with 124 Wing Signals, RAF. Back in Devon, his old Home Guard comrades continued to defend the county under Colonel Spread, who had a terrible sacrifice to make, as Frank Kellaway remembered: 'Poor old chap [Colonel Spread], he lost three sons in the war'.[54]

Conclusion: The British people

'Enemy aliens', middle-aged veterans of the First World War, women, boys, and young men waiting for call up to the regular armed forces – all these were to be found in the ranks of the Home Guard. The accounts of their service that the individuals gave help illustrate the way that the force drew on a wide variety of the British people. For these individuals, too, Home Guard service was a key element in their experience of the Second World War.

Part IV

Equipping the Home Guard

Chapter 7

Rifles to Rockets

Arms for the Home Guard

The Home Guard was equipped with an extraordinary range of weapons. In the early days of the LDV, many volunteers had no weapons at all, and went on patrol with walking sticks or home-made coshes and clubs. However, by the end of 1942, the force was well equipped with personal weapons, and would go on to man anti-aircraft guns and rockets, as well as coastal artillery batteries. In addition, a range of weapons was developed especially for the Home Guard which aimed at providing it with equipment characterised by simplicity and minimum cost – a not entirely successful strategy. This wide variety of weaponry has attracted some attention, and a number of writers have provided accurate and detailed accounts of the Home Guard's armoury.[1] Finally, the Home Guard used a range of vehicles, both unarmoured 'soft-skins' and armoured vehicles, including locally produced 'emergency' armour.[2]

The purpose of this chapter is to provide an overview of the progressive arming of the force over its lifetime, from the early days of desperate improvisation to the position where the Home Guard was a well-equipped defence force. Given the range of equipment, both officially issued, and developed locally, not all weapons are covered here. Particular attention is paid to the Home Guard's anti-aircraft and coastal defence weaponry, which has received comparatively less attention elsewhere. In these roles, the Home Guard showed that they were as capable as regular troops in operating heavy equipment, and, once again, enabled the Army to release men from Home Defence for active service outside the United Kingdom.

1940: coshes and shotguns

Remembering his early service in the LDV, Norman Longmate described an older boy at his school, Christ's Hospital:

> lovingly whittling down a large piece of wood into a club, with string wound tightly round it to form a handle, and as the final touch, a set of heavy football-boot studs screwed into the 'business' end. Any German he encountered at close quarters was not merely

likely to retire hurt, but looking as though he had been badly trodden on in a particularly vicious rugger scrum.[3]

The problem faced by almost all the LDV in May 1940 was twofold. Firstly, it was an entirely new force, with no existing supply structure to call upon. Secondly, the Army was itself short of almost all types of weapons, and, after the debacle of the withdrawal from France and Belgium, had very little in the way of any equipment – particularly artillery, armour or transport – most of which had been abandoned or lost in France. With no existing supplies, and little immediate hope of new equipment, most LDV units were left to their own devices when it came to weapons and other equipment. Charles Graves' contemporary account gave a picture of the problem, and the LDV 'solution':

> Improvisation, not to say scrounging, was particularly necessary in connection with weapons. The 49th Lancs. Battalion Home Guard borrowed a quantity of old Snyder rifles from Belle-Vue Zoological Gardens, Manchester, which had been used in the Crimea and the Indian Mutiny. The 55th County of Lancaster Battalion Home Guard armed each man on duty with a 6ft spear and a heavily weighted truncheon made by employees of Manchester Collieries Limited, who formed a large proportion of the personnel. The Marylebone Company of LDVs scrounged four dozen SMLEs [Short Magazine Lee Enfield rifles] from Drury Lane Theatre, where they were used by the chorus boys in patriotic tableaux. The 10th Norfolk (Norwich City) Battalion Home Guard paid a call on a local museum and borrowed not only firearms on exhibition there, but also a pedigree sentry box. The 77th County of Lancaster Battalion Home Guard acquired fifty Martini Henry carbines from a local Boys' Brigade unit, much to the latter's annoyance. The 11th Battalion Salop Home Guard declined the offer of a muzzle loader, but acquired several revolvers and a number of Crimean War cavalry carbines covered with rust [...] 'J' Zone [...] records the acquisition of many strange fowling pieces and blunderbusses, together with twenty-four cutlasses which led the way to the formation of a Cutlass Platoon commanded by an old naval rating.[4]

Although this picture was not entirely uniform across the UK, with the force in Northern Ireland being able to draw upon existing police stocks of modern rifles and ammunition,[5] and some LDV volunteers in Kent being quickly issued with rifles,[6] it was the usual experience for the new LDV volunteers. Even if units were able to find old but functioning weapons, there was frequently the problem of a lack of ammunition, meaning that the weapons were only of 'dummy purpose' use. William Weightman was in the force in Durham, in what became the 11th Battalion Durham Home Guard, and remembered that, as late as 1941, 'we were issued with some very large Italian rifles for which we had no ammunition, and these were for exercise purposes [...] I think they had been made at the end of the 19th Century, and possibly captured by the Abyssinians'.[7] It may well have been that these weapons were, in fact, British war booty from the spectacular defeat of the Italians in North Africa or East Africa in early 1941. Even when modern rifles were issued, ammunition was in short supply or nonexistent, with one volunteer in Hull in 1940–1941, explaining, 'we had a rifle to share [a Lee Enfield]. One [volunteer] brought it home one week, another, another week, to clean it. No ammunition. One rifle between two of us'.[8]

It was not only in the UK that private sources of weaponry were scoured to supply the ill-equipped LDV. As Martin Mace has described, there was also an 'unofficial Lend-Lease' programme established, whereby weapons were donated by private individuals in the USA for the LDV.[9] In the summer of 1940, the 'American Committee for the Defense of British Homes' was established, with its headquarters in New York, and 364 local committees across all forty-eight states of the union. The aim was to collect weapons, ammunition, binoculars, steel helmets and other equipment to be sent, free of charge, to the British Home Guard. In addition, funds were raised to buy more weapons and equipment. The American committees advertised widely, and approached individuals, businesses and police forces for weapons. An advertisement in the National Rifle Association of America's journal, *American Rifleman*, stated: 'Send a gun to defend a British home. British civilians, faced with threat of invasion, desperately need arms for the defense of their homes. [...] You can aid by sending any arms and binoculars you can spare'.[10] When the campaign was drawn to a close, in June 1942, the final tally was 25,343 weapons sent to the UK, comprising, 5,133 rifles, 6,337 donated revolvers and 13,763 revolvers bought with donations, 110 Thompson sub-machine guns, and 2,042,291 rounds of ammunition.[11] In addition, 16,322 steel helmets and 2,993 binoculars and telescopes were collected and sent to the Home Guard.[12]

Rifles and automatic weapons

The Home Guard Training Manual was published in 1940; edited by John Langdon-Davies, and including chapters by Major J A Barlow of the West Yorkshire Regiment. This pocket-sized book was based on 'War Office

Instruction Books', and three of the twelve chapters covered rifles, automatic weapons and grenades. The chapter on rifles identified the main rifles in use at the time:

> You, as one of the Home Guard, may be armed with any one of the following rifles:
>
> (a) The .303″ British Service rifle (SMLE).
> (b) The .303″ pattern Dec. 14 rifle (P14).
> (c) The .303″ Canadian Ross rifle (Ross).
> (d) The .300″ USA 1917 model which looks almost exactly like the British P14, having been copied from it (Model 17).
> (e) The .300″ USA Springfield rifle (Springfield).[13]

Major Barlow went on to explain that as further supplies of American rifles arrived, so the Home Guard would be increasingly equipped with them. This issue was, naturally, of paramount importance, and the War Cabinet was kept informed of developments. Anthony Eden reported, on 17 June 1940, that:

> The LDV's were at the moment largely a 'broomstick' Army. Rifles were being provided for them as quickly as possible. We had a supply of rifles which had been kept in store since the last war, and which were now being reconditioned. Another 500,000 rifles were ready to leave the United States. According to the original intention, these would have been divided equally between this country and France, but arrangements were now being made which would ensure that the whole consignment came to us.[14]

There were, clearly, some small consolations to be had from the rapid fall of France. That summer the British government bought 615,000 P17 rifles from the USA. These were followed by a further 119,000 of the weapons in 1941, in addition to 138 million rounds of .300 ammunition.[15] The fact that the P17, although based on a .303 British weapon, fired a .300 round meant that all these rifles had to be clearly marked with a red band around the 'furniture' of the weapon, to prevent the accidental use of .303 ammunition. The US rifles had been in store since the Great War, and were distributed to Home Guard units still packed in thick grease. One Home Guard, Frank Kellaway, a member of the 8th Battalion, Devonshire Home Guard, remembered the early days of scrounged weapons, followed by the arrival of American rifles:

> Well, in the beginning, it was local shot guns and the like. The bank manager [. . .] he got his revolver that he had left over from

the First World War. But then, one day, I think it was 350 rifles, left over from the 1914–18 war, they were delivered to me, at least, I went to the station to collect them. In big cases, about the size of a coffin, ten rifles in a case, all packed away in grease [...] Fortunately, we'd got a sergeant-major instructor who had been attached to the old drill hall in Holsworthy, and he came to help with these things, and we organised it at the back of the shop [...] A lot of volunteers, there must have been 25, 30 volunteers, women, and all sorts, and Sergeant Towzer would take all these rifles out and swab them down with paraffin, take them all in pieces, and pass the parts on, and they went round the yard in a horse shoe shape, and came out at the end all clean and ready for use.[16]

In this way, this rural Home Guard unit was uniformly equipped with an effective infantry weapon. Although these First World War vintage weapons were not as highly regarded as the SMLE, they were still potent, and enabled a large percentage of the force to be uniformly equipped – an important factor in terms of supply. If some considered the American rifles to be 'rather cumbersome', and with 'a difficult bolt action for rapid fire'[17] they were, nonetheless, better regarded than the Canadian Ross rifle, which was issued, in much smaller numbers, to the Home Guard. The Ross Rifle was first issued to the Royal Canadian Mounted Police in 1905. Although it used a .303″ round, it was different from that used in the SMLE. Further, the Ross Rifle had a tendency to jam easily, and was very susceptible to dust and dirt; these attributes making it a poor battlefield weapon. As a result, its use during the Great War, was restricted to training, and second line use. Small numbers of these rifles were issued to the Home Guard, who, while appreciating the weapon's usefulness for range training, regarded it as 'unsuitable for Service conditions', and 'a 'heavy ill-balanced brute to lug about'.[18]

The rifle that all Home Guardsmen wanted was the standard British service rifle of the period – the Short Magazine Lee-Enfield (SMLE). John Brophy, an under aged volunteer in the Great War, eulogised the SMLE in a particularly English fashion in *Britain's Home Guard*:

Old sweats felt youth flow back to their muscles and minds when, after an interval of more than twenty years, they again held in their hands the smooth, proportionate contours, beautifully finished and balanced, of the SMLE – the Short Lee-Enfield rifle which was the standard infantry arm throughout 1914–18. It is an expensive weapon, the metal parts surfaced like silk, and the butt and stock made of walnut wood; it is the product of skilled craftsmanship, the easiest and lightest of all military rifles to handle, the most practical for active service. It 'comes up' as sweetly as a favourite cricket-bat. No one who has ever used the Short Lee-Enfield is likely to be satisfied with another type, except perhaps for fancy shooting on a range.[19]

The SMLE was one of the finest bolt-action rifles ever produced, firing a .303″ round, with a ten round detachable box magazine, weighing just over 8lb, and was an effective and accurate weapon out to 1,500 yards, well beyond normal battlefield range. The Mark I was introduced in 1903, and successive Marks remained in British army for nearly six decades, and continued to be manufactured in India and Australia until the end of the 1950s. Some fortunate Home Guards were issued with the SMLE from the outset, the most notable being the Ulster Home Guard who were issued with the rifle as it was already the standard Ulster Special Constabulary weapon.[20] However, for British Home Guard units, the US P17 became the standard rifle, with the SMLE only being held by unit armouries in very small numbers, largely for training familiarisation purposes. The priority in 1940 had been to replace the third of a million SMLEs lost to the British Army during the evacuation from France,[21] and refurbish those that the evacuated army had brought back with it.

The Home Guard was issued with a range of automatic weapons, including British and US pattern Lewis guns, US Browning Automatic Rifles (BARs), US Thompson sub-machine guns, Vickers medium machine guns, Sten sub-machine guns, and the Hotchkiss machine gun. The first automatic weapon issued to the force in any numbers was the Lewis light machine gun (LMG). Dating back to 1910, this American designed weapon was widely used on land, sea and air during the Great War. By 1940, it was regarded as obsolete by the regular forces, and had largely, though not entirely, been superseded by the Bren light machine gun in Army service, although the Lewis continued its frontline service with the Royal Navy and the merchant marine for longer. The Home Guard received both British made weapons, manufactured by the Birmingham Small Arms (BSA), and US weapons, imported in 1940. In typical fashion, the American supply for the Home Guard was far from straightforward. Not only did most US Lewis guns take a .300 round, rather than the standard British .303 round, but the American weapons came from two sources, one being for aircraft. Major Barlow explained that the .300 Stripped Lewis was a modified aircraft pattern weapon: 'These guns started life as aircraft observers' guns in US planes. They came over here with no sights, no bipod, no radiator casings and only a spade handle grip instead of a butt'.[22] The stripped down Lewis guns needed extensive modification before they could be issued to the Home Guard:

> The first few thousands had normal Lewis gun spare wooden butts fitted, instead of the spade grip. A ground battle-sight was fitted for a range of 400 yards. In view of the shape of the wooden butt and the consequent position of the head and eye, the line of sight could only be arranged to be sufficiently high to clear the [top mounted] forty-seven-round magazine. Later consignments have been fitted with a skeleton butt with a wooden check rest. The shape of this butt was so arranged to permit of the eye being in such a position that the line of sight clears the higher ninety-seven-round magazine. Neither type of conversion caters for a bipod rest in view of the fact that these weapons are intended for the Home Guard only. They will normally be used therefore from behind prepared cover.[23]

The remarks concerning the lack of bipod, which was linked, by Major Barlow, to the Home Guard's static, point defence role, illustrates contemporary military thinking about the role and functions of the Home Guard in 1940. Later in the war, as the Home Guard developed its role to include fighting patrols, automatic weapons were issued on an enhanced scale to give the force greater offensive power. In Northern Ireland, for example, during 1943, 500 additional Lewis guns 'which had been loaned by the RUC Inspector-General to the Army', were returned and issued out to the country units with particular harassing roles, on the basis that each company would have two at its disposal. Where possible it was issued at a ratio of approximately one per platoon.[24] Although the Lewis gun was not as effective as the latest light machine guns like the Bren, or the German MG34, it was still a proven battlefield weapon, and provided many Home Guard units with their first automatic infantry weapon.

Another American weapon issued to the Home Guard in 1940 was the Browning Automatic Rifle (BAR), a weapon that did not really have an equivalent in British service. It was developed towards the end of the First World War for the American Expeditionary Force. Although it was classed as a rifle, it was, perhaps, better described as a light LMG, capable of being fired on single shot, or in fully automatic mode. However, as the box magazine held only twenty rounds, only the shortest of fully automatic bursts could be fired. As Major Barlow advised his Home Guard readers:

> The weapon should be rested on cover if possible [it weighed over 19lb] or else fired in the open like a rifle. Normally, the weapon

should be used for firing single shots, the fully automatic capacity only being employed in an emergency. Besides avoiding waste of ammunition, this disguises the fact that an automatic weapon is present, until the enemy is too close to do anything about it.[25]

In US squad tactics, the role of the fire team was to support the BAR gunner, unlike the role of an LMG in British service, such as the Bren or the Lewis, whose role was to support the rifle armed section. Nonetheless, the BAR provided the Home Guard with a much welcomed extra battlefield capacity, and, in the US armed forces the BAR was always popular, and saw active service with them until 1957.

A famous wartime image of Winston Churchill showed the Prime Minister in a pin-striped suit, chewing a cigar, and toting a Thompson Sub-machine Gun (SMG), the 'Tommy gun'. This SMG, firing a .45 round, loaded into eighteen, twenty or thirty round box magazines, or fifty or 100 round drum magazines, was famous to cinema goers around the world in the inter-war period as the weapon of choice of Hollywood gangsters. It was this cultural reference that enabled German propagandists to make use of the Churchill image to boost their claim that Churchill was nothing more than a Chicago style 'hood'. The Tommy gun was the first sub-machine gun to be issued to the Home Guard, with the first weapons arriving from the USA in the summer of 1940. It was a very popular weapon, as it was quickly appreciated that it was a deadly close combat weapon, firing a powerful round. The Home Guard actually received priority in the issue of the Tommy gun, but within a year it began to be withdrawn from the force, to be reissued to the regular army, and, in particular to new commando formations.

The Thompson sub-machine gun was replaced by a far different SMG, and one that was, at first, received with dismay by the Home Guard. This SMG was the Sten gun, which, eventually would gain fame across Europe as a key weapon of Resistance fighters, to whom it was dropped by tens of thousands by the RAF.[26] The Sten marked a change from the usual British practice of highly engineered weapons. Instead, the Sten was built to be as cheap and easy to produce as possible. To many Home Guardsmen this was met with horror: 'They were said to cost thirty shillings each and I do not doubt it', commented one Cornish officer. 'It is inaccurate over fifty yards and apt to be dangerous in the hands of an untrained man.' 'Its breeding might be described as by Woolworth out of Scrap Heap', agreed another Home Guard in Devon. 'It works . . . I am told, after being thrown into a river and dragged through mud'.[27]

The Sten did, indeed, cost thirty shillings (£1.50) to make, and having only six components, it was easy to mass produce, often by companies with no history of weapons manufacture. The Mark I version did not have a safety catch, which made the weapon particularly dangerous to the user. Dropping this mark of Sten frequently led to the weapon discharging all the thirty-two rounds in the magazine. The magazine was made of low grade metal, and could easily be damaged, leading to problems with feed, and stoppages. The weapon was only really accurate to around sixty yards, which frequently proved, as Resistance fighters found out, to be suicidally close. However, it was easy to use, light at just over 6½lbs, fired a powerful 9mm round, and was, above all, cheap and quick to manufacture, with more than two million of the Mark II being manufactured. This, and later Marks of the weapon, incorporated improvements, including a safety catch, and changes to the butt, but the Sten remained the epitome of an emergency, mass produced, total war weapon.

The Home Guard were issued with a variety of heavier automatic weapons, mostly in the medium machine gun (MMG) class. These included the Vickers MMG, the Browning MMG, the Hotchkiss (a LMG), and the Marlin MMG. The Vickers was the British Army's standard MMG from its introduction into service in 1912, until the 1960s, when it was replaced by the General Purpose Machine Gun (GPMG). The Vickers was a British development of the Maxim machine gun. Water–cooled, weighing 40lb, and usually fired from a tripod mount, the weapon was sturdy, reliable, and capable of long periods of sustained fire. In the Great War, it was the Vickers that gave truth to the Machine Gun Corps' Biblical motto, 'Saul killed his thousands; David his tens of thousands'. However, as the Vickers remained in front line service with the regular army, only small numbers of the weapon were issued to the Home Guard. Instead, the force had to rely on a variety of other machine guns for support firepower. The Browning M1917A1 was the USA's equivalent of the Vickers, and, like most other American infantry weapons fired a .300 round. In the summer of 1940, the first of 10,000 Brownings arrived from the USA, and many were issued to the Home Guard. Small numbers of British manufactured Hotchkiss machine guns were also issued to the force. These were First World War era French machine guns, built under licence in Britain, and utilising a .303 round. In Home Guard hands, the Hotchkiss, which was one of the first LMGs, was usually used for static defence, mounted on a tripod. In October 1940, for example, Hotchkiss machine guns were 'issued to Belfast City to help provide defence of the city limits. The outer perimeter had 50 guns allocated to it, while the inner perimeter had one allocated to each road-block manned by the U[lster] H[ome] G[uard]'.[28] Austin Ruddy has drawn attention to a further MMG issued to the Home Guard, the American .300 M1918 Marlin. This was a First World War aircraft and tank weapon, but in

1940, 17,000 were sent to the UK. Once again, being chambered for the .300 round meant that they were issued to the Home Guard, and 'fed with a 250 round belt and mounted on an improvised mounting, the Marlin was issued in limited numbers making it practically forgotten today'.[29]

By the early autumn of 1940, the War Office estimated that, on the most positive reckoning, the 1,682,303 volunteers in the Home Guard, would have under 847,000 rifles, 46,629 shotguns, and 48,750 automatic weapons. In other words 'even under ideal conditions at least 740,000 Home Guards would have no personal weapons'.[30] Worse, the prevalence of non-standard, and US .300 weapons, meant that the supply of ammunition was a serious worry. It was in this context of a shortage of weapons and ammunition that cheap, innovative weaponry was developed for the force, and even greater efforts were made to arm it with conventional weapons. More weapons were imported from the USA, weapons like the Sten came into being, and 'by the start of 1943 [...] almost 900,000 rifles, 30,145 shotguns, 23,630 BARs, 248,234 Sten guns, 12,895 Thompson sub-machine guns, and over 20,000 Lewis, Browning, and Vickers light and heavy machine guns' were in the hands of the Home Guard.[31]

Anti-tank warfare

Hugh Slater was a veteran of the International Brigades, and had risen to Chief of Operations on the International Brigade Staff. Before that, he had commanded the anti-tank battery of the 15th International Brigade, equipped with Soviet built 37mm anti-tank guns. In his 1941 book, *Home Guard for Victory!*[32] Slater gave his Home Guard readers anti-tank warfare advice. He concluded, somewhat optimistically:

> Even the most simple and seemingly ineffective form of opposition to a tank may be dangerous to the crew inside it. For example, an ordinary 12-bore shot gun fired against the bullet-proof glass visor will star the glass and force him to use his reserve glass. When that also is starred and the periscopes have been destroyed, he has got to look through the small slits in the steel plate.[33]

The German Blitzkrieg on Poland and Western Europe had not only raised the spectre of a Fifth Column, but also the far more tangible threat of armoured warfare. Both threats occupied the minds of the Home Guard, and there was a widespread realisation that the force desperately needed some anti-armour capability. It was out of the question that the Home Guard should, in the aftermath of Dunkirk, be equipped with the regular army's standard anti-tank weapon, the 2pdr anti-tank gun, so the force had to be equipped with a variety of extempore and emergency weapons. These included a large range of anti-tank grenades or bombs, along with 'sub-artillery' designed specifically for the Home Guard.

The first anti-tank weapon to be used by the Home Guard was the petrol bomb, more commonly known at the time as the 'Molotov Cocktail', and even the '*Chiang-Kai-Shek*' cocktail. The former name referred to the weapon's use by the Finns against the Soviets during the 'Winter War' when the Soviet Union was Nazi Germany's co-conspirator and aggressor, while the latter name referred to the use of petrol bombs in the defence of Shanghai against the Japanese. In his account of petrol bomb use by the Home Guard, Martin Mace identified the first official reference to the weapon, on 5 June 1940, at a meeting of senior LDV leaders. At the meeting, the Commander-in-Chief Home Forces, General Ironside, said:

> I want also to develop this thing they developed in Finland, called the Molotov Cocktail. It is a bottle filled with resin, petrol and tar, which if thrown on top of the tank will ignite, and if you throw half a dozen more on it you have them cooked. It is quite an effective thing. If you can use your ingenuity, I give you a picture of a [road] block, with two houses close to the block overlooking it. Out of the top window is the place to drop these things on the tank as it passes the block. It may stop for two minutes there, but it will be quite effective.[34]

General Ironside had previously confided to his diary, 'The LDV going well. I must get them armed with Molotov Cocktails in all the villages of England. The only way to deal with a tank'.[35] The Molotov Cocktail quickly became a staple weapon in the LDV's armoury, with volunteers frequently told about the weapon's successes in the Spanish Civil War and the Russo-Finnish war. However, in both wars, conditions had been such that this primitive weapon had, perhaps, had more success than it could have had in an invaded Britain in 1940. In Spain, the close infantry-tank co-operation that was the mark of successful armoured warfare had not been perfected. Indeed, the Republicans had frittered away their qualitative advantage, given by the latest Soviet tanks, precisely by their failure to train infantry and tanks together. However, in 1940, the Germans were masters of close co-operation. General Ironside's picture of a conveniently lone German tank stopped by a road block being bombarded at close range by LDV petrol bombs, ignored the reality that German armour would be accompanied by infantry trained to neutralise just such a threat. Finnish successes against the Red Army were also a result of poor Soviet infantry tactics, but, in addition, the Soviets were compelled to advance into Finland along a limited number of roads which were closely invested by thick forest. In these conditions, the slow moving columns of Soviet armour could be ambushed by faster moving Finnish troops. Neither the Spanish, nor the Finnish case, was, then, a good model for Britain in 1940.

Despite the limited usefulness of the Molotov Cocktail, manufacture of the weapon was undertaken on an enormous scale, using any type of bottle that came to hand. One popular Home Guard activity was the preliminary stage in the preparation of beer bottle petrol bombs, that is, the emptying of the original contents. Home Guard and army units manufactured petrol bombs of a wide variety of types. Most required the user to ignite a rag at the neck of the bottle before throwing. This was another weakness of the weapon, as the rag could be blown out by the act of throwing, or the neck portion of the bottle, including its fuse, could break away from the tar/naphtha/petrol mixture in the main part of the bottle on contact with a tank. In the latter case, the Home Guard were instructed to encase the bottle in a wire cage, and to overcome the former problem, an official, self–igniting petrol bomb was developed, and some six million were issued to the force by August 1941.[36] Frank Kellaway remembered collecting and storing these petrol bombs, known as the No. 76 Self-Igniting Phosphorous (SIP) grenade, or AW (Albright and Wilson) bomb:

> We had those Molotov Cocktails [...] ginger beer bottles filled with a mixture of stuff, [and] there was some rubber in it as well. As soon as air got into it, it would burst into flames, and the rubber would burn and would stick to things. I had to go to the station and collect these things, and store them under the staircase where our flat was, over the shop. It would have been a pretty rumpus if one had gone off! You only needed to get air at this stuff, crack a bottle, and it was terrific! [...] They were supposed to stick on the side of tanks, or, if you got near enough, in the tank.[37]

This bomb, manufactured by Albright and Wilson of Oldbury, the main manufacturer of white phosphorous,[38] was a great improvement on the home made petrol bomb, but was, as Kellaway remembered, potentially extremely dangerous for users, even during storage. In fact, the warning notice on each crate of SIP grenades recommended that they be stored 'in cool place, under water if possible'.[39] The SIP grenade was manufactured in two variants, 'a red-capped type for throwing and a green–capped type for launching from the Northover Projector',[40] and, containing phosphorous, could not be extinguished but burnt until all the fuel was consumed.

The Home Guard was issued with a large range of other grenades and bombs, designed, for the most part, to be used against armour. David Orr has provided a useful directory of these grenades and bombs, ten in all, some of which were issued only to the Home Guard, and others which were also issued to the regular forces.[41] What is of interest is that Home Guard was issued with bombs that had been rejected by the regular army on safety grounds. The No. 74 ST grenade was a bomb that was initially designed for the regular army as an anti-tank weapon. This grenade was more commonly known as the sticky bomb, as the charge, jellified nitro-glycerine was in a glass, later plastic, sphere, which was covered in stockinette coated in sticky adhesive. The idea was that 'upon throwing, the striker was released to initiate the delay fuze and on impact the glass flask shattered, allowing the jellified filling to impact on the target where the adhesive held it until the fuze burned down to the detonator'.[42] Although an effective weapon, the use of unstable nitro-glycerine, the danger of the glass sphere prematurely breaking, and the tendency of the adhesive to adhere the bomb to other things, including throwers, as well as enemy tanks, all led the regular army to reject it. However, not untypically, Winston Churchill, in his enthusiasm for the Home Guard, had the bomb manufactured for them. Other bombs, such as the No. 75 Hawkins grenade, which could be thrown, or more effectively, laid as a light anti-tank mine designed to damage tank tracks, and the No. 82 Gammon Bomb, were used by both the regular army and the Home Guard. The former saw widespread use in North Africa, and, indeed, much later against the British in Aden; while the latter was used to some effect by British airborne troops at Arnhem.[43]

All these weapons were limited by the need to be thrown by the user, and it was recognised that the Home Guard lacked any form of effective weapon with which it could engage the enemy at a distance. There was some issue of the EY Cup Discharger, which was a rifle attachment designed to enable the No. 36 grenade (the famous 'Mills Bomb'), and, for anti-armour use, the No. 68 grenade, which used the shaped charge principle to enhance the force of an explosion, enabling the weapon to penetrate between 30–50mm of armour. However, the maximum effective range of the cup discharged No. 68 grenade was around 75 yards, and there was a need for a longer range, and heavier, weapon for the Home Guard. This need was met by some innovative types of 'sub-artillery'.

Three Home Guard 'heavy' weapons were developed: the Northover Projector, the Smith Gun, and the Spigot Mortar, also known as the Blacker Bombard – all species of sub artillery. These weapons aimed to provide a cheap, simple, yet effective anti-tank capability. The development of these weapons can also be linked to the development of defence planning. The move away from a linear view of defence lines running across the country, which informed thinking in the summer of 1940, towards the Defended

Localities (DL) model of defence, saw a change in the Home Guard's role. The DL model defence was similar to the defended 'islands' model adopted by the French during the second stage of the Battle for France. By then, it was too late for France, but, as a response to armoured warfare, it was a better model of defence than the linear model. The Home Guard's main role in the DL scheme was to man key defended areas, known as Nodal Points. This involved manning pillboxes, roadblocks, and strong points. To enable the force to effectively defend these areas, heavier weapons than machine guns and personal weapons were needed. It was this need that was met by the sub-artillery.

The Northover Projector was designed by a Home Guard officer, Major H Northover, and in appearance it resembled a drainpipe of just under four feet in length, mounted on a base plate and tubular legs. It was a smooth-bore weapon, designed to 'propel grenades [including the SIP] using a small explosive charge of black powder as a propellant'.[44] This effectively made the Northover Projector a type of primitive cannon, although that does not appear to have diminished some Home Guards' enthusiasm for it, as Norman Longmate remembered that the Northover was Christ's Hospital's pride, though firing it was 'a treat reserved for the masters' platoon'.[45] However, like many Home Guard weapons, it was potentially dangerous to the user, and, utilising black powder, it would have effectively been a one shot weapon, with a cloud of white smoke giving its position away as soon as it was fired. As Henry Smith of the Ministry of Food Home Guard remembered:

> The principal purpose for which it was designed was to discharge glass bottles containing a phosphorous mixture [the SIP] which burst into livid flames, giving off quantities of suffocating smoke upon exposure to the air. When dealing with this ammunition [...] the least lovable characteristics of the Northover Projector became apparent. Unless the utmost care was exercised in loading and firing there was a natural tendency for the shock of discharge to break the glass bottles in the breech, whereupon the gun, and sometimes the gunner and troops standing leeward were liable to burst into flames.[46]

Yet the gun gave the Home Guard the capacity to accurately fire an anti-tank 'round' to around 150–200 yards. Given the effect of black powder, however, it would have been difficult to fire ranging shots, and the weapon would have been best deployed in a fixed position, pre-registered on target areas. By August 1941, over 8,000 Northover Projectors had been issued to the Home Guard, and by the end of the war, 21,000 had been manufactured, at the cost of £10 each – cheapness being the most successful part of the design.[47]

The Smith Gun was, like the Northover Projector, a smooth bore weapon, but was much more recognisable as an artillery piece. It could fire anti-tank and anti-personnel rounds. It was capable of penetrating 80mm of armour at 50 yards, was accurate between 100 and 200 yards, had a maximum range of more than 1,000 yards, and could be towed behind a small car. The official view of the weapon was that it was a 'simple, powerful and accurate weapon which, if properly handled, will add greatly to the fire power of the Home Guard',[48] and 4,000 were manufactured. In fact, small numbers of the weapon were also issued to the regular forces, particularly the RAF for airfield defence purposes. However, safety concerns along with mediocre performance, led to it being withdrawn by the RAF after only a year in service. The safety issues surrounded faulty fuses fitted to Smith Gun ammunition, which led to accidents, and gave it a bad reputation, leading to it being withdrawn in some areas.

The final piece of Home Guard sub-artillery was the Spigot Mortar, or the Blacker Bombard. This was yet another weapon that owed its acceptance for the Home Guard to Churchill. The inventor, Lieutenant-Colonel L V S Blacker had little success in interesting the War Office in his various designs, but, during a demonstration of his Spigot Mortar at the Prime Minister's country residence, Chequers, on 18 August 1940, 'it is alleged that the first shot nearly killed General de Gaulle, and this enthused Churchill so much that he issued a production order for 2,500, the quantity based on a ratio of one per company at that time'.[49] Unlike the Smith Gun, the Spigot Mortar was not really a mobile weapon, weighing 405lb, and mounted on four heavy tubular legs that needed to be staked to the ground, it was best pre-sited. Interestingly, the remains of the fixed sites for the weapon, usually covering some road, rail or canal feature, can still be seen around the country. They are easily recognised by the stub of the mounting pin, in stainless steel, projecting from concrete firing bases, although the fire pits and sandbags that surrounded them are usually long gone, or buried. The mortar could fire two types of mortar bomb, a 26lb anti-tank bomb, and 14lb, high explosive, anti-personnel bomb. The main drawbacks of the weapon was that the slow muzzle velocity and limited accuracy of the weapon, and it was, in effect, yet another 'one shot' weapon. Not all Home Guards took to the weapon, with, for example, 'Chick' Fowles, who served with the 8th, City of London, Royal Fusiliers, Home Guard, remembering:

> I [went] on a course, out at Woodford, North London [...] we had
> to go to quite a few weekends. We eventually finished up firing

this thing [the Spigot Mortar]. It was very frightening, there was a huge bang, and we had to take all sorts of precautions. I did hear, later on, that they had several accidents with this thing, and it wasn't considered to be a very good weapon.[50]

However, the anti-armour round was very heavy, and would have had a devastating effect. The Spigot Mortar was, probably, the most effective anti-tank weapon that the Home Guard was commonly issued with, and from 1941 was produced in large numbers, enabling, for example, 'Cambridge's defenders [to be] equipped with 92 of them, [while] the Chatham garrison had 111'.[51]

Towards the end of the war, the Home Guard was, increasingly issued with more standard anti-tank weaponry. These included the 2pdr anti-tank gun, which, by the time of its Home Guard issue in 1943, was obsolete as an anti-tank weapon, but still had some anti-armour uses. The force also received the .55" Boys Anti-tank rifle, which had, at the outset of the war, been the infantry's standard anti-tank weapon, but was quickly shown to be of little use in the role for which it was intended. Some Home Guard units were also issued with 75mm artillery reconfigured for the anti-tank role, while Home Guard on airfield defence duties manned the famous 25pdr field gun, which could be used in the anti-tank role. But these were exceptions, and, for most Home Guard anti-tank warfare was characterised by hand-thrown, and often dangerous weapons of limited combat value, supported by cheap, but none too effective, Home Guard sub-artillery.

Armour

In 1940, the Home Guard spirit of scrounging and improvisation saw the emergence of vehicles that, to Home Guard eyes at least, qualified as 'armour'. In some cases, the force was able to draw upon obsolete armoured vehicles. This was the case in Northern Ireland where the fact that the force in the Province was part of the Special Constabulary, allowed it to draw upon Lancia armoured tenders from the period of the Anglo-Irish War. Similarly, other units were fortunate enough to be able to equip themselves with obsolete armoured cars, and once the crisis of 1940 had passed, some Home Guard units were officially equipped with 'emergency' armour of the post–Dunkirk period. But the Home Guard also made efforts to equip itself with 'home-made' armour; a flavour of the fantastic variety of which has been captured by Martin Mace in *Vehicles of the Home Guard*. Typically, civilian cars were the basis of improvised 'armour', utilising boiler plate, mild steel, or, in some cases hardened armour plate. In most cases, these improvised armoured cars would have struggled to provide protection against rifle or machine gun fire, but, in some units, considerable energy and ingenuity was expended on building these vehicles. For example, Colonel Tickler, of the eponymous Berkshire jam company, drew on his company's resources to make a number of armoured cars for the Maidenhead Home Guard,[52] as did Morris Motors in Oxford, for its own defence force.[53] However, it was not just the Home Guard which was forced into improvising armour in 1940, the regular armed forces, in the aftermath of Dunkirk, were also compelled to fall back on emergency armour. Utilising non-strategic materials, a range of protected vehicles were built, including the Bison, the Armadillo, and the Beaverette. These vehicles were used by the Army and the RAF, and as they received more conventional armour, their emergency vehicles where handed over to the Home Guard.

The basic idea behind the Bison was to mount a concrete pillbox structure on 6 × 4 or 6 × 2 truck chassis, creating a mobile defence point. The vehicles were built by the Concrete Company Limited, and were largely issued to the Home Guard, with 'several hundred' finally seeing service.[54] The idea of a protected or armoured box on a truck mounting was also the basis of the Armadillo vehicle, which was issued to the RAF for airfield defence, and the Home Guard. The fighting compartment of this vehicle was made of a double skinned wooden box, the space between the skins being filled with pebbles and gravel. Perhaps surprisingly, trials showed that 'these structures offered its occupants complete protection against small arms fire'.[55] The real advantage of the Armadillo, however, was that it was very quick to manufacture, something that was of importance in the summer of 1940. The later mark of the Armadillo replaced the wooden walls with more conventional armour. All models of the vehicle were armed with Lewis guns and rifles, which were fired through sliding hatches in the face of each wall of the box structure.

It was not until the introduction of the Beaverette that the Home Guard received a standard, conventional armoured vehicle. In the aftermath of Dunkirk, Lord Beaverbrook, who, as minister of aircraft production, was concerned with the defence of vital aircraft factories, initiated production of an armoured car that was subsequently named after him – the Beaverette. As with Home Guard local improvisations, the basis of the Beaverette were standard car chassis, most commonly the Standard, or the Humber Super Snipe. 'Fitted to the car chassis was a body of mild steel to a maximum thickness of 0.35in. A layer of 3in thick oak planks bolted behind the steel reinforced the frontal armour. Both the Mark I and Mark II had an open roof'.[56] Armament was provided by a Bren gun, or Boys anti-tank rifle, fired through a slit in the frontal armour. Later Marks were fully enclosed, and included a small turret, and, in total, 2,800 Beaverettes were manufactured.

The response of some Home Guard units to their perceived need for armour led to a range of improvised vehicles, protected to one degree or another. This response to the crisis of 1940 had its official parallel in the emergency armour – the Bison, Armadillo and Beaverette – that equipped both regular forces and, increasingly, the Home Guard. Both the government and the Home Guard were thrown back, in the post-Dunkirk equipment shortage, onto improvisation. For the Home Guard, however, the emergency programme did, nonetheless, provide the force with some mobile armour that enabled it to reinforce static defensive positions.

Anti-aircraft

By late 1942, it appeared that the threat of German air attack was greatly diminished. In consequence, the War Office decided that 50,000 anti-aircraft gunners could be switched to other roles. However, there was a desire to maintain the numbers of anti-aircraft guns and searchlights. The chief of Anti-Aircraft Command, General Sir Frederick Pile, was able to get Churchill's agreement to use Home Guard and women from the Auxiliary Territorial Service (ATS) to crew anti-aircraft equipment, with regular army personnel as cadre elements.[57] As a result, 'by May 1942, over 11,000 Home Guard volunteers were being trained as anti-aircraft gunners',[58] and within a year, 111,917 Home Guard were in anti-aircraft units,[59] a figure that would eventually rise to 141,676 by the late summer of 1944.[60] The main anti-aircraft guns in use were the Vickers 3.7in. Mark 1 heavy anti-aircraft gun, and the far less numerous 4.5in. gun. There were also a small number of First World War vintage 3in. guns. For defence against low level air attack the main weapon was the 40mm Bofors gun.[61] There were shortages of all these weapons throughout the war, with production of the heavy guns, in particular, being slow. A simpler anti-aircraft weapon was required, and this came in the form of the 3in. rocket projectile which entered service in 1941. In his account of Britain's air defences, Alfred Price described the weapon:

> Each rocket projectile was 6ft 4in. long and weighed 54 pounds. These fin-stabilised rockets did not rotate in flight, and for that reason were called 'Unrotated Projectiles', 'Ups' for short. The UPs were fired in salvoes of 128, on the indications from GL [gun laying] radar, to produce a 'shotgun' effect. After launch each rocket accelerated to about 1,000mph in 1½ seconds, then coasted on to its maximum engagement altitude of 19,000ft. The 22-pound warhead was fused to explode at a pre-set time after launch.[62]

The rocket batteries were also known as 'Z batteries' and many were manned by the Home Guard.

Roy Barclay joined the Home Guard as a sixteen-year-old volunteer in 1940. As an apprentice at Charles Hill and Sons shipyard in Bristol, he joined the yard's own Home Guard unit, which was attached to the Royal Artillery, and provided crews for rocket batteries sited around Bristol. The Home Guards spent three nights a week at the rocket battery sites around the city; 'we used to go about seven o'clock, get there [the battery site] about eight, and we used to leave about eight o'clock the next morning, come back and carried on the normal work in the shipyard'.[63] Barclay believed that there were three or four rocket sites around Bristol, manned by Home Guard, under the command of regulars from the Royal Artillery. Each battery consisted of twelve rocket launchers, with each launcher crewed by two men. Another teenage Home Guard rocket crewman was Ronald Elliott, who joined the force in South Shields, where he was a temporary clerk in the Town Hall. South Shields was, like Bristol, a shipbuilding and repair centre, and was similarly equipped with rocket batteries. Elliott explained the siting and use of the rockets:

> We had the site which is off Highfield Drive in South Shields, on the top of the cliff. There were two fields there, and they had this pattern of anti-aircraft rocket launchers, and they were in a sort of square with so many at intervals, so that you had a grid, and each crew had two of them. And what the aim was was to fire all of these rockets into the air into this grid formation to catch any aircraft that were coming in over the sea. And they fired rockets about five or six feet long which were loaded onto racks at each side. It span round, did the whole contraption, the operator was in the middle, and he had a rocket on each side of him. You set the fuse, which determined how high the rocket went before it actually exploded, and you turned the whole machine around to give it a direction, and you set the elevation – and these were all given to you by a control, and they were tuned into anti-aircraft defences, and they sent us information. And everybody set their fuses, and elevation, and the direction, and, at a given signal, sent all these rockets off into the air. And I think we shot down one aircraft at one time. It was part of the anti-aircraft protection, rather like balloons.[64]

In comparing the rocket batteries with balloon defence, Elliott was, in all probability, accurately assessing the value of the weapon. Anti-aircraft artillery expended large amounts of ammunition to bring down enemy aircraft, but the rocket batteries were even less effective. Nonetheless, they were an integral part of a sophisticated anti-aircraft defence system. Another Home Guard, Joseph Yarwood, who had seen active service with the Royal Army Medical Corps (RAMC) on the Western Front and in Egypt during the First World War, also served in a rocket battery, but in a plotting control role. The Home Guard battery that Yarwood served in was one of those sited around Plymouth, on a cliff top, overlooking the sea approach to the port. Yarwood's role was 'in the plotting room. We [would] get the messages for them [the rocket crews], and we would pass them on to the guns [i.e. rockets and guns at the same site], the range and the bearing, and to what angle the rockets were to be'.[65] Yarwood was on duty one night when the Luftwaffe mounted a heavy attack on Plymouth:

> We were there on this particular night, when we had a very severe attack, and what was making me particularly anxious was the fact that a lot of the stuff was dropping down near my house. And we engaged those raiders at least 20 times, it was an all-night do. We were tracking them along the sky, and giving the readings to the men on the guns [and rockets], so they could set the rockets or sights accordingly, and then we got so far, instead of getting the order to fire, we were back to square one, and we'd be tracking another lot. And that's what we did all night. Never fired.[66]

In fact, despite repeated raids on Plymouth, Yarwood was never on duty when the rockets were fired in anger. This was also the case for Roy Barclay, although he was later to see action in both the Merchant Navy and the Royal Navy. The lack of action experienced by some Home Guard anti-aircraft units, something that became the typical experience as the Luftwaffe's attacks on the UK lessened, led to problems of absenteeism. By late 1943, for example, 'low morale and absenteeism [was] a major problem: in one Glasgow rocket battery the average rate of absenteeism was 20 per cent'.[67] Although the last large air raid was mounted on the night of 10 May 1941, against London, air attacks on the UK would continue throughout the war. Sneak, hit and run raids were mounted by fighter bombers on coastal towns and targets, and raids by medium bombers continued, spasmodically, throughout 1942 and 1943. These included the *Baedecker* Raids of April and June 1942, which targeted York, Norwich, Canterbury and Exeter in retaliation for the RAF's destruction of Lübeck. But in the first four months of 1944, the Luftwaffe mounted the 'Baby Blitz', or *Operation Steinbock*, deploying more than 500 bombers in raids across Britain. By then, the RAF night fighter defences and Anti-Aircraft Command, including its Home Guard gunners, was a well-integrated, effective defence. '*Steinbock* cost the

Luftwaffe more than 300 planes. For every five people killed on the ground, the raiding force had lost about one bomber and four crewmen killed, wounded or captured. The defending night-fighter squadrons and gun batteries ensured that although the bomber force could inflict serious losses, it suffered almost equally heavy losses itself'.[68] In these raids, Home Guard gunners played an active, combatant role.

Coastal batteries

Prior to the First World War most coastal defence artillery had been in place to defend the major ports of the UK. The thinking behind this approach was that the Royal Navy was sufficiently strong to maintain a powerful Home Fleet that could quickly deploy to any part of the UK's coastline and defeat any attempted invasion force. German navy bombardment of the North-East of England partially changed that, as did the need to protect targets from unexpected attack by fast torpedo boats. Despite some improvements in coastal defences in the inter-war period, 'Britain faced the beginning of the Second World War, with, essentially, the same coast defences with which it had weathered the previous one'.[69] However, the rapid collapse of France, Belgium and the Netherlands brought home the need for a much-improved coastal artillery defence system, and the emergency battery programme was embarked upon. Old naval guns, mostly of 6in. calibre were taken from navy stores and used to strengthen existing gun sites and create new ones. In just over a year, from May 1940, nearly 100 emergency batteries were established, 'extending the continuous chain [of guns] around the coast as far as north Devon, and to add in discrete locations on the English north-west coast, such as Fleetwood'.[70] The 6in. guns had ranges between 14,000 and 24,500 yards, depending on whether they were Mk 7 or Mk 24 models. Larger calibre, 9.2in. counter-battery pieces had a range of 36,700 yards, and there were super-heavy, 18in. guns mounted in Kent to counter German guns in the Pas de Calais.[71] In addition, 4.7in. and 6pdr quick-firing guns were in use.

As the war progressed, the Home Guard provided gunners for many of the coastal guns, particularly in the emergency batteries. William Aikman was educated at Bradford Grammar School, and had just completed his first year as an undergraduate at Queen's College, Oxford, when he was called up as a regular Royal Artillery officer shortly before the outbreak of war. He went to France with No. 5 Battery, 1st Heavy Regiment, RA, as part of the British Expeditionary Force (BEF) in 1939. Returning after Dunkirk, Aikman served as a gunnery instructor with the South-West Sector of Southern Command from 1943–44. During this time, the Home Guard came to play a major role in providing the manpower for Britain's coastal artillery, and Aikman was closely involved with this process. As a staff officer, he had the oversight of coastal artillery on the south-west coast of England. He explained that by 1943:

> Most of them [the emergency batteries] were now being manned by Home Guard. There would be the regular component of the officers responsible for the unit, and there would be staff who would occupy key roles, and the Home Guard would be there, so the battery would be on four hours' notice [...] And I would go there to see if the permanent staff were coping with what they had to cope with. I would be there to see the practice, seawards, conducted.[72]

Aikman's role enabled him to gain an accurate and detailed picture of the capabilities of the Home Guard gunners. He was absolutely sure that the Home Guard gun crews were competent and effective:

> The Home Guard were competent [...] they were trained on the equipment, and they were competent to do it. And they were trained to do it. I can remember one battery, where the man who was in control of the battery observation, of the range finder. His civilian job had been as a brigadier. He was certainly taking upon [himself] a brigadier [role], and not a bombardier in charge of the range finder. Yes, they [the Home Guard] were able to fire and service the equipment; I have no doubt at all. They were trained to do it, and were there to do it.[73]

The 6in. and 4.7in. guns that the Home Guard gunners used were largely drawn from First World War stocks, guns taken from decommissioned British warships. But other sources had been drawn upon, including old French and Japanese naval guns. It was the latter that were responsible for a fatal incident that Aikman witnessed, one that shows, yet again, that Home Guard sacrificed their lives in the defence of the UK. Aikman had gone to inspect a Home Guard coastal battery at Torquay bay. The battery was to demonstrate their competence in a live fire exercise, a 'practice seawards'. Aikman remembered:

> So we had this practice seawards, and I was there, and my brigadier from Plymouth was there, and also my senior brigadier was there from Wilton, the RA Southern Command [...]. The practice seawards was proceeding normally, as far as I was concerned in the control tower, with the officer who instructed the shoots [...]. And we were surprised that a shell did not fly normally through the air, and landed short of the target. It seemed that

there had been a premature explosion, not of the shell, but of the cartridge before the breech mechanism was fully locked, so much of the blast of the propellant had come back into the gun emplacement, killing three men outright, and three others died of their injuries [. . .] and this was a considerable disaster [. . .]. On the night of the explosion, I can remember that my brigadier from Plymouth, in order to convince the Home Guard of the safety of the equipment, insisted that there should be a further firing from the other gun, which was done.[74]

Aikman was put in charge of the enquiry into the accident, and, as it transpired, the guns had a rather chequered safety record:

It was an emergency battery, it was equipped with naval guns, 4.7in., that had been made in Tokyo under licence from Vickers Armstrong [. . .] and I sent to Bath, where the naval artillery people were, and they came down, and I learnt from them that this was the third time it had happened on the 4.7in. gun. The naval people were rather pleased that it had now happened on a land mounted gun, because that meant that they could see the bits, because on the previous occasions they had taken place on merchant ships, and the bits had finished up in the sea.[75]

Aikman was upset by the deaths of the Home Guardsmen, particularly the fatally wounded men whom he had interviewed in hospital before their deaths. The exact cause of the accident was not established, but the deaths of the men gave a grim edge to one Home Guard's half-humorous comment that 'a Home Guard weapon was one that was dangerous to the enemy and, to a greater degree, to the operator'.[76]

If the danger of a full-scale invasion had greatly receded by the time the Home Guard formed the key element in the coastal artillery defence of the UK, raids by German light naval forces were not unknown. In these cases, it was Home Guard gunners who were in the frontline. In the run up to the western allies' invasion of Normandy, German air and sea raids intensified. The Home Guard manned coastal batteries around Plymouth had been issued with 40mm Bofors light anti-aircraft guns to strengthen the port's air defence against what turned out to be, in Aikman's words, 'several spectacular raids'. In addition, Aikman was in the fire control tower at Pendennis Castle in May 1944 when a German E-boat force was picked up on inshore radar. Pendennis Castle is one of the elegant Tudor 'paired castles' – its twin is St Mawes Castle – built in the 1540s to repel any attempted French or Spanish invasion.[77] Four hundred years later, these forts were still part of England's defence against invasion, and when the radar picked up the raiders, Home Guard manned 6in. batteries opened fire at the fast attack boats and drove them off. By this time, around 7,000 Home Guard were serving with coastal artillery, and more manned coastal searchlights that formed part of the batteries.[78] In Aikman's view, these men were 'efficient and competent',[79] and the Home Guard contribution enabled the army to release regular gunners for the invasion of Western Europe.

Conclusion: the development of a fully armed force

A volunteer in the LDV in May, 1940, may have started his military career 'armed' with a heavy walking stick, but, by the time the force was 'stood down' in 1944, he might have progressed from that to Molotov Cocktails, American P17 rifles, Lewis guns, anti-aircraft rocket batteries, or 6-inch coastal defence artillery, by way of armoured cars and spigot mortars. The Home Guard was issued with a remarkable variety of weapons, some a good deal more effective than others, and some difficult and dangerous to use. The Home Guard's armoury was a unique mixture of the extempore, the scrounged, and the orthodox, but, as Home Guard service on the coastal batteries illustrates, the force was competent and ready to defend the United Kingdom.

Chapter 8

Cloth Caps and Steel Helmets

Uniforms for the Home Guard

The appearance of the Home Guard underwent dramatic changes in the force's short history. In the earliest days of the LDV, most volunteers were not, in fact, uniformed at all, but wore civilian clothes. This was problematic for a number of important reasons. Lacking uniforms, the LDV were in contravention of international law – having the appearance of *franc-tireurs* they were, as German radio was quick to point out, open to being executed if captured. Further, the lack of uniform was, as the government knew, hardly conducive to the maintenance of morale or discipline among the volunteers. And, for the volunteers, concerned about their status among their fellow civilians, it left them open to ridicule, especially if they were on duty armed only with coshes, walking sticks and shotguns. Initial remedies came in the form of local improvisation, old uniforms held by ex-servicemen, and the ubiquitous armband. In some areas, such as Northern Ireland, uniforms were quickly made available, but the real solution to the problem was in the hands of the UK government. Surplus pieces of uniform kit were available, notably side caps in army khaki, and fatigue uniforms from the regular army, but it was some time before the force really took on the appearance of a properly constituted military organisation.

The story of uniforms for the LDV and Home Guard is complex, and reflects the competing demands on wartime production, the changing importance and role of the force, and local conditions. The Home Guard wore a range of uniforms, and exhibited a variety of rank, proficiency and unit insignia, which reflected the changing status of the force as the war progressed. In addition, waterborne Home Guard often wore more naval elements of kit with khaki items, and women in the Home Guard, never issued with official uniforms, frequently wore a mix of civilian and military clothing giving them the appearance of a paramilitary militia. The intention here is not to provide an exhaustive account of uniforms, badges and kit issued, acquired, and worn by the Home Guard, but to examine some of the stages by which the force was transformed in appearance from a type of volunteer militia, with little to distinguish itself from the civilian population, to one that had every appearance of an arm of the UK's defence forces.

The question of uniforms and marks of distinction was not, however, merely one that concerned the outward appearance of the Home Guard, but was also related to fundamental questions of discipline, organisation, and effectiveness.

May 1940 – What to Wear?

The nineteen-year-old Dundee LDV recruit, William Scroggie, joined the force as soon as it was established. As a young, middle-class, white-collar worker employed by the famous Dundee publishers and printers, D C Thomson, Scroggie went on patrol wearing 'a sports jacket and a pair of flannel trousers, with a distinctive forage cap'.[1] The forage cap was, in fact, the most widely available uniform item at the outset, also known as the Field Service (FS) cap, it was a fore and aft cap in khaki, and the only uniform item that was available for distribution to the LDV in May 1940. The Under Secretary of State for War, Sir Edward Grigg, informed the House of Commons on 22 May that 250,000 Field Service caps were available for the LDV.[2] As with much of the kit that the LDV was to receive in 1940, the surplus FS caps were often of odd sizes, and many volunteers were to find that their heads were either far too small or grossly over-sized when it came to finding a cap to fit. Further, even the 250,000 FS caps available left the majority of volunteers without even that small indicator of military purpose.

Lacking even enough forage caps, the immediate solution to the uniform problem was to authorise the wearing of armbands by volunteers. Both government issue and locally produced armbands were used. The earliest official armbands were in white, bearing the black letters LDV, and were worn on the right arm above the elbow. Not enough of these could be manufactured or issued, and locally produced versions were widely made. There were also versions of the LDV lettering, with, for example, the unit at Portsmouth dockyards wearing armbands with the lettering 'DDV' – for Dockyard Defence Volunteers.[3] Cyril Punt, a merchant marine and Royal Navy veteran of the Great War, and, later a RNVR officer who served on minesweepers in UK coastal waters, and off Norway, from 1941–1945, joined the LDV in Team Valley, Tyneside in May 1940, and remembered the locally produced armbands, which, interestingly, were made with white lettering on a black armband, reversing the official colours :'All the women were making black armbands with white tape – "L" "D" "V" – printed on them. [We were told] "you wear these every time you come on duty". [. . .] Just this black band, with LDV on it'.[4] Cyril Punt went on duty wearing his civilian clothes, his white and black armband, and carrying his merchant marine revolver, while the seventeen other volunteers in his platoon carried shotguns. The Team Valley armbands were, perhaps, a little more tactically discreet than the official white armbands, something that the authorities soon appreciated, leading to a new issue of khaki armbands with the LDV lettering in black. This became the standard armband for the LDV, but they were frequently issued with additional stamps and marks. For example, the primary importance of maintaining the security of communications meant that Post Office and railway volunteers were issued with LDV armbands bearing identification stamps in addition to the letters LDV. These stamps often bore issue numbers or the wearer's National Identity number, designed to keep track of *bona fide* armbands issued to these key workers. In addition, armbands were also seen bearing rank details, with, for example, Southern Railway LDV armbands sometimes carried red stars above the LDV lettering, denoting rank.[5] The armband continued to be issued and worn even after other uniform items were made available. When the LDV became known as the Home Guard, new armbands were issued with 'Home Guard' in black on khaki. The wearing of armbands seems to have been unpopular once uniforms were issued, and it was normal to see the section of the armband bearing the title 'Home Guard' cut out and stitched directly to the right arms of uniforms. What many sartorially minded Home Guards really wanted were Regular Army style shoulder titles, not civilian style armbands.

Denims and Battledress

The first uniform that many volunteers were issued with was surplus Army fatigues – loose fitting, coarse cloth blouses (short jackets) and trousers that the Army called 'denims'. In the same announcement in which Sir Edward Grigg had told the House of Commons that FS caps were available, he also said that 90,000 sets of what he called 'overalls' had also been issued to the LDV. These were the denims, and, like the FS caps, the fortunate, or not so fortunate, volunteers who received them were frequently surprised to discover that there appeared to be something wrong with their body shape and size. The denims had been introduced for the Regular Army in 1939, and had been designed to wear over the battledress uniform, introduced in the same year, to protect it when carrying out dirty tasks. The denims had, therefore, never been intended for wear on their own, neither were they designed for anything but fatigues. For the Home Guard, the ill-fitting, ugly denims soon became notorious. The 23rd Middlesex Battalion of the Home Guard discovered that the denims were not exactly what they were hoping for, and the poor sizing problem was exacerbated by the manner of issue:

> Uniforms as they arrived at Platoon were divided by four and sent to the four Sections. It was thus impossible to fit any man. Three pairs of trousers large enough for Göring would arrive with three

blouses small enough for Goebbels. It did not matter much, however, as denim never was made to fit human beings. The first parade of the Section after the issue of denim was a sartorial triumph. The necks of the blouses, whatever the size of the blouse itself, were like horse collars and disclosed an array of necks and underwear.[6]

Despite the unpopularity of the denims, the initial intention was that they would constitute the basic uniform issue for the force. The Home Guard, however, realised that not only were the denims the antithesis of military smartness, they were, more importantly, not as serviceable as the Regular Army issue serge battledress. Further, the denims were seen by many Home Guard as being yet a marker of their inferior status in the defence of the UK. For the government, the question involved cost and the availability of both the denim material and the serge battledress. On 14 August, 1940, the Secretary of State for War, Anthony Eden, informed the War Cabinet that the supply of denim material was now sufficient to provide denim uniforms for all the Home Guard in the near future. However, the time needed to manufacture the uniforms meant that many volunteers would still be without uniform for the foreseeable future. As an interim measure, Eden recommended that Regular Army battledress be released to the Home Guard. This would result in 'a mixture of uniforms, but this was preferable to allowing any considerable period to elapse before the issue of uniform to the Home Guard was completed. The result of the step now proposed might well be that ultimately the whole of the Home Guard would have to be provided with battledress'.[7] The cost of providing battle dress for the Home Guard was estimated to be about £1million, and the War Cabinet approved this recommendation, 'subject to Treasury consultation'. This decision marked the change away from denims for the Home Guard, with standard British Army battledress being gradually issued to the force from the autumn of 1940 to the spring of 1941. Home Guard units still held stocks of the denim uniforms, at a rate of one set for every four men, but for use as originally intended – as fatigue overalls. The changeover was welcomed by all the Home Guard, and Charles Graves' contemporary record of the force included one volunteer's grateful farewell to the denims:

> *Adieu, thou threadbare boiler suit of green*
> *My Denim dress! Alas! You have not been*
> *(Candour avows it) such a perfect boon*
> *That I need weep to part from you so soon;*
> *In short, your fit impels me to confess*
> *You make me look a very nasty mess.*

Mark how the tunic, scanty at the waist
Which ripening years with kindly curves have graced,
And tempts my family to ribald mirth;
As for the collar – see the tortoise hide
A startled head by drawing it inside
His roomy shell, where he may rest unharmed –
E'en thus can I take cover when alarmed.
The nether half of this sartorial jest
Doubles the part of trousering and vest
By spreading from the armpits to the heels,
And in the middle publicly reveals
Such vast and wrinkled stern as one may mark
Upon a pachyderm at Regent's Park.[8]

Two other items of uniform – greatcoats and army pattern steel helmets – were also in extremely short supply in 1940. As an interim measure, the force was issued with shower-proof capes in waterproof khaki serge to wear in cold and wet weather. These had been specifically manufactured for the Home Guard, and, like the denims, seemed designed to be an antidote to smart turnout. As army greatcoats, 'Greatcoat, Dismounted, 1940 Pattern', became available for the Home Guard, so the cape was phased out. The lack of steel helmets for the force was seen to be particularly problematic as the tempo of German air raids increased in 1940–41. Steel helmets had been issued to Air Raid Precautions and other civil defence organisations, and could be bought privately, but the issue to the Home Guard was in short supply. Home Guards on duty during air raids often felt particularly vulnerable from falling shrapnel, and the officer commanding in the Croydon area noted, for example, 'I regret to say that on more than one occasion, I had difficulty in the middle of the night with groups of Home Guards in public shelters, who declined to go on sentry duty on the grounds that they could not face what were referred to as "showers of shrapnel"'.[9] Eventually, as with other essential pieces of kit, every Home Guard was issued with a steel helmet.

Black and Blue

Not all Home Guards wore khaki, with waterborne units frequently wearing some naval-style items of uniform in navy blue, and, in the case of Northern Ireland, the LDV initially wore black uniforms. Although the United Kingdom government had not included Northern Ireland in the plans to establish the LDV, the Ulster government was quick to establish the force itself, as an adjunct to the Royal Ulster Constabulary.[10] In fact, Northern Ireland's long experience of organising large-scale, auxiliary and para-military forces, a product of the troubled history of the whole island of Ireland, meant that the LDV in the province was quickly the most effective in the UK. Not only were modern weapons available, but so too was an organisational structure that was lacking in Britain. Further, although there were examples of localised co-operation between private industry and the LDV to provide uniforms – the case of Sir Montague Burton's provision, in collaboration with the local corporation, of 1,500 battle-dress uniforms for the Harrogate LDV being the most famous[11] – Northern Ireland accomplished this on a large scale. The question of uniforms for the new force was solved extremely quickly in the Province. The leading historian of Ulster's Home Guard, David Orr, described how 20,000 new uniforms were made and issued within a month:

> On 1 June 1940 300,000 yards of denim was purchased in Belfast and rushed to the dyers to be dyed black – some believe that it was meant to be dark green [the colour of the RUC's uniform], but had turned out black. A conference was called of all the tailoring establishments in Belfast, who offered their complete equipment for making the Defence Force uniforms; machines set to make women's and children's clothing had to be altered and switched [...] Three weeks after the initial order was given for a uniform to be made, 6,400 men were clothed, and six days later the number had risen to 10,000 and within a month 20,000. This was an amazing undertaking at any time, given that uniforms had to be delivered to villages all over Northern Ireland and subsequently to the men.[12]

The Northern Irish volunteers quickly took on the appearance of a uniformed and armed defence force, in their black denim blouses, trousers and side caps. Buttons on the uniforms came from a variety of sources, and included Army general service, RUC, and even old Royal Irish Constabulary buttons. The side caps sported the harp and crown badge of the RUC.

Before the spring of 1941, however, the Ulster Home Guard (UHG) began to metamorphisize into a force that looked more like its British counterpart. In December 1940, for example, during the bitter winter of that year, the War Office issued 30,000 khaki great coats to the volunteers. This, unfortunately, meant that the force was then uniformed in black and khaki – a reminder of the 'Black and Tans' of the Anglo-Irish War. However, the great coat issue was the first move to completely uniforming the UHG, like the Home Guard in the rest of the UK, in army khaki battledress, the first issue being in April 1941. Army boots and leather, Home Guard pattern, anklets were also issued at the same time as the greatcoats

The extensive, and vital docks and harbours of Northern Ireland saw the establishment of a waterborne unit of the force – the UHG (Belfast) River Patrol. This unit was 'formed from members of the Belfast Harbour Police, expert yachtsmen and employees of Belfast Harbour Commissioners and performed similar duties to those undertaken by similar mainland units, patrolling the Belfast Harbour area at night by motor boat'.[13] Across the UK, waterborne Home Guard units were formed, from the lakes of Cumberland to the dockyards of the country's ports, via inland waterways and canals. In many cases, the uniforms of these units reflected, in part, their 'naval' nature. One of the most famous of these units was the Upper Thames Patrol (UTP). This force pre-dated the establishment of the LDV, being established at the outbreak of hostilities in September 1939, with the co-operation of the Thames Conservancy.[14]

> The Patrol operated on the non-tidal waters from Lechdale to Teddington, a distance of 125 miles. Patriotic owners of motor launches came forward and lent their craft and in the majority of cases were able themselves to join the Patrol. Very quickly the requisite number of personnel became available. A high skill of watermanship being required, the Upper Thames Patrol receive special instructions as to this, in addition to the normal training received by Home Guard Battalions.[15]

Photographs show waterborne units, particularly in the LDV period, wearing yachting caps, pea jackets, roll neck sweaters, and LDV armbands. One UTP volunteer on the Thames at Reading remembered that his uniform was 'army battledress, seaman's blue roll-neck jersey, blue peaked cap, sea boot socks and Wellington boots'.[16] The Ulster Home Guard (Belfast) River Patrol eventually wore standard battledress and a navy blue peaked cap with constable's or officer's pattern cap badges, bearing a fouled anchor and crown.[17] The UTP also had their own cap badge bearing fouled anchors surmounted by the heraldic shields of the City of London and the Thames Conservatory topped with a King's Crown.[18]

Uniformed Women in the Home Guard
The history of the UTP sheds more light on the role of women in an unofficial capacity from the earliest days of the Home Guard. A contemporary report in Graves' *The Home Guard of Britain* provides details of the role of women in the shore patrols of the UTP, which were established

in June 1940. The officer commanding of 'A2 (Shore) Company, UTP' explained the genesis of the shore companies of the waterborne force:

> As far as the Shore Companies were concerned, it [the UTP] suffered from two handicaps which were never overcome: no one could be induced in spite of many efforts on my part to lay down exactly how far inland the 'banks' were to go, which seemed to promise a good deal of friction with the LDV of several counties; and, secondly, we started recruiting some weeks after every one else. I suggested that all men living within, say, three miles of the river should be automatically transferred to the Shore Companies of the UTP, but this, I venture to think, quite reasonable idea was turned down with the comment that, if I could persuade any men to transfer, I might do so *provided* I did not thereby tread on the toes of any of the county Commanders.[19]

This, of course, proved to be an extremely difficult task to manage, and in a six week period, only 'scattered pockets of men' had been recruited for the Shore Patrol. The solution lay in motorizing these groups of men, but that required drivers. The officer commanding A2 (Shore) Company UTP found the answer with women keen to join the Home Guard:

> In the course of my wanderings I had come across dozens of women who were anxious to do something beyond the rather colourless activities of the WVS; and had even most illegally roped in one invaluable one as my sort of office second-in-command, a lady to whose efficiency the Company owed much of its success [. . .] I was given *carte blanche* to recruit as many women as I liked [as drivers] or could; but, unfortunately, some rather important points were forgotten. In the event of invasion it would be unlikely for any women, apart from MTC, etc., to be allowed on the roads at all. No women were at that time allowed in the Home Guard, as it had now become. But of all this I was blissfully ignorant. With the help of my second-in-command, I held a meeting at Wallingford on August 29 [1940], recruited about forty women (the first, I believe, ever recruited for the Home Guard), designed a uniform, organized map-reading classes (at which they proved extraordinarily good) and evolved a scheme for mobilization of the whole Company.[20]

This is a fascinating account of the recruitment and role of women, and women's desire to be involved in active defence, at the outset of the force's history, at a time when no women were officially allowed in the LDV/Home

Guard. Unfortunately, no details of the uniform that was designed by the anonymous officer are given, but there are other descriptions of uniforms worn by 'illegal' women Home Guards.

Women working in government ministries were frequently absorbed into their workplace Home Guard units, usually in a support capacity, undertaking, for example, administrative, communications and catering tasks. However, some women were involved on an equal footing with their male colleagues. Mary Warschauer was a cipher clerk at the Air Ministry in London in 1940, and joined the ministry's Home Guard.[21] The women wore the same uniform as the men – 'we wore air force blue, navy blue dungarees and little Glengarry type hats'.[22] Interestingly, Lois Baker, another clerk at the Air Ministry, also remembered that 'the only uniform [of] "Dad's Daughter's Army" were allowed was a navy blue boiler suit, navy "fore and aft" cap, service tin hat and respirator'.[23] Photographic evidence also indicates that, in the earliest days of the force, unofficial women LDV volunteers wore, like their male comrades, improvised uniforms. The UTP again provides evidence of this, with a well-known photograph showing a woman at the wheel of a motor boat with two male volunteers. The woman wears an Auxiliary Fire Service ski-type cap, or, perhaps a Mechanised Transport Corps (MTC) cap, with an unidentified cap badge, and a dark blue or black armband bearing the white lettering, 'UTP'.

In April 1943, the government finally announced that women would be able to serve in the Home Guard in non-combatant roles, under the title 'nominated women', later known as 'Women Home Guard Auxiliary' (WHGA). No uniform was to be issued, and women were only to wear a round, gold coloured plastic badge bearing the letters 'HG'. It seems that many women did, in fact, wear just the badge attached to their civilian clothes. However, photographic and oral history evidence shows that plenty of women did, in fact, wear uniform. Some wore complete Home Guard uniform, as a photograph of the Women's Home Guard Auxiliary unit, Goole, Yorkshire in 1943 illustrates – with seventeen women in a formal photograph with the unit's commanding officer, all wearing battledress and FS caps.[24] The presence of the commanding officer in the photograph, and the perfect turn out of the women, suggests that, in this case, the Home Guard unit was fully supportive of its women members wearing full Home Guard uniform. More typically, women seemed to have put together their own WHGA uniform, either closely modelled on the standard uniform, or distinctive in itself. For example:

> Winifred Watson, full-time Home Guard secretary in Wingham,
> Kent, wore an ATS-style tunic and skirt. Eunice Lowden's unit in

the City of London wore dark trousers, white shirts with epaulettes and shoulder flashes, dark ties and forage caps, their round badges pinned to their chests; and Mollie Dale in Smethwick and Jeanne Townend in Goole, new entrants after 'recognition', wore ATS-style greatcoats and army-trousers, and a battle dress top.[25]

Interestingly, photographs show WHGA wearing berets, an item of kit not worn by male Home Guards, who wore the FS cap, or, in Scotland, the Tam O'Shanter. The typical intention of WHGA appears to have been, when putting together a uniform for their service, to mix what military items they could find with civilian clothing that imitated, in colour and fabric, military wear. For example, a composite WHGA illustrated in Martin Brayley's *The British Home Front*, shows a woman wearing her badge on an FS cap, a khaki shirt with epaulettes and breast pockets, khaki tie, a brown corduroy skirt, and a large khaki cloth side bag, as dictated by her role as a stretcher bearer, which is indicated by red on white 'SB' armband.[26]

Badges and designations

The LDV started life with little in the way of uniform, and nothing, beyond the armband by way of any sort of insignia. There were, at the outset, no commissioned or even NCO ranks, and, hence, no system of rank badges comparable to that of the Regular Army. Instead, in June, 1940, a series of 'appointments', were recognised. These appointments, which roughly corresponded to commissioned and NCO ranks, were to be displayed on uniforms (if the volunteers possessed one at that stage) using a system of dark blue cloth stripes on the shoulder for appointments including and above platoon commander, and by chevrons for section commander. This rank structure was partially revised in August, 1940, with more detailed instructions as to the display of appointments. The system is summarised in Table 8.1.

There was a low-level of resentment among the Home Guard that they had not been granted more formal status in respect of commissioned and NCO ranks. This concern was expressed by some senior figures in the force, with, for example, Sir Hubert Gough, a renowned retired general, and organiser of the Chelsea LDV from the outset, writing in a letter published in *The Times* on 21 August 1940: 'Everybody knows that the exercise of leadership in battle and ordinary discipline cannot be enforced in any military unit without a properly constituted body of officers and NCO's whose authority is acknowledged by all concerned'.[28] Some Home Guards, however, were keen that the force remained distinct from the Regular Army in terms of its internal structure, and wished to maintain its strong volunteer

Table 8.1   Officers and NCOs Rank Markings, LDV, 1940.[27]

LDV appointment markings, as per Army Council Instruction 653, 24th June 1940

Appointment	Markings
Zone Commander	Four dark blue cloth stripes on each shoulder strap
Battalion Commander	Three dark blue cloth stripes on each shoulder strap
Company Commander	Two dark blue cloth stripes on each shoulder strap
Platoon Commander	One dark blue cloth stripe on each shoulder strap
Section Commander	Three worsted chevrons worn on one sleeve

Home Guard rank markings as set down in Army Council Instruction 924, dated 15th August 1940

Appointment	Markings
Zone Commander	One dark blue cloth stripe 2″ deep on each shoulder strap
Group Commander	Four dark blue cloth stripes 3/8″ deep on each shoulder strap
Battalion Commander	Three dark blue cloth stripes 3/8″ deep on each shoulder strap
Company Commander	Two dark blue cloth stripes 3/8″ deep on each shoulder strap
Platoon Commander	One dark blue cloth stripe 3/8″ deep on each shoulder strap
Section Commander	Three worsted chevrons worn on one sleeve
Squad Commander	Two worsted chevrons worn on one sleeve

ethos, something that was felt might be undermined by the granting of commissions, badges of rank, army style discipline, and saluting. The saluting issue was a good example of this tension, as Charles Graves highlighted:

> In most cases free submission to authority was willingly given, but as an example of instruction may be quoted: '*Saluting*: There is no authority which orders that members of the LDV should salute. The matter has been left to the personal dictates of the individual. The view is held, however, that it would be in accordance with the high standard of bearing and general individual efficiency of the LDV if volunteers when in uniform preserved the universal custom of the Services and paid the usual military marks of respect to all officers in uniform'.[29]

The issue of the general discipline of the force was one that was central to the question of commissioned ranks. Examples of Home Guard volunteers resigning, sometimes *en masse*, over officer appointments and resignations, reflected the informal, voluntary nature of the force in 1940, but were not seen by the more militarily and traditionally minded as being evidence of good discipline.[30] The pressure for a more formal establishment of the Home Guard, combined with manpower problems,[31] led, in December 1941, to compulsory Home Guard service and conscription to the force, but, before that, the regularisation of ranks had been addressed.

The impetus to the changes came, as so often, from Churchill. At a Cabinet defence committee meeting on 3 September 1940, the Prime Minister 'stressed the importance of ranks for [Home Guard] officers'.[32] As a result the Army Council established a sub-committee, chaired by Sir Edward Grigg, joint Under-Secretary of State for War, to look at the training and organization of the force. It reported in October, and noted that 'the Home Guard was above all an asset to national morale and ought to be supported as such. [It] was also agreed that there were real problems with the current semi-independent and disparate nature of the force. "The time has arrived when more direct control and administration as distinct from guidance are required" '.[33] This led to the superseding of 'appointments' to Home Guard commands, and the creation of Regular Army style ranks. For the government and the army, the changes brought the Home Guard further under central control, and diluted some of the aspects of what was a volunteer force that had been seen as potentially problematic. For the Home Guard, it was another important step towards the regularisation of its position. In March, 1941, the Home Guard were instructed that the rank structure, and badges of rank, would henceforth correspond to that of the Regular Army.[34] The old system of blue stripes was replaced by the stars and crowns of regular, commissioned ranks.

Frank Kellaway, a Home Guard officer in the 8th Battalion, the Devonshire Home Guard, remembered when he and one of his platoon commanders went to Plymouth in 1941, prior to his unit's issue of army rank badges, to attend a demonstration of the Spigot mortar. For the demonstration, Kellaway had been issued, for the first time, with the single crown badge of a major. Returning to his home town on the Sunday evening, Kellaway remembered:

> It was a lovely summer evening, and, on our way back, we went up round Plymouth Hoe, just to have a look at the Sound [...] and, of course, there were barrage balloons out. Plymouth, in the old days, was almost like a home town, I had an aunt living there, and I used to spend a lot of time there. And Fred and I had got out of the car, leaning over the wall looking out over, and I was thinking, more or less, about the good old days that I had in Plymouth before the war when I was younger, and a couple of very smart marines came striding along the pavement [...] and came up with

a terrific salute, and I said to Fred, 'My goodness, who do you think those chaps are saluting?' 'Us, you silly bugger! You're the senior officer, return the salute!'[35]

This incident not only illustrates the surprise of a civilian-minded Home Guard officer, but also the degree to which, with army rank badges, that the Home Guard of the early summer of 1941 could look indistinguishable from other elements of the UK's military. The outward transformation, at least, of the force from ill-uniformed volunteers wearing distinctive rank badges, to a regularly uniformed and organised adjunct of the Army was almost complete.

Other outward signs of the increasingly formalised position and status of the Home Guard took place in 1940, as the question of cap badges was dealt with, along with shoulder titles and battalion flashes. The question of affiliation and the right to wear the cap badges of county regiments was an important one for many Home Guards. Popular attachment to local regiments was strong, and 'August 3 was a red-letter day in the history of the Home Guard. The various units were affiliated to County Regiments, armlets were issued with the badges of these Regiments printed on them, and an issue was promised of actual regimental badges'.[36] The majority of units took the cap badge of their local regiment. However, exceptions have been identified, including those of Huntingdonshire, Radnorshire, Rutland, Caithness and Sutherland, the Palace of Westminster, and the 1st American Squadron. In the latter case, these US citizens in their own motorised Home Guard unit wore a cap-badge featuring an eagle with the USA 'Union Shield' upon its breast.[37] In addition, the Upper Thames Patrol kept its own cap badge, while the Ulster Home Guard wore the RUC cap badge. Home Guard units that had been organised by function, such as the Post Office and railway units, wore a variety of regimental cap badges as their personnel were spread over wide geographic areas. In addition, there were exceptions such as the Windsor Castle company of the Berkshire Battalion of the Home Guard, which wore the badge of the Grenadier Guards, as did the Buckingham Palace company, by special permission of the King. The London area Home Guard units wore not the old badges of the London Regiment, but those of the King's Royal Rifle Corps, East Surrey, Queen's Royal West Surrey, or Queen's Own Royal West Kents. Finally, the 3rd Inverness-shire Battalion of the Home Guard wore the caribou cap badge of the Newfoundland Forestry Unit – the famous 'Sawdust Fusiliers' who came from both Newfoundland and Canada to boost the UK's production of timber.

The Home Guard were also issued, from late 1940 onwards, with shoulder titles, usually of the style worn by the Regular Army, a curved khaki cloth badge with embroidered or printed 'Home Guard', which was worn at the top of the uniform sleeve. The majority of shoulder titles 'seem to have been manufactured privately for purchase by individual battalions, and thus the exact style and colouring varied considerably'.[38] As with other signs of army uniformity, the granting of shoulder titles was welcomed by the Home Guard: 'That was a big moment for us. At last we were being granted the appearance of professional soldiers, with a shoulder designation just like that of the Foot Guards'.[39] From the beginning of 1941, a system of identification for individual units was also developed, but one that contained numerous examples of eccentric codes. The badges were usually in the form of khaki rectangles bearing blue letters and numbers. So, for example, the code 'WR' above '56' stood for the 56th West Riding (Barnsley) Battalion.[40] A variety of unusual letter codes have been identified, for example, 'ABK', which stood for the Kincardineshire Battalion of the Aberdeenshire Home Guard, and while 'NRY' stood for the North Riding, 'SRY' stood for the Southern Railway.

Conclusion: rags to riches
The typical LDV volunteer went on patrol in May 1940 wearing civilian clothes, and, at best, armed with a shotgun, or, perhaps, a service revolver keepsake from an earlier war. By stages, from FS cap to battledress, via unsightly denims and locally manufactured 'LDV' armband, the Home Guard was transformed into a well-equipped part-time soldier, indistinguishable from other arms of the British Army. The apogee of Home Guard turn-out saw volunteer and conscripted Home Guards wearing a modern uniform, and fully equipped with personal weapons that would have enabled him to take an effective part in the defence of the UK. That sartorial transformation had also marked the transformation of the force from a volunteer body, imbued with all the positive and negative attributes of such a force, to a regularised, disciplined defence force.

Part V

Understanding and Remembering the Home Guard

Chapter 9

'It All Happened Before'

Understanding the Home Guard

The Home Guard, more than any similar force in modern British history, represented a people in arms. By July 1940, there were 1,166,212 volunteers in the LDV.[1] This number declined slightly over the winter of 1940/41, but in the summer of 1942, the figure stood at 1,565,000 serving in the Home Guard, and, following the introduction of conscription to the force, the figure was around 1.8 million by early 1943.[2] Compared with earlier organisations in the British military volunteer tradition, the Home Guard involved a much greater segment of the population:

> Whereas the Rifle Volunteers in 1861, at the height of their strength, made up 0.8 per cent of the total male population, and the volunteers of the VTC in 1917 about 0.7 per cent, in June 1941 the total membership of the volunteer Home Guard, in relation to the adult male working population not engaged in essential police or civil defence work, or in the regular armed forces, was 19.6 per cent. That meant that about one out of every five men not otherwise engaged was enrolled in the force (not to mention the thousands of women engaged in unofficial support duties).[3]

The LDV came into being at a time of national emergency, when it looked as if the volunteers who enrolled might, in a very short space of time, find themselves face to face with an invader. The sudden birth and rapid growth of the force, combined with the *ad hoc* nature of much of its initial organisation, recruitment, and equipment, meant that, from the outset, the precise function of the force was fluid. Further, what the LDV and early Home Guard was, exactly, was unclear. Some argued, with a particular eye on the recently ended Spanish Civil War, that it was a new type of People's Army or People's Militia; others saw it as a guerrilla force in the making, while others felt that it was simply yet another example of the long volunteer military tradition, that it had, in fact, 'all happened before'.[4]

This chapter looks at some of the contrasting views about what the Home Guard was, what it stood for, and how differing perceptions of its wider social and political significance influenced views about its proper military role in the defence of the United Kingdom. The emphasis here is not on the official, government or army, views of the meaning and role of the force, but on the views of others concerned with the Home Guard at the time. In particular, the arguments of a small, but significant group of left-wing Home Guard enthusiasts in the 1940/41 period are examined. I have grouped these writers and Home Guard activists under the heading of 'Home Guard Socialists', and examine their arguments for a politicised 'People's Army' approach to the Home Guard.[5] By contrast, other contemporary commentators saw the force as being in a long tradition of the defence of the British Isles from external invasion. This view tended to reflect a cross-class stress on national unity and patriotism (something that the Home Guard Socialists also stressed, but in a particular 'Popular Front' fashion). How accurate these contrasting interpretations of the force were is a moot point, but there was some truth in each of them.

The Home Guard Socialists

The mobilisation of the people, the rapid expansion of a wide range of auxiliary units, and the feeling that many of the politicians who had led Britain into war were, at best, incompetent, and, at worst, Nazi sympathisers, created a sense of the need for a rapid reassessment of social, economic, political, and military norms. When *Guilty Men*,[6] a polemic against appeasement, was published in July 1940 (selling over 220,000 copies, and being reprinted twelve times that July alone), it looked as if a new, patriotic, anti-Nazi and socialist discourse was going to dominate the political landscape of Britain under siege. To contemporary commentators, British political and social life was in flux, and the feeling among many was that there was scope for radical change within Britain. For some, particularly on the left, Britain was not only faced with the probability of invasion but also by the possibility of social revolution. Yet, by the winter of 1941, writing in the American *Partisan Review*, George Orwell offered a damning analysis of the failure of much of the left to capitalise on the situation, in particular to capitalise on the creation of the Home Guard:

> The personnel of the Home Guard is not quite the same now as it was in the beginning. The men who flocked into the ranks in the first few days were almost all of them men who had fought in the last war and were too old for this one. The weapons that were distributed, therefore, went into the hands of people who were more or less anti-Fascist but politically uneducated. The only leavening was a few class-conscious factory-workers and a handful

of men who had fought in the Spanish Civil War. The Left as usual failed to see its opportunity – the Labour Party could have made the Home Guard into its own organization if it had acted vigorously in the first few days – and in left-wing circles it was fashionable to describe the Home Guard as a Fascist organization.[7]

Orwell went on to note that the Communist Party of Great Britain (CPGB) forbade its members from joining the Home Guard, in keeping with its opposition to the war, which would continue until Hitler broke his pact with Stalin with the invasion of the USSR in June 1941. However, Orwell did identify, for his American audience, two key members of a small, but very active group of ex-communists and Spanish Civil War veterans who had seen both military and political potential in this mass organisation:

> The chief educative force within the movement [the LDV/Home Guard] has been the training school which was started by Tom Wintringham, Hugh Slater and others [. . .] Their teaching was purely military, but with its insistence on guerrilla methods it had revolutionary implications which were perfectly well grasped by many of the men who listened to it.[8]

Orwell was correct in identifying Tom Wintringham and Hugh Slater as key players in the training of the Home Guard in 1940, particularly at the Home Guard training school at Osterley Park, but he was inaccurate in his assessment that they restricted themselves to 'purely military' teaching. For such men also saw in the Home Guard the potential for the force to make a significant contribution to the radicalisation of British political and social life.

Both Tom Wintringham and Hugh Slater were Spanish Civil War veterans, as were other members of a loose grouping associated with Wintringham, who had been the commanding officer of the British battalion of the International Brigades in February 1937, before being wounded. Other figures with a background in the International Brigades included F.O. Miksche, and Bert 'Yank' Levy, who both worked with Wintringham on Home Guard training. In addition, there were other Home Guard educators and publicists, who could broadly be described as being on the left, and were concerned with the military and political implications of the organisation. These included the *Sunday Pictorial* journalist and columnist, Major John Langdon-Davies who had covered both the Spanish Civil War, and the Winter War between Finland and the USSR, and described himself as 'an anti-Fascist journalist'. Another journalist, novelist, and a veteran of the Great War, was John

Brophy, who was a close friend of the famous First World War memoirist, and Second World War pacifist, Vera Brittain. Langdon-Davies wrote the standard handbooks, *The Home Guard Training Manual* (1940), and *The Home Guard Fieldcraft Manual* (1942), while John Brophy authored *A Home Guard Drill Book and Field Service Manual* (1940). Brophy also wrote a best-selling tribute to the Home Guard, *Britain's Home Guard; a character study* (1945). This very popular account of the movement was illustrated by the war artist Eric Kennington (famous for his portrait illustrations in T E Lawrence's *Seven Pillars of Wisdom*). Kennington's colour illustrations of Home Guards complemented Brophy's text by showing Home Guards in their wider civilian context. Portraits showed, for example, 'Sergeant Stokes, Huntingdonshire Home Guard' in his farmworker's clothes,[9] while two facing portraits showed 'Melvin Jones, miner', and 'Corporal Melvin Jones, Monmouthshire Home Guard'.[10] Kennington's illustrations were a very graphic portrayal of the idea of the Home Guard as a citizens' army. All the Home Guard enthusiasts, like Wintringham, Slater, Miksche, Brophy, Langdon-Davies, and Levy, played an important part in the popularising of a left-wing analysis of the military and political significance of the Home Guard. Their contribution to the training of that organisation was notable, especially in the 1940–1941 period, and their widely read books, pamphlets and articles on the role and character of the Home Guard were unique in that they postulated an active, political significance to this military movement.

The historiography of left-wing involvement in the Home Guard is limited, and largely focused on the life and writings of Tom Wintringham. David Fernbach, in the early 1980s, put Wintringham's contribution to the Home Guard in the context of his Marxism, his Spanish experience, and, interestingly, in attempts by the left in the 1980s to develop a credible, non-nuclear defence policy for the UK. Fernbach's 'Tom Wintringham and socialist defense strategy' remains the most detailed consideration of Wintringham's ideas. Hugh Purcell, in his ground-breaking biography of Wintringham, *The Last English Revolutionary*, produced a readable life of a remarkable man, rightly characterised by Purcell as being an '*English revolutionary*'. Finally, S P MacKenzie in his, *The Home Guard*, devoted some space to the involvement of a range of left wing figures with the Home Guard, thereby putting Wintringham's efforts into a wider context. MacKenzie's chapter, 'A People's Militia? 1940–1', focuses primarily on Wintringham's struggles with the War Office and the Army, as they sought to minimise the impact of the Osterley Park group of socialists, but says less about the specific ideas of those activists.[11] What characterised Wintringham and the other socialist enthusiasts for the Home Guard was the combination of practical involvement in Home Guard training, allied to the development in lectures, newspapers, books, and pamphlets of a specifically socialist analysis of contemporary military imperatives. In the period 1940–1941, these enthusiasts developed an approach to the defence and transformation of Britain that can usefully be termed Home Guard socialism.

An alliance of the progressive classes

The idea of the Popular Front dominated Home Guard socialism. For the CPGB, as with other communist parties that took their line from the Comintern (the umbrella organisation for all Moscow-affiliated parties), the Popular Front had been just one more tactic in a roll-call of tactics that had marked the evolution of Moscow-led communism since the early 1920s. Following Lenin's recommendation to the Bolsheviks to think always of 'tactics, comrades, tactics', communists were happy enough to cynically shift from one position to another if it was deemed tactically necessary. In 1935, the Comintern instructed Moscow-affiliated communist parties to abandon their previous sectarian policy, 'class against class'. Reacting to the failure of the German Communist Party in the face of Nazism, the Comintern instructed its followers 'to overcome, in the shortest time possible, the survivals of sectarian traditions which have hindered them in finding a way of approach to the Social–Democratic workers'.[12] No longer was the British Labour Party to be dismissed as 'social fascist', instead the CPGB strove to create a 'united front' with the Labour movement – something that the Labour Party studiously ignored. Nonetheless, the Comintern's *volte face* enabled British communists to emerge from the isolation of 'class against class' and reach out to a wider audience than they had for the previous seven years. For the leadership of the CPGB this move was, above all else, merely a tactical move, but for many of their followers, the 'united front', or Popular Front period, was also driven by the desire to create an effective alliance of anti-fascists from among the progressive classes.

For the Home Guard socialists, such as men like Tom Wintringham, who had been a very early member of the CPGB, the Popular Front had real meaning. Wintringham himself was from a long-established middle class family, had been privately educated, and, after service in the Royal Flying Corps in the Great War, had taken a shortened war service degree at Balliol College, Oxford. Similarly, Hugh Slater, another of the key Home Guard socialists, an International Brigades' commissar, and the commander of the British battalion's anti-tank gun unit in Spain, was privately educated at Tonbridge School and the University of London. For communists like these, the Popular Front had a direct appeal, and seemed to take shape in Spain, when a small but vocal minority of middle class communists and anti-fascists volunteered to fight with the International Brigades, alongside the workers who formed the majority of the international combatants. Yet there were notable class tensions among the British volunteers, as James Hopkins pointed out in his detailed study of the British in the Spanish Civil War.[13] Hopkins noted that the fifth commanding officer of the British battalion, Fred Copeman, grouped most of the young students, graduates, and self-educated workers together in the anti-tank gun unit, as a deliberate act of class segregation aimed at reducing class tensions in the battalion. Although Slater, who commanded the unit, was regarded by most as being a very effective soldier, Hopkins argued that Slater's:

> ability to understand and gain the co-operation of his working class subordinates was severely limited. A Durham miner who had been with the battalion from the start, and was described as a 'good proletarian type' was forced to leave the Anti-Tanks 'because of differences with Slater'. Another comrade in the Anti-Tanks, Jim Brewer, despised the young officer.[14]

There was a feeling among many of the working class volunteers who came in contact with Slater, that he made no 'effort to disguise his contempt for working men'.[15]

If the day to day reality of campaigning with the International Brigades was not as free of class tension as might have been hoped, it was in Spain that some of the British volunteers for the Republic came to feel that the realities of the Comintern's tactics were much worse than tensions between individuals. Foremost among these was George Orwell, whose experiences fighting with the POUM (*Partido Obero de Unificación Marxista* – a revolutionary, anti-Stalinist communist party), and his witnessing of the Barcelona 'May events' in 1937, when the Communists systematically suppressed anarchist and anti-Stalinists, led him to the conclusion that the communist idea of the 'Popular Front' was nothing more than a betrayal of the revolution in Catalonia, and the implementation of fascism by another name. Orwell later referred to the Popular Front in Spain as being like 'a pig with two heads or some other Barnum & Bailey monstrosity'. Interestingly, other anti-fascists in Spain who later formed the core of the Home Guard socialists took the communist line that the crushing of the POUM and the anarchists in Republican Spain by the socialists and communists was merely the crushing of an attempted 'Trotsky-fascist' coup. As a leading member of the International Brigades, and a member of the CPGB, Tom Wintringham accepted this line. Another of the Home Guard socialists of 1940–1941, John Langdon-Davies, also followed the communist view in his reporting for the *News Chronicle*, alleging that the anarchists and the POUM were the tools of fascist *agents provocateurs*. Writing about the 'May Days' in Barcelona for the *News Chronicle*, Langdon-Davies commented:

> This has not been an Anarchist uprising. It is a frustrated *putsch* of the Trotskyist POUM, working through their controlled organisations, 'Friends of Durruti' and Libertarian Youth ... The tragedy began on Monday afternoon when the Government sent armed police into the Telephone Building, to disarm the workers there, mostly CNT men. Grave irregularities in the service had been a scandal for some time [...] By Wednesday evening, however, it began to be clear who was behind the revolt. All the walls had been plastered with an inflammatory poster calling for an immediate revolution and for the shooting of Republican and Socialist leaders. It was signed by the 'Friends of Durruti'. On Thursday morning the Anarchist daily denied all knowledge or sympathy with it, but *La Batalla*, the POUM paper, reprinted the document with the highest praise. Barcelona, the first city of Spain, was plunged into bloodshed by agents provocateurs using this subversive organisation.[16]

Ironically, Langdon-Davies was himself later to be denounced by the Communists as 'anti-Soviet' for his reporting from Finland during that country's amazing stand against the USSR during the Winter War of 1939–40. During that war, of course, the Soviet Union was a co-conspirator with Nazi Germany in the dismemberment of central Europe and the Baltic states.

Yet, despite their differing interpretations of the reality of the Popular Front in the late 1930s, the key Home Guard socialists believed that a successful defence of Britain had to lie in an alliance of the progressive classes. Further, following the Hitler-Stalin Pact, the CPGB had performed yet another *volte face*, and abandoned the idea of a Popular Front. But by then, none of the Home Guard socialists were members of the CPGB, most having been expelled from the party, in Wintringham's case because he refused to end his relationship with the American anti-fascist, Kitty Bowler, whom the CPGB regarded as a Trotskyist spy.

A patriotic, anti-Nazi defence

The Home Guard socialists stressed that victory over Nazism would be a result of the efforts of the entire British people. Their appeals were made to all those who wished to engage in a patriotic, anti-Nazi defence of Britain. That defence, to be effective, was to be built upon a socialist programme, one that would be of benefit to all patriots, including what Orwell characterised as 'the great mass of middling people, the £6 a week to £2,000 a year class who will defeat Hitler if class privilege is wiped out and socialism brought in'.[17] This was the class that Wintringham saw as being the 'meritocratic class', the technicians that ran modern industry, and had, in his opinion, strong anti-Nazi sympathies.[18] The obstacles to the successful defence of Britain and the ultimate defeat of Nazism by the progressive classes, were seen to come from pro-Nazi sympathisers in high places, and those who put the interests of private capital before those of Britain, the British people, and the war effort. In his best-selling Penguin Special, *New Ways of War* (July 1940), Tom Wintringham argued for the expansion of the Home Guard to four million men, creating a people in arms, which was, he claimed, both a revolutionary idea, and a patriotic and quintessentially British idea. Those who opposed such an idea were, he implied, incompetent, or worse:

> There are those who say that the idea of arming the people is a revolutionary idea. It certainly is. And after what we have seen of the efficiency and patriotism of those who ruled us until recently, most of us can find plenty of room in this country for some sort of revolution, for a change that will sweep away the muck of the past. But arming the people is also completely part of the tradition of the British.[19]

George Orwell, a sergeant in the Home Guard, complained about the class structure of the movement, which he termed the 'Blimp' mentality after the famous character of 'Colonel Blimp', but also noted that the force was, 'in the lower ranks [...] extremely democratic and comradely'.[20] Further, the events of 1940, at home and abroad, contributed to a new, essentially left-wing, political outlook that crossed classes:

> The political discussions that one hears in [Home Guard] canteens and guard rooms are much more intelligent than they were, and the social shake-up among men of all classes who have now been forced into close intimacy for a considerable time has done a lot of good.[21]

Sergeant Orwell was, as his friend, the writer, Sir V S Pritchett noted, a man who saw the war 'as a fight against the [British] governing class as well as a fight against the Nazis'.[22] For these socialists like Orwell, the Home Guard was both an instrument, and the concrete expression of, a real 'Popular Front', one built upon patriotic, progressive, anti-Nazism.

The Home Guard socialists argued that the movement was an essentially British phenomenon, and that such a people's militia had a long and distinguished pedigree in British history. However, from the Home Guard socialists' standpoint, previous manifestations of the popular defence of Britain were important not just because they attested to the enduring patriotism of the population, but also because those manifestations could be fitted neatly into their narrative of a popular, people's movement. Bert 'Yank' Levy, a Canadian who fought with the British battalion at Jarama, was another of Wintringham's comrades at the Osterley Park training school. Levy had served with Royal Fusiliers in the Near East during the First World War, and then, by his own account, had been involved in the Sandinista revolt in Nicaragua in the 1920s.[23] He was captured on the second day of the British battalion's action at Jarama, and a photograph exists of Levy with other captured British machine gunners being guarded by Nationalist *Guardia Civil*. He taught classes in 'unconventional warfare', which formed the basis of his Penguin Special, *Guerrilla Warfare* (1941, with an introduction, and, it appears, some input from Wintringham himself).

In *Guerrilla Warfare*, Levy referred to a range of precursors to a projected Home Guard guerrilla defence of Britain. He made a direct connection between the 'heavily armoured forces' of William the Conqueror and those of Hitler, holding up Hereward the Wake as a model of resistance to the Home Guard, albeit one, as Levy admitted, who failed to defeat the invader. There were unfortunate parallels here, too, between the failure of the Republicans in the face of Nationalist military prowess during the Spanish Civil War; indeed, Levy himself had only been in action for a day, as part of a medium machine gun company, before being captured by the Nationalists, and had certainly had no Spanish experience of the sort of irregular warfare tactics that he later enthusiastically recommended for the Home Guard. Wintringham drew also upon the Anglo-Saxon *fyrd*, and the raising of volunteers throughout British history, to underpin his argument that the people should be armed:

> It is in fact part of the British Constitution, and the *fyrd* of Anglo-Saxon times, the militia or volunteers of latter periods, have often been called 'the Constitutional Force', because it is part of the fundamental law of this country that each able-bodied citizen can and should have arms for training for defence.[24]

This attempt to co-opt the traditional, patriotically imagined history of England (as opposed to Britain or the United Kingdom) was interesting as it represented the recognition that patriotism, or, indeed, nationalism was a powerful motivating factor. The same story of England's, and, sometimes Britain's, history was also utilised by more conservative and traditionalist supporters of the Home Guard. By basing their argument that the people should be armed in their reading of English and British history, the Home Guard socialists were attempting to strengthen their call for an organisation that they imagined had the potential to become a force like the militias in the Spanish Civil War. At the height of the invasion fear in June 1940, Orwell wrote, in a letter to *Time and Tide*, that, 'at such a time our slogan should be ARM THE PEOPLE'.[25] Many socialists saw this as being the key to creating a revolutionary situation, or, at least, to helping to shift the balance of power from the state to the people. As Orwell put it in the *Evening Standard*: 'That rifle hanging on the wall of the working class flat or labourer's cottage is the symbol of democracy'.[26] And one of the common complaints that the Home Guard socialists had in 1940, as the force became better equipped, was that its members were, at first, forbidden to take their weapons home with them. This, they argued, made no sense militarily; nor, they might have added, politically, but it ignored the fact even by Autumn of 1940, at least 740,000 out of nearly 1,700,000 Home Guard were without personal weapons of any sort, and ammunition was in short supply for all weapons.[27]

Models of resistance

The Home Guard socialists were also able to draw upon a wide range of contemporary, and near contemporary, examples of the sort of organisations and types of warfare that they felt the Home Guard could emulate. All these proselytisers drew upon the examples of T E Lawrence and the Arab Revolt, the Irish war of independence, the Spanish Civil War, aspects of the Sino-Japanese War, the Winter War between Finland and the USSR, and, later, partisan activity on the Eastern Front. Such conflicts provided examples of militia, irregular, and guerrilla warfare. John Langdon-Davies in his lecture, 'Why the Home Guard?', drew upon his experience of the Winter War, and upon some slightly more exotic examples of the sort of warfare that he felt the Home Guard was capable of:

> There is another kind of war – 'Small War' or 'Guerrilla', and here everything is very different. This is the kind of war which the Spaniard has fought for centuries amid his mountains – the Finn amid his frozen lakes and forests. This in a way is the kind of war the Chicago gangsters and G-men fight incessantly in the suburbs of that great city [...] this is the kind of war which was waged in the marshes of the Chaco Canyon in South America.[28]

'Yank' Levy, in *Guerrilla Warfare*, made particular reference to the Irish war of independence, noting that 'the Irish were the first guerrillas to fight against an army that largely manoeuvred by vehicle', something that was of direct relevance to a Home Guard faced by a potential invasion by what was thought of as being a highly mechanised army.[29] Levy also made extensive reference to the Arab Revolt, and Orde Wingate's role in organising 'Jewish irregulars in Palestine'. Levy's advice to the Home Guard was to read fictional accounts of the campaigns in Ireland, Spain and China, namely O'Malley's *On Another Man's Wound*, Hemingway's *For Whom the Bell Tolls*, and Edgar Snow's *Scorched Earth*.

Guerrilla warfare was not the only focus of the Home Guard socialists. They also developed an analysis of the operation of blitzkrieg, and suggested a wide variety of military methods to combat the tactic. These military methods were closely related to a political analysis of the implication of armoured and mechanised warfare, and, in turn, were tied to their arguments for socialism and a people in arms. In *New Ways of War*, Tom Wintringham took as his starting point an analysis of blitzkrieg, and offered his response to that strikingly successful method of waging war. But it was a book by a former officer in the Czechoslovak army, the International Brigades and the regular Republican Army, F O Miksche, *Blitzkrieg* (1941), that provided the most thorough analysis and critique of the tactic. Wintringham was involved in the translation and provided an introduction to *Blitzkrieg*, in which Miksche gave a detailed account of German tactics that had brought such stunning success in Poland, western Europe, and at the time of publication, on the Eastern Front. He then proposed both defensive and offensive tactics with which to combat the blitzkrieg method. Where his analysis was most pertinent to the Home Guard enthusiasts was in relation to his theory of 'web defence'. This proposed that blitzkrieg could be successfully met by defence in great depth, built around 'islands of resistance', that were, in effect, all-arms defensive positions, interlinked, and possessing the capacity to take operational initiative without reference to a higher chain of command. This type of defence against the German concept of blitzkrieg had been adopted, with local success, by the French in the latter stages of the Battle of France, but too late to make any difference to the outcome in the summer of 1940.

Nonetheless, Miksche's analysis had a particular attraction for the Home Guard enthusiasts, and Wintringham, in his introduction, highlighted this element of the book. Whatever this type of defence was called – total defence, 'web defence', defence in depth – it gave a key role to the Home Guard. As Orwell noted in late 1941:

> The strategic idea of the Home Guard is static defence in complete depth, i.e. from one coast of England to the other. The tactical idea is not so much to defeat an invader as to hold him up till the regular troops can get at him.[30]

This, of course, was the army's view of the role of the Home Guard once it had taken over much of the static defence role, particularly in inland areas of the UK.

Military roles for the Home Guard

Over time the role of the Home Guard changed, both in the views of the government, the army, and the Home Guard socialists. The army was, throughout the Home Guard's existence, keen that it fulfilled two main functions, that of local reconnaissance and the defence of local areas. But many Home Guards wanted to have more active roles; aiming to increase their own mobility, or prepare for guerrilla warfare should their local areas be occupied. Writing at the end of 1941, Orwell commented on changing perceptions of the Home Guard's role. He identified six different roles: in 1940, the key roles had been to combat sabotage and the Fifth Column, while guarding against airborne assault. This was followed, once the summer invasion scare was over, by a move towards making the Home Guard into ordinary infantry. In 1941 the emphasis changed again, as events in North Africa and Crete suggested that the Home Guard should concentrate on anti-tank warfare, and, once more, on countering paratroopers. Then, with the emergence of Soviet Partisans in the areas of the Soviet Union rapidly overrun by the Germans, Home Guard volunteers seemed to have a potential role as guerrillas.[31] Whatever the precise function of the Home Guard, one constant for the socialists was that it should have an active, central role in the defence of Britain, providing aspects of defence that only an armed population could provide.

Writing in 1945, John Brophy, in his *Britain's Home Guard*, outlined the events of 1940 that led to the spontaneous organisation of men into self-defence groups, followed quickly by Anthony Eden's appeal for men for the Local Defence Volunteers. For the Home Guard socialists the fact that groups of men had come together prior to Eden's broadcast, especially groups of trade unionists who began to organise factory-based defence, was yet another example of the way in which patriotic, anti-Nazi workers were ahead of the government in the struggle to defend Britain. Brophy explained the particular fears of the summer of 1940:

> The Home Guard came into being in May 1940, before Dunkirk.
> At that time Norway had been overrun, and Denmark annexed in a
> single casual gesture. Rotterdam had been blasted into submission
> by air bombardment, and parachute troops, disguised or in their
> proper uniforms, were paralysing the communication centres of
> Dutch resistance, in co-operation with the 'fifth column'. These

were the enemies the Home Guard was designed first and foremost to meet and overcome – the parachutist and the fifth column.[32]

Langdon-Davies, in his lectures of the winter of 1940, also laid great emphasis on these two elements, arguing, inaccurately, that the fall of Norway was almost entirely due to Quisling and his fifth column, while paratroopers and airborne troops were, more accurately, blamed for the fall of Holland. The fifth column threat loomed large in 1940, and led to the internment of 'enemy aliens' (often refugees from Nazi Germany, or long-time residents of the UK), IRA men, around 1,000 members of the British Union of Fascists, and a few renegade Scots and Welsh nationalists. The paratroops fear lasted much longer, being given a further boost with the fall of Crete to German airborne forces in May 1941. The Home Guard enthusiasts were quick to point out that whether it was fifth columnists, paratroopers, or armoured and mechanised assault, the Home Guard had a role, as it could provide constant, if limited, coverage, across the whole territory of Britain, against any of these threats, something that regular forces could not. Further, the Home Guard socialists believed that the movement contained within it a large number of men who wanted social change, and that their effectiveness as a defensive force was tied to that radicalism. John Brophy, who had been an underaged volunteer in 1914, and had written two best-selling novels about the Great War, *The Bitter End* (1928) and *The World Went Mad* (1934), referred to the fact that the overwhelming majority of the initial LDV volunteers had been men from the Great War, who had maintained an idealistic desire for social change:

> This [...] hope for a radical impetus to social, economic, and political improvement survived the disillusionments of the battle-field, the parade-ground, and the field hospital [of the First War] better than the poetic and youthful idealism of selfless patriotism.[33]

This was a reflection, perhaps, of the celebrated First World War 'martyr', Edith Cavell's view that 'patriotism was not enough', and it was certainly the view of the socialists that patriotism met anti-Nazism, and a desire for social change, in the Home Guard.

Social radicalism and the people's defence
Defence against saboteurs, paratroopers, or armoured assault, all required, in the socialists' view, a different mindset in the Home Guard than in other, more traditional, military formations. Wintringham repeatedly argued that the unit of command had been steadily reduced by historical developments in warfare. In the face of modern war, characterised by the disruption of the

chain of command, widely dispersed encounters on a huge, non-linear front, and by a host of unorthodox tactics, soldiers had to be able to be their own leaders. Writing about his experiences in Spain, Wintringham commented: 'I drew the conclusion that in defence as well as in attack the initiative of the subordinate commander and of the ordinary soldier is the most vital quality to be cultivated'.[34]

Further, the Home Guard socialists envisaged the Home Guard being involved in guerrilla war should Britain be invaded and partly occupied. In all these cases, they argued, it would be important for Home Guard soldiers to be trained to operate on their own initiative. For this to happen, however, the Home Guard had to be fully imbued with a sense of democracy and the desire for social progress. This linkage of military effectiveness with social radicalism was at the heart of the Home Guard socialists' message. 'Yank' Levy argued that effective guerrilla resistance could only emerge from among people who benefited from a democratic political culture. His view was that, for guerrillas to be effective, they had to be imbued with independence of action and a freedom to use their initiative which arose most effectively under democratic systems. He contrasted this with what he felt was the inability of fascist or Nazi systems to produce effective guerrilla movements:

> We in Britain can go much farther than can the Germans, when it comes to the development and utilization of guerrilla methods, for both attack and defence. There are ways open to us which are closed to the Nazis. For we are men of democratic tradition, fighting for freedom, and guerrilla warfare is essentially the weapon of free men – a guerrilla band functioning efficiently under compulsion is inconceivable. Fascism or Nazism – and they are fundamentally the same – set out to destroy in men the very qualities which are most prized in guerrilla fighting. Free men, hating oppression, with freedom of initiative and arms in their hands – these make the ideal guerrillas. Therefore in the democratic countries there is far larger scope for the development of regular warfare along lines derived from guerrilla warfare. There are new ways of war which in this country and in Europe we can adopt, if we will – ways of war which the Nazis cannot and dare not use.[35]

Levy foresaw guerrilla warfare in Britain in stark terms, and clearly felt that there were few among the population who should not be involved in this type of warfare. For example, in addition to writing about the killing of Quislings and prisoners, he also mentioned, approvingly, an article from

Soviet War News, which covered the exploits of two Soviet Young Pioneers, whom Levy called 'Boy Scouts', aged twelve and fourteen, who had killed numerous German motorcyclists with wire stretched across roads. In an interesting aside, Levy noted, 'the British Boy Scouts who demonstrated how this should be done at Osterley, when we had not enough older instructors, were about the same age'.[36] There might have been a degree of propagandistic boasting in this, but, in reality, this was a dangerous path to go down. Certainly, under-aged combatants took part in the war across Europe, most notably the Boy Scouts of Poland in the Warsaw Uprising of 1944, and the youngsters of the Hitler Youth in 1944–45, but there was an important ethical question that had to be addressed (and was not addressed by Levy) in leaving children open to reprisals at the hands of a ruthless opponent. Further, the effectiveness of guerrilla war in defeating an enemy engaged in total war was a moot point. Successful guerrilla activity during the war was always related to the progress of large-scale, conventional military forces fighting on established front. For example, in the summer of 1944, when it was clear that the Axis would be defeated in Europe, the Italian Partisan movement (which was, at that stage around 80,000 strong) established two 'Free Zones' in Northern Italy. In response, the para-military and security forces of Mussolini's Italian Social Republic, and its German allies, crushed both zones in bloody battles that nearly saw the extinction of the Partisans.[37] Similarly, even in France, immediately following the Normandy invasion, elements of the French resistance which attempted the same policy of taking on Vichy French and German forces in large-scale actions on the Glières plateau, and at Vercors, were heavily defeated.[38] The much celebrated Partisans of Marshall Tito in Yugoslavia also fared badly in a succession of Italian military sweeps against them, even though the Italians were often using second-line troops. It was not until the overall, conventional, military situation forced the Germans to abandon Yugoslavia that the Partisans made real headway. Guerrillas had a role, but they were only ever effective in support of conventional military forces. If Britain had been invaded, the window for such guerrilla activity would have been small, and, in the event of the defeat of Britain's regular forces, continued recourse to guerrilla activity would have been tragically futile. Nonetheless, it can be argued that, on one level, the real point was, for Levy and the other Home Guard socialists, that the Home Guard represented the entire British people in arms, as Hugh Slater argued:

> The Home Guard is itself half civilian. It is a people's army. How useful it can be in the military sense depends wholly on the extent to which it reflects the needs, the desires, and the aspirations of

the ordinary British people. Its purpose is a democratic one – to win the war against Fascism. The Home Guard must, therefore, be thoroughly permeated with democratic ideas, methods and attitudes.[39]

Probably unknown to any of the Home Guard socialists, the government did, in fact, put in place a guerrilla army, designed to harass occupying forces. This stay-behind force was the Auxiliary Units, or Auxunits, made up of a mixture of some regular soldiers, and Home Guard. Secret bases, known as Operational Bases (OBs), were set up in 1940 and stocked with arms and equipment. Men with good local knowledge of their home areas formed a unique guerrilla force in waiting. The Auxunits were a reasonably substantial force with, for example, 300 men in Somerset serving in forty-four Auxunits using fifty OBs. However, they were not, as men like Levy would have wanted, a large, people's guerrilla force.[40]

The final chapter in Wintringham's *New Ways of War* was quite explicit about the nature of these democratic ideas stating, 'what we need, in order to be strong, is a planned use of men, machines, and factories: in other words what we need is socialism.'[41] Further, he went on to state, 'that since we need socialist measures for victory, these measures will be best carried out by socialists'.[42] This socialist programme was to be protected by a four million strong Home Guard (in fact, the Home Guard's peak membership was around 1,800,000) that would be largely responsible for the defence of Britain, while the regular armed forces were deployed overseas. In addition, just as the Home Guard socialists proposed that socialists should be running the war at a macro level, they also stressed the role that the ordinary Home Guards could have in strengthening socialism, and the link between the Home Guard and socialists, at the local level. In preparing the defence of local areas, Hugh Slater argued, it was not sufficient for Home Guard units to be fully familiar with the geography and topography of their home area, they also had to be familiar with key people in that area. One of the fundamental duties of the platoon commander was that, 'he must know, and work in co-operation with, the Police and ARP services, Post Office, *Trade Unions, Shop Stewards*, and, of course, the regular army command in the neighbourhood'.[43]

In the summer of 1940, the Home Guard socialists had a direct influence on the training of the force. Its rapid creation, and the need for training, enabled Tom Wintringham and his comrades, backed by Edward Hutton and *Picture Post*, who funded the enterprise, and the Earl of Jersey, who owned Osterley Park and its grounds, to create the innovative Home Guard training school at Osterley Park. This was, in S P MacKenzie's view, 'an instant success, and news of it rapidly spread through word-of-mouth and the press'.[44] Five thousand Home Guards passed through Wintringham's training school on three day courses.[45] The school became a model for others, and although the War Office and the Army eventually managed, by May 1941, to wrest control of Osterley Park from the Home Guard socialists, their message continued to be read by the huge audience for their books, pamphlets and newspaper articles. For these enthusiasts, the Home Guard was a Popular Front in arms, patriotic, radical, anti-Nazi, and capable of advancing the British people's cause on the Home Front. As Wintringham wrote in the *Picture Post*, 17 May 1941:

> The future of the Home Guard is to be recognised as demo-cracy's answer, and an effective answer, to the Nazi technique of aggression. If we choose only to copy totalitarian methods we shall never catch up or surpass the Nazis. But if we set free and mobilise the initiative of our people in a democratic way, in a way similar to that in which this defensive army of volunteers was raised and trained, I believe we shall find and develop ways of taking the offensive also, new methods of war, which the Nazis are doomed by their ideas and their organisation never to be able to understand or copy.[46]

For the British, the period from the German invasion of Holland in May 1940, to their assault upon their erstwhile allies, the Soviet Union, in June 1941, was a period dominated by the expectation of Nazi invasion. Out of that expectation emerged the Home Guard, a force created so rapidly that it presented a notable group of revolutionary, patriotic, anti-Nazis with the chance to strengthen the defence of Britain, and, they hoped, enhance the radicalism of a large part of the British people. For these Home Guard socialists the threat of invasion, and the need for a democratic, socialist, patriotic, and anti-Nazi analysis of military and political imperatives was an opening for their unique contribution to Britain's war effort. In their extensive involvement in the practical and theoretical training of the Home Guard, Britain's 'People's Army', the Home Guard socialists created a fascinating, and, perhaps, influential, theory of a British Popular Front in arms.

It All Happened Before

If the Home Guard socialists saw the force in radical terms, and as a possible stage in a revolutionary transformation of British society, there were others who saw the Home Guard as being firmly within a long tradition of volunteer defence, a tradition that was essentially, national, patriotic, and conservative.

Further, although the early days of the force appeared, to the Home Guard socialists, to offer a chance to influence strongly, if not control, the direction of the organisation, the reality was that, even in the fluid situation of the late spring and early summer of 1940, the force reflected the hierarchical, class based nature of British society. Ex-officers and NCOs of the Great War, other ex-servicemen, middle-class tradesmen, school masters, solicitors, factory managers and even clergymen, formed the 'officer' class of the LDV, and very quickly, the superstructure of Territorial Associations and Lord Lieutenants came into play. Where the Home Guard socialists did have an impact, most famously at the Osterley Park training school, the Army was quick to neutralise that influence and incorporate the basic idea into its own system of Home Guard training.[47] Books and articles by Home Guard socialists were undoubtedly read by many tens of thousands of Home Guards, but it is reasonable to assume that their primary interest was in the tips and advice that writing gave about military matters. A contrasting interpretation of the meaning of the Home Guard was that which stressed continuity with the past, with a continuing tradition of instinctive patriotism, of which the Home Guard was simply the latest manifestation.

John Radnor's *It All Happened Before; the Home Guard Through the Centuries* was a contemporary popular history of the force, published in 1945, although written before the war's end. It was a profusely illustrated book, with attractive line drawings by R T Cooper, which graphically underpinned Radnor's central message. That message was:

> There is nothing more typically and historically English than the large army of spare-time soldiers now called the Home Guard [...] Its members, old and young, have fairly represented the spirit of the nation in good times and bad [...] Their history, in fact, *is* the history of England's wars and those of the United Kingdom of Britain.[48]

This stress on tradition and continuity above all else was emphasised by the illustration at the top of the first page of chapter one, which showed Alfred the Great facing King George VI, and bore the legend, 'From FYRD to HOME GUARD, 871–1940'. Radnor's understanding of the Home Guard was that it represented the same cross-class, national, patriotic alliance that had come to the fore at times of national crisis throughout the long history of England, and, the shorter history of the United Kingdom. He argued:

> This book [...] ventures to point a good many historical morals while at the same time aspiring to tell a story as fine as anything English history – now, of course, British history – can show.

British loyalty to tradition, which is an easy-going word for history, may be said to be instinctive, in the blood, and to require no vocal or verbal stimulus. Reading, learning, and inwardly digesting facts undoubtedly have had little to do with it, a fact which must be a sore trial to the propagandists, patriotic and subversive alike. All walks of life, however, and the very extremes of military age and experience, have gone to make up the modern Home Guard, as they have made up all the 'Home Guards' before it. Present and Past are linked by invisible but powerful bonds [49]

This is a classically conservative analysis of English and, to a much lesser extent British, national characteristics, arguing that it is not in any way 'theoretical' or vocal, but, rather, instinctive and unspoken. Further, in all ages, 'all walks of life' have combined, in this view, to defeat the external enemy. Radnor's account of that historic cross-class alliance nonetheless saw generations of part-time military volunteers combine together under arms in ways that reflected their social status in civilian life. Again, the illustrations in *It All Happened Before* underline this argument. The frontispiece, for example, shows 'a man of the *fyrd* with a Saxon *thegn*' standing on a cliff top looking out to sea. The 'man of the *fyrd*', the common man, is quite clearly listening to orders from his noble countryman – the classes combine in defence of their homeland, but, unlike the lessons the Home Guard socialists would have had Home Guards draw from national history, the class order is not undermined. However history was interpreted, there was undoubtedly an awareness that the Home Guard was another example of the long volunteer tradition, and of the history of militia musters. Charles Graves gave a fascinating example of this awareness of national continuity, by referring to the militia muster rolls of 1545:

Very many of the names of the LDV of 1940 are those of descendants of the men mustered in 1545. In the Faringham Platoon of the 19th Battalion of the Kent Home Guard there were seven men lineally descended from the men who were mustered in the days of King Henry VIII. Here are their names:

Scudder	spelt	Skudda in 1545
Goodwin	spelt	Goddwyng in 1545
Hills	spelt	Hylles in 1545
Alchin	spelt	Alchorn in 1545
Gillis	spelt	Gilles in 1545
Middleton	spelt	Mydleton in 1545
Aldridge	spelt	Aldregh in 1545

These names figure extensively in the 1545 roll. In one village alone there were three Skuddas:

Will Skudda (the elder)   Pykeman
Will Skudda (the younger)   Archer
Ned Skudda   Bylman.[50]

The message was clear – this was an old country that had withstood crises before, and would again, because it was the same people on the same land, with the same instinctive patriotism.

The reality of the Home Guard was that the cross–class, but hierarchical view of the force was nearer the truth than any hopes that it might be a People's Militia along the lines of the various left-wing militias of Republican Spain. George Orwell's famous description in *Homage to Catalonia*, of the militias of Barcelona in 1936, was of para-military units in which the middle-class had no place, and, indeed, which had been responsible for the killing of large numbers of that class. By contrast, accounts of the founding of LDV units at the beginning of the force's history, in the period before the army took full control, when, if at all, the Home Guard socialists' wishes might have become reality, suggest that, in fact, the class system asserted itself from the outset. For example, John Bone, a volunteer in the Chislehurst Home Guard in Kent remembered that the major in command was a publisher.[51] Cyril Punt who joined the LDV on Tyneside at the very outset, remembered that not only was the local coal magnate, Lord Lampton's land agent appointed as the commanding officer, the same land agent, Colonel Scott-Owen, told the new LDV volunteers that Lord Lampton and he had picked out 'the men that they were going to nominate to take charge and [. . .] organise their little districts'.[52] Factory units also reflected class and work hierarchies, for example, Hawtin Mundy, a Great War veteran who was an officer in the Wolverton Works Home Guard (a metal works employing 5,000 people) remembered that the commanding officer was a Colonel Hagley, who was also the firm's managing director.[53] In rural units too, class hierarchies asserted themselves, with Frank Kellaway remembering that his unit, the 8th Battalion Devonshire Home Guard was, in May 1940, organised and led by men who were firmly in the middle class. Talking about the creation of the LDV in his small home town, Kellaway said:

> we had a meeting, and amongst the people there was Dr Evans, who was a great friend of mine, and a bank manager, who had been a captain in the First World War [. . .] Anyway, Dr Evans, and this chap, Baker, Norman Baker, bank manager at Lloyds Bank, it was decided that he should be the head one, and that

Dr Evans should be assisting him, and the rest of us were just ordinary volunteers.[54]

Kellaway, himself a businessman, also noted that the area commander of the LDV was a Colonel from the Great War.

The military connection was also strong, with a good many of the officers and men having had previous military experience, and not only in the Great War. The core of the LDV was provided by men with military backgrounds. An example of this can be found in the papers of Herbert Allsopp, a Cambridge University graduate, and physics master at Wellingborough School, a Captain in the school's OTC (and, therefore, in the Territorials), and its officer commanding, who was to become the commanding officer of the 7th Battalion Northamptonshire Home Guard. At the beginning of July 1940, Allsopp organised 'special training' for ex-servicemen volunteers from each of the four companies of his LDV unit. Each company provided Allsopp with a list of eight men available for this extra training, and the lists show the range and variety of ex-service experience to be found in this Northamptonshire LDV force. For example, the men from 'C' company had the following military backgrounds, and ranged in age from 37 to 49:

Royal Field Artillery Great War service, aged 44
Royal Tank Corps six years in RTC, and six years in the Reserves, aged 37
Royal West Kent Regiment five years service, aged 41
Northamptonshire Regiment seven years service, aged 48
Infantry five years service, aged 41
Northamptonshire Territorials five years service, aged 37
Army and Reserve eight years service, aged 48
Northamptonshire Regiment five years service, aged 49.[55]

The men from the remaining three companies exhibited a similar background, combining what appears to be Great War experience with additional service in the regular and reserve forces. Of course, as the Home Guard developed, so younger men came increasingly to the fore, as they served in the force while waiting call-up to the regular forces, or, for those in reserved occupations, made their military contribution to the war effort. However, throughout its history, the Home Guard always possessed a strong leavening of military and combat experience.

Conclusion: People's Militia or a Nation in Arms?

The Home Guard socialists were a small, but active and vocal group, whose writings can still easily be found in second hand bookshops around the country. They represented a range of left-wing opinion, ranging from ex-CPGB activists like Wintringham to centre-left anti-Nazis like Langdon-Davies, and anti-Soviet radicals like George Orwell. They were not, in the end, successful in their attempts to foster a four million strong People's Army, as the government and the army outflanked men like Tom Wintringham; but the Home Guard socialists were, in 1940–41, a notable aspect of Britain at war. It is difficult to assess the impact of the Home Guard socialists on the political culture of Britain during and after the Second World War. It is true, however, that this small group of veterans of the Spanish Civil War provided training, along with military and political education for thousands of Home Guards. Through the Osterley Park training camp and their widely read publications, the Home Guard socialists sought to bring a form of politically radical military training to the British people, something that had not, perhaps, been attempted since Cromwell's New Model Army. Nonetheless, the LDV and the Home Guard was, in fact, much more in the traditional, volunteer mould that informed Radnor's *It All Happened Before*. The force was a representation of the UK at war. It was cross-class, national, and anti-Nazi. It did not, however, fundamentally challenge traditional, hierarchical, class or military norms. It was a creature of its time, in that it meshed together conservative, patriotic instincts, with the long tradition of voluntary military service in defence of the country, while being flavoured by the democratic, anti-Nazi mindset of the United Kingdom, and its Empire, singing its great historic swansong. In his history of the Home Guard in Scotland, Brian Osborne finished his account by quoting Major J D Butler, second in command of the 7th Fife Battalion of the Home Guard. Butler's view of the history of the force can stand as a final thought on its true nature:

> Only the men were the same and it mattered not at all whether they were veterans who had made the Home Guard or the younger men who had been made by it. They ran true to type and produced a truly citizen army, the like of which had not been seen in history.[56]

Chapter 10

Gone but not Forgotten

'Stood ready to defend our homes'

On Thursday 17 May 1945, King George VI replied to his Parliament's addresses of congratulations following Victory in Europe. The King summed up Britain's and its Empire and Commonwealth's struggle over the preceding years:

> The gallantry of the Army which fought in Europe against over-whelming odds in 1940 and the miraculous rescue from Dunkirk will ever be remembered. In the years that followed, the Army, with the Home Guard, stood ready to defend our homes against the invasion. All of this time the powerful instrument was being forged which, with the Forces of the Empire and Commonwealth, at first alone and later with our Allies, drove the enemy from Africa and then landing on the shores of Sicily and Italy, and later on the Normandy beaches, swept victoriously across Europe.[1]

It was a tale as epic as any in the long history of England, Britain, and the Empire, and it was one in which the Home Guard had an honourable place. But unlike the defeat of the Armada in 1588, or Napoleon in 1805 and 1815, this war was not a precursor to Imperial expansion, but, rather, a swansong that marked the end of one period of Britain's history and the beginnings of another. The general election of July 1945, when the Labour Party under Clement Attlee, swept to victory with forty-eight per cent of the poll, as opposed to Churchill's Conservatives' forty per cent, marked that change. Building on the wartime experience of planning, and a heightened wartime sense of national cohesion, allied to the limited socialism of the Attlee government, a new deal was struck between the British state and people, and, indeed, between an impoverished Britain and its fading Empire.

The survival of Britain, and parliamentary democracy, and the defeat of Nazism, if not totalitarianism, had depended, for much of 1940 and 1941 on the determination of the United Kingdom to defend itself. That determination was, in many respects, symbolised by the LDV and the Home Guard. As a symbol of the country's will to resist, the force was undoubtedly important, especially in the period, from June 1940 until June 1941, when the UK stood alone in Europe. As the Home Guard developed, becoming increasingly better trained and armed, it took on a significant domestic role in plans for the invasion of western Europe, but the impetus that had created and sustained the force in its early days – fear of invasion – was no longer a powerful motivator. To some, the value of the Home Guard declined just as it became a more credible military force. The question that hung over the force, during its lifetime and after, is just how effective would it have been had the United Kingdom been invaded? This chapter examines views about the value and effectiveness of the Home Guard, looks at the brief re-birth of the idea of volunteer home defence in the 1950s, and reviews the ways in which the Home Guard is remembered in the UK.

Island fortress and unsinkable aircraft carrier

The period from the fall of France to the invasion of the Soviet Union was the only period when, realistically, the British people faced the possibility of invasion. It was during this period too that, victories against Italy in East and North Africa notwithstanding, the British armed forces had few successes beyond the crucial, history defining, one of the Battle of Britain. During this period, the UK's capacity for offensive action was limited, and its armed forces were essentially being rebuilt after the efforts of the summer of 1940. It was at this time, too, that the LDV/Home Guard was, paradoxically, of the greatest value and yet of the least effectiveness in military terms. This was the period when the UK saw itself as an 'island fortress', garrisoned by a determined people, supplied by an extensive Empire and Commonwealth with materials and men and women who flocked to defend the 'Mother Country'.[2] The existence of the LDV/Home Guard matched perfectly with this mindset, and the heroic view of 'Britain alone'. The establishment of the force in May 1940, enabled hundreds of thousands of Britons to express their determination to defend their country against invasion. It created an organisation that seemed to provide a partial answer to what were seen as new aspects of warfare – airborne assault and an organised 'enemy within' in the form of the Fifth Column. In the first case – parachute, glider and air landed troops – there was a clear threat. The German assault in the West had seen notable, and battle-winning, use of airborne troops in Denmark, Norway, the Netherlands and Belgium. Although the Germans had far fewer paratroopers and airborne troops available than the British feared, there was a threat of a sudden attack almost anywhere in the country. The need for early warning of airborne assault gave the LDV their first task, and their first nickname – 'The Parashots'. In a similar fashion, the fear of the Fifth Column, which reached almost hysterical proportions in the early summer of 1940, was also partially nullified by the creation of a force that was always on the lookout for these seemingly ubiquitous, but unseen, allies of Nazism. Although there was, in fact, no Fifth Column, the LDV nonetheless helped reassure the population that things were being done to face the threat. In this, the LDV had a positive impact on the morale of the nation. In fact, the role that the force had in maintaining morale was one that the government, and, in particular, the Home Guard's champion, Winston Churchill, was aware of, and placed great store in. These early LDV days marked the first steps in the force's life, and 'during this period, the LDV/Home Guard's military role was insignificant, but the government hoped the force could provide Britons with a greater sense of security and raise their spirits'.[3] The military effectiveness of the force was to grow throughout its short history, and it continued to provide large numbers of men, and some women, with an outlet for their patriotic desire to contribute to the war effort, over and above the contributions they were making in their daily lives. In his study of the Home Guard on Tyneside, Craig Armstrong concluded that:

> the greatest contribution that the civil defence organisations [i e. the Home Guard] made to the regional war effort was in the boost to morale that they gave to the general public, by giving reassurance that they were being actively protected and watched over, as well as providing an outlet for energy for many men who would otherwise have possibly felt, often quite wrongly, that they were not contributing to the military war effort.[4]

It might be noted that their 'energy' was something that Home Guards, and many others, gave of all that they had. The author's grandfather, George Jackson, who had served throughout the Great War as an infantryman in the King's (Liverpool) Regiment, and was fifty-nine at the outbreak of the Second World War, worked long wartime shifts as a ship's joiner on the Liverpool docks, and served for more than three years as a Home Guard in the Mersey Docks and Harbour Board Home Guard, which included service throughout the Liverpool blitz.

As the LDV/Home Guard steadied itself on its young feet, so it rapidly became better organised and better equipped, and was fully incorporated into the Army's defence plans for the United Kingdom. David Yelton has argued that this was a 'second phase' for the force, from summer 1940 until summer 1941, when there was:

> a growing emphasis on the military duties of the force, which was necessitated by both the threat of German invasion and the public's recognition of the initial weakness of the LDV. This year also saw a corresponding growth in respect for the Home Guard

as Britons came to consider the force to be a distinct and valued part of the nation's defenses.[5]

By the spring of 1941, the Home Guard was reasonably well-equipped with rifles and automatic weapons, was increasingly better uniformed and trained, and had taken over much of the static, area defence role from the Regular Army. As a result, the Army was better able to continue its rebuilding programme, effectively training and equipping a new army that would soon, by the end of the year, see victory in North Africa, while beginning the long preparation for the invasion of western Europe. The Home Guard not only patrolled local areas, guarded key assets and vulnerable points, such as telephone exchanges, bridges, railways and factories, but also formed an integral part of the static defence system built around nodal points. An example was Pevensey Castle on the Saxon Shore, Sussex, a defence stronghold since the third century, which was refortified in the summer of 1940. Its defence in July 1940 was in the hands of the 4th Battalion, the Duke of Cornwall's Light Infantry, and sixty-five men of the 21st (Eastbourne) Battalion, the Sussex Home Guard.[6] A key defensive position, sitting directly in the path of the proposed assault of the German 9th Army, had the invasion occurred, those men of the Eastbourne Home Guard would have been among the first to fight and die in defence of their homeland. Pevensey Castle was later classified as a centre of resistance, and it was such defensive centres that, as the war continued, were increasingly in the hands of the Home Guard. The defences of Littleport, Cambridgeshire, on the banks of the canalised River Great Ouse, for example, were built around the Home Guard. In 1941 the network of pillboxes, roadblocks, mines, anti-tank ditches, weapons pits and trenches defending the area were manned by 100 men from 2nd Battalion Ely Home Guard, equipped with ten spigot mortars, 200 anti-tank grenades, and 200 anti-tank mines.[7] This was the sort of core, defence role that the Home Guard played for the remainder of its existence, and one that they were increasingly better trained, equipped and prepared for.

The Home Guards themselves were confident that their improved training and equipment would have enabled them to give a good account of themselves against the invader, and that they would be able to carry out their role of slowing down the German advance, thereby buying time for the Regular Army's mobile forces to position itself for counter-attack. Training improved rapidly, and included weekend 'schools', longer camps, and specialist courses, short attachments to regular units, as well as the weekly evening and Sunday parades which usually involved a training element. Veterans of the Great War, such as Welshman, John Mill, who had served on the Western Front with the Rifle Brigade from 1916–18, and was a major in the Neath Home Guard, were clear that 'the Home Guard would have given a good account of themselves if they had been called on. They weren't like "Dad's Army", they were well trained, I can tell you that now. Very well'.[8] Some Home Guard were less sanguine about the force's capabilities, for example, Michael Bendix, who served in the Eton College Home Guard from 1940–43, believed that 'probably, it [Home Guard] would have been of nuisance value, but I'm not quite sure that they were equipped to deal with armour'.[9] That comment was made in the light of his subsequent service with the Coldstream Guards in Normandy and North-West Europe, and probably reflected the severe fighting there when the early wars years characterised by blitzkrieg had been replaced by bitter battles of armoured attrition. Nonetheless, in the context of the Home Guard's role as a guard and area defence force, playing, especially in inland areas of the country, a first line of defence, the force was a key element in the defence of the United Kingdom. In addition, it was an increasing presence in coastal artillery and anti-aircraft batteries. It played a valuable function in freeing up large numbers of regular military personnel who were redeployed in the preparations for the invasion of Western Europe. Ironically, as the Home Guard's military importance and effectiveness grew, in this 'third phase' of its history, 'pride and morale in the force declined as Britons came to resent both the pedestrian duties of and growing military discipline in the Home Guard'.[10] It was fears surrounding morale that led, for example, to the government to prompt the widespread celebrations of the Home Guard that marked its third anniversary in 1943, with 'Home Guard Sunday' and military parades throughout the country. Just over a year later, the Home Guard went on to heightened alert, as the Normandy invasions took place, and the force faced possible German raids and spoiling attacks on England. These, of course, did not take place, but the Home Guard continued in its defence duties, and its Civil Defence support role, until stand down in November 1944.

There were two messages of thanks from the King to his Home Guards to mark stand-down. The King made a radio broadcast on the evening of 3 December, and the written message was released on 14 November. This message was drafted by P J Grigg, but was heavily revised by the Prime Minister, and the final version bore an unmistakably Churchillian stamp:

> For more than four years you have borne a heavy burden. Most of you have been engaged for long hours in work necessary to the prosecution of the war or to maintaining the healthful life of the nation; and you have given a great portion of the time which

should have been your own to learning the skills of the soldier. By this patient, ungrudging effort you have built and maintained a force able to play an essential part in the defence of our threatened soil and liberty. I have long wished to see you relieved of this burden, but it would have been a betrayal of all we owe to our fathers and our sons if any step had been taken which might have imperilled our Country's safety. Till very recently, a slackening of our defences might have encouraged the enemy to launch a desperate blow which could grievously have damaged us and weakened the power of our own assault. Now, at last, the splendid resolution and endurance of the Allied Armies have thrust back that danger from our coasts. At last I can say that you have fulfilled your charge.

The Home Guard has reached the end of its long tour of duty under arms. But I know that your devotion to our land, your comradeship, your power to work your hardest at the end of the longest day, will discover new outlets of patriotic service in time of peace.

History will say that your share in the greatest of all our struggles for freedom was a vitally important one. You have given your service without thought of reward. You have earned in full measure your country's gratitude.[11]

The LDV had been a necessary, and, one might argue, an almost inevitable creation in May 1940. People had already begun to organise local patrols in various parts of the country, particularly on the south coast of England. Further, the long tradition of volunteer military defence organisations that stretched back, in the modern period, to the eighteenth century and fear of French invasion provided an historical memory of the desire to defend country and homes. Once given official shape and backing, the force became a national movement in an exceptionally short space of time. It was a sign, if one was needed, that the British peoples were still determined, and that they did not regard the war as lost, despite the cataclysmic events of the spring and early summer of 1940. The Home Guard was an interesting response in a country that had a strange attitude to the militarism and the military. Despite a general sentiment that, unlike Germany or France, the British were anti-militarist, the popularity of a range of volunteer and para-military groups (including, for example, the university and schools' Officer Training Corps, the Boy Scouts and Girl Guides, rifle clubs, the First Aid Nursing Yeomanry, and even the Boys' Brigade, Church Lads and Jewish Lads' Brigades), and, particularly since the Great War, pride in County

Regiments, meant that the notion of a volunteer military force was well received in most quarters. On these foundations, the government was able to build a force that made a noteworthy contribution to the United Kingdom's war effort. The idea of an area defence force that was permanently in place and available for both continuous routine guard duties, in addition to having the potential for rapid mobilisation was a sound one. Not only did it obviate the necessity of regular forces undertaking a duty that had a marked tendency to lead to the slow demoralisation of regular troops, but it also gave those unable to make a regular military contribution to the war effort a military role.

The basic soundness of the concept was also reflected in the establishment of 'Home Guards' in other countries on both sides of the conflict. For example, the Australian government, faced in February 1942, with the possible threat of Japanese invasion, founded a Home Guard on the UK model. The New Zealanders were quicker off the mark, creating their Home Guard in August 1940, which reached a total of 124,194 effectives in March 1943.[12] On the other side of the fence, too, the concept was widely utilised. For example, among the multitude of armed collaborationist para-military organisations established across occupied Europe, the Belgian 'Rural Guard' (*Garde Rurale* in Wallonia, and the *Boerenwacht* in Flanders) was created in June 1941 to protect farms, crops and agricultural supplies. By May 1942, it had a total membership of 66,000 men.[13] Other, more active, more militarised, and better armed, German and state-sponsored collaborationist para-militaries, such as the Dutch *Landwacht Nederland* (which, in a later guise, fought the British and Allies at Arnhem), or the Vichy French *Milice Française* (which fought the French Resistance), also fitted the broad category of volunteer defence organisations, albeit in a heavily politicised form. Finally, the German *Volkssturm*, established in September 1944, played an identical role to that intended for the Home Guard, and were a notable element in the last ditch defence of Germany.

The performance of *Volkssturm* units varied greatly, but, particularly on the Eastern Front, the *Volkssturm* often fought tenaciously against the Red Army, in attempts to buy time for escaping German refugees. The *Volkssturm* was established in September 1944, in the aftermath of the failed July bomb plot against Hitler. The intention was to enrol six million men and boys in the force, made up of four 'levies'; although it is unlikely that the force ever reached that number. The first and third levies consisted of fit men between the ages of twenty and sixty, while the third levy consisted of sixteen to twenty year olds. Most of this levy consisted, in fact, of sixteen year old members of the Hitler Youth. However, as the war approached, then entered the Reich, much younger boys, often members of the *Jungvolk*, and girls, also joined the *Volkssturm*. Finally, the fourth levy consisted of unfit men from the ages of twenty to sixty, in addition to volunteers over sixty.[14] Like the Home Guard in 1940, this emergency defence force was equipped with a hotchpotch of weaponry, and a range of uniforms as well as civilian clothing. Training, too, was mixed in its duration and effectiveness. This was reflected in their performance on the battlefield. There was a tendency for *Volkssturm* on the western front to perform poorly, putting up token shows of resistance before surrendering to British, Canadian, or US forces. However this was not always the case:

> Even on the western front, Allied troops were often horrified to discover that they were fighting, and killing, women and children. Lieutenant Colonel Roland Kolb of the US 84th Division battling towards the Elbe reported coming across boys aged 12 and even younger manning artillery pieces. 'Rather than surrender, the boys fought until killed,' he remembered. Major James Hollingsworth of the US Second Armored Division recalled with horror another incident near Bielefeld in which, during a tank battle with a Panzer training unit, his .50 calibre machine-gun shot up a truck loaded with soldiers all of which, when they looked at the ripped-up bodies, were found to be women.[15]

The role of young boys, and girls, in the defence of Germany was notable, if dreadful. One historian of the Hitler Youth in 1944–45, has commented: 'it can be established that the Hitler Youth proved its worth in battle in East Prussia, no matter how this combat deployment was viewed then and is viewed today'.[16] Gerhard Tillery, who was a nineteen-year-old German soldier on the eastern front, defending Berlin against the Red Army, remembered one occasion when Hitler Youth went into action:

> We had only been going a few minutes when we were rounded up. A unit of 15- and 16-year-old Hitler Youths had deployed here, even though not all were armed. All soldiers going past were rounded up by them and taken into their ranks. There were hardly any machine guns, but one thing you had to give them was their spirit, which was something seldom seen. They simply could not wait for the Russians to come. They knocked out several Russian tanks at ranges of four or five metres, and when the Russians realised that the resistance here was particularly strong, they brought up more tanks as reinforcements. Although the youngsters suffered severe losses, we only withdrew when the Russians came at us from three sides.[17]

The combination of youth, old age, and a determination to defend one's homeland was also a noticeable feature of the Home Guard. Perhaps there was an indicator in the defence of Germany of the sort of defence that the Home Guard would have put up had the UK been invaded.

Home Guard redux?

Although the Home Guard was stood down at the end of 1944, and disbanded on 31 December 1945, it was not the last that was heard of the force in the UK. The force was re-established in 1952, and had a short and troubled existence until it was stood down again in December 1955, and finally disbanded in July 1957. The impetus for the re-creation of the Home Guard was, as in 1940, fear of Fifth Column activity and airborne assault, but this time the enemy was communism and the Soviet Union. The Labour government of 1945–50 considered the re-establishment of the force, concerned, as it was, about the loyalty of the Communist Party of Great Britain (CPGB) to Moscow. The CPGB regarded the post-war world as being divided into two camps – 'the imperialist camp and the democratic [i.e. Soviet] camp'[18] – and its loyalty was to the 'democratic' camp led by the USSR. Harry Pollitt, the general secretary of the CPGB until 1956, regarded Stalin as a personal friend, and the CPGB's policies routinely marched in step with those dictated by Moscow. Further, once the short post-war honeymoon between the former allies that had defeated the Axis powers was over, the west and east settled down into two armed blocs. The British assessment was that if the Soviet Union invaded western Europe, the Red Army would quickly sweep to the Channel ports, and that the UK would be threatened by 20,000 Soviet paratroopers.[19] The combination of a disciplined, ideologically motivated political party, with a strong presence in key industries, for example the engineering industry and the docks, with the threat of a military power geared to offensive operations, seemed, once more, to require an armed defence force capable of defending vulnerable points and assets against sabotage and surprise assault.

The calls for a new Home Guard grew stronger with the outbreak of the Korean War, and by the October 1951 general election the Conservatives had come out strongly in support of the Home Guard idea, which they rapidly put into place following their election victory. The initial 1951 plan was that a peacetime cadre of 600,000 Home Guards would be recruited, to be boosted by a further 400,000 in the event of war. However, cost considerations soon reduced this proposed figure to 125,000 peacetime effectives, but problems were still envisaged in terms of uniforming that much smaller number. The proposals came under attack from a number of MPs, and even *The Times* 'on 22 November [1951] devoted a leading article to demolishing the whole idea'.[20] Interestingly, at least one of the MPs who were most vociferous in opposing the Home Guard, Labour MP, Stephen Swingler, was a secret member of the CPGB, and had been identified by the Labour leadership as a Soviet asset in the House of Commons.[21] Nonetheless, the plans went ahead, and recruiting began for the force. It was soon apparent that the real problem was a lack of interest on the part of the British public:

> In the age of the hydrogen bomb and successive crises which never actually resulted in full-scale war, the Home Guard appears to have struck the man in the street as both anachronistic and unnecessary. By 18 February 1952, only 28,120 men had registered to join, and by March recruiting was still yielding under 4,000 volunteers per month – a far from encouraging response given the target figure of 125,000.[22]

The men and women who did join were a combination of those with wartime military experience and people too young to have served in the Second World War. David Carroll has given a brief account of two volunteers, Roger Ray, a prep school master at Ashfold House, lying between Horsham and Haywards Heath, and Peggy Wightman, a Home Guard radio operator in Norwich.[23]

Despite the enthusiasm and efforts of people like Roger Ray and Penny Wightman, the reborn Home Guard could not overcome the central problem that it faced, namely that few people saw it as necessary. The result was that the organisational structure had to be repeatedly rejigged to try and accommodate the fact of very low numbers, and, increasingly, the force became one of many officers and few soldiers. By early 1953, there were 9,000 Home Guard officers, but only 20,000 other ranks,[24] and Roger Ray remembered that:

> To carry out [our] duties of helping to defend airfields, combating airborne and seaborne raids, protecting vulnerable points against sabotage and rendering help to Civil Defence, the ten men [of our unit] were kept on their toes. In charge of this army, half of them ex-wartime men, was Captain Richard Sykes, joint headmaster of the school. Promotion was fairly rapid and I think there was only one private when we disbanded in 1956.[25]

Repeated attempts to improve recruiting, at both local and national level, were unsuccessful, and the final nail in the Home Guard's coffin came when a defence review in 1955 argued that with the arrival of the hydrogen bomb, it was unlikely that there would be a prolonged, full-scale European war that would necessitate the sort of defence that a Home Guard could play a role in. In December 1955, the Home Guard was stood down for the second, and final, time.

A very British celebration

The BBC television programme, *Dad's Army*, ran from 1968 until 1977, with the eighty episodes watched by a large segment of the British public. The programme's 'viewing figures exceeded 13 million in 1969, after which the show attracted an average of over 12 million viewers per week from 1969 to 1975, with a peak of 18 million in 1972'.[26] *Dad's Army* was sold to television companies in thirty countries, and has been repeatedly re-shown on British television. The impact of the programme on popular perceptions of the Home Guard, and the British war effort, has been profound. The term 'Dad's Army', which was not used during the war, has a high recognition value. A number of books on the force have used 'Dad's Army' in their titles, and the marketing department of Pen and Sword Books was insistent that it be used again in the title of this book.[27] In the minds of many people, *Dad's Army* was not just a well-liked comedy series, but a reasonably accurate portrayal of the Home Guard.

The historians, Penny Summerfield and Corinna Peniston-Bird, analysed the appeal of the television programme in relation to historical and popular perceptions of the Home Guard.[28] They argued that, despite the short re-birth of the Home Guard in the 1950s, there was little in the way of historical or cultural commentary on the wartime force after the end of the war. In consequence, the creators of *Dad's Army*, Jimmy Perry (who had served in the Home Guard from 1941–1944) and David Croft, had a clear field when it came to representing the Home Guard for post-war generations. The way in which they did represent the force is interesting, and hinges on the degree to which the programme was intended to be satirical. Perry and Croft insisted that they were not mocking the Home Guard, or the United Kingdom's war effort, but it may have been that there was a satirical element, which could have had origins in Perry's links, as an actor, with the left-wing theatre group 'Theatre Workshop' in Newham, East London. Theatre Workshop was the creation of two ex-Communists, Joan Littlewood, and her one time husband, the folk singer (and wartime British Army deserter), Ewan MacColl. The theatre company was an innovative and influential one, and, most notably, was responsible for the 1963 play *Oh! What a Lovely War*, which made a highly successful transition to the West End stage and the cinema screen, greatly affecting popular perceptions of the Great War in the process. Yet the satirical elements of *Dad's Army* were overshadowed by the more sympathetic portrayal of the Home Guard heroes of 'Walmington-on-Sea', and in the minds of the British viewing public, it became not only a much enjoyed comedy, but also an affectionate celebration of one aspect of the country's war effort.

Although the Perry and Croft, and the BBC, received large postbags about the programme, there was very little in the way of criticism from former members of the Home Guard. However, the sound archives of the Imperial War Museum do contain reminiscences of Home Guards that include protests about the picture of the force created by *Dad's Army*. For example, one veteran from the Great War, Hawtin Mundy, said about *Dad's Army* that it was:

> a real laugh. I enjoyed it, everyone enjoyed it. But it was a long, long way from the real thing. The youth now, or anyone who just watched it, have the impression that it was a card, or just a joke. But it was not. Not by a long, long way.[29]

The problem was that the settings of the programme – vehicles, uniforms, hair styles, props, and contemporary references – were generally very accurate, so that many people assumed, even given that it was a comedy show, that the level of competence exhibited by the cast of *Dad's Army* was also a reflection of reality. It was this that seems to have annoyed former Home Guards, who were proud of their standard of turnout and their training. An officer from B Company the City of London Post Office Home Guard, and a veteran of the 3rd Battalion, The London Regiment (The Post Office Rifles) in the Great War noted:

> The unit was formed by nearly all ex-Post Office riflemen [from the Great War]. The commanding officer was an ex-sergeant who was in the Post Office Rifles. As a matter of fact, I rather resented the programme 'Dad's Army', because it ridiculed the Home Guard. I know I had a chuckle myself, occasionally, at it, but we were a very, very smart unit. We were trained and drilled at Wellington Barracks at everything, weapons, machine guns, everything they had.[30]

Similarly, a member of the Newbury Home Guard said:

> The Home Guard, a lot of people I think have just got the wrong impression from a certain television programme. Because it was **never** like that. They became quite a professional unit. Remember at least a year before the European War finished that one of the training exercises we went on was in the same manner as the regular forces – Battlefield Inoculation – we had live bombs thrown at us, and live ammunition shot over our heads.[31]

This is an interesting point, for although there was progression over the long lifetime of *Dad's Army*, the emphasis was more on the atmosphere of the early days of the LDV, when improvisation and amateurism (in its most negative sense) than in the latter stages of a more efficient, better armed, better trained, and younger force. For *Dad's Army*, of course, the imperative was the comic situation, rather than accurate history.

Despite the justified complaints of some ex-Home Guards, *Dad's Army* came to symbolise a humorous and nostalgic view of an extremely dangerous period in history, when the United Kingdom was involved in a war of national survival. *Dad's Army* was a gently comic series that characterised a particular national sense of being able to laugh at the British peoples' own efforts. Its enormous reach was enabled by the limited numbers of television channels available in the 1960s and 1970s, and by the BBC's then still extant role as a national institution. It was such a popular programme, that it had a notable (if distorting) impact in the popular understanding of the Home Guard, and the British war effort. Summerfield and Peniston-Bird's conclusion about the role and impact of *Dad's Army* has, in this respect, much to recommend it:

> The Second World War is [in *Dad's Army*], by implication, a just war against a real (though mostly unseen) enemy. It is waged by well-meaning but not very competent people, who muddle through and triumph in the end, not because they are well organised or more efficient than the enemy, but because they are (somehow) intrinsically better. As with the Home Guard, so with the British at war, the *Dad's Army* interpretation could be read either as criticism or as celebration. It was this feat of cultural mastery that enabled *Dad's Army* to make an indelible mark not only on the history of the Home Guard but on representations of home defence across time, and to have a profound influence on understandings of the British war effort.[32]

Home Guard remains

As a boy in the early 1970s, the author, accompanying his father in a viewing of a dusty, empty, but still part-furnished house, came across a chest of drawers that contained just two things: an 'LDV' armlet, and a cut down 'Home Guard' armlet. These mementoes of someone's Home Guard service would be comparatively rare finds today, but there are more permanent artefacts that serve as reminders of the Home Guard. The immense effort that went into the construction of defence works in 1940–41 has left many remains in the built landscape of the UK that have associations with the

Home Guard, and the war on the Home Front. Some 28,000 pillboxes were constructed during the Second World War, and in recent years, there has been increasing interest in the recording and preservation of surviving modern defence structures, not just from 1939–45, but also from the Great War and the Cold War periods. In addition, the relatively new discipline of modern military archaeology has led to the some innovative projects to uncover the buried remains of Home Guard defence in the Second World War.

The father of contemporary interest in twentieth century British defence structures was Henry Wills, a Salisbury press photographer, who embarked on a project to record as many pillboxes as possible. Advertising in local and national newspapers for collaborators to help identify and record these structures, Wills was able to record some 5,000 pillboxes in his *Pillboxes: A Study of UK Defences 1940*, which was published in 1985.[33] A number of groups of enthusiasts, such as the Fortress Study Group, the UK Fortifications Club, and the Pillbox Study Group also extended knowledge of surviving structures, and in the early 1990s, various local pilot studies, sponsored by the Royal Commission for Historical Monuments of England, Historic Scotland, and the Pembrokeshire National Park all contributed to the developing study of these artefacts in the landscape of the UK. The next stage in the development of this field of study came in the mid-1990s:

> a full survey of the whole of Britain and Northern Ireland [...] the Defence of Britain (DoB) was born. All the national heritage bodies had combined with the Council for British Archaeology, and were supported by funds from the National Heritage Lottery Fund. Networks of volunteers were supported in recording sites, and contributing them to a central database, using an agreed thesaurus. Over 13,000 sites were recorded during the Project's life between 1995 and 2002 [...] This research was collated into volumes of commentaries, appendices, gazetteers and sources under 11 separate subject headings [...] and each of the 11 topics is currently in the process of being commercially published as discrete volumes.[34]

The most useful book currently available is William Foot's *Beaches, fields, street, and hills ...; the anti-invasion landscapes of England, 1940*, published by English Heritage and the Council for British Archaeology in 2006, which contains a wealth of detail about field fortifications, and the Home Guard's role in manning them.

Many people are aware of defence structures in their own localities. These are usually the concrete pillboxes found throughout the UK, but include other remains, such as concrete anti-tank cubes or cylinders, loopholed walls, and odd pieces of concrete, that, to the untrained eye, appear to have no obvious function, but, for example, are the bases of Home Guard weapons such as the Spigot Mortar. However, what is usually not clear is how these remains fitted into the complex, inter-connected defence works of the period. Anti-tank ditches have long been filled in, sandbags have rotted and disappeared, road blocks are gone. The result is that surviving pillboxes often appear to be strangely marooned in the landscape, with little tactical sense being obvious. To fully understand the purpose of these structures research into documentary sources, and the use of archaeological techniques is necessary. One innovative archaeological project – 'Digging Dad's Army' (DDA) – is currently underway as part of the East and South-East London's People's War Project (ESELPWP). The ESELPWP aims to use 'research into official and community archives, oral history, and archaeological recon-naissance, survey, excavation, and recording to explore the militarised land-scapes and popular experience of modern conflict between 1914 and 1945'.[35] The DDA project has already uncovered forgotten aspects of defence in the area of Shooter's Hill, which has been broadcast on the popular television programme *Time Team*, and is accessible on the project's internet blog.[36] This type of work, combining documentary, oral history and archaeological research has the potential to rescue a good deal of highly detailed history of the Home Guard's contribution to the country's defence. The DDA's team believes that:

> We have maybe ten years where we can still tie studies of the Home Guard and its archaeology to the recollections of witnesses who actually took an active part in the movement as young adults. We have perhaps as long again if we are recording the memories of those who were children seeing, if not always fully understanding the facilities and activities of the Home Guard. We do have a starting point for this process. The Defence of Britain Project and subsequent work has been very good at providing a skeleton of information about the infrastructure, the hardware of the anti invasion preparations and the Home Guard. Now we need to put the flesh and blood on the skeleton while we still can. It is as if we arrived at Hadrian's Wall two generations after it ceased to function and with some of the soldiers and their families still living there to record as witnesses. No archaeologist would pass up that opportunity.[37]

The fact that projects like the DoB and the DDA combine professional historians and archaeologists with small armies of volunteer enthusiasts is a nice parallel with the combined efforts of volunteers and professionals in the defence of the UK from 1940–45.

The sincerest form of flattery

The interest in a nostalgic celebration of Britain's wartime experience seems to be a constant in contemporary Britain. Television programmes set against a wartime backdrop are perennially popular. For example, ITV's *Foyle's War*, set in wartime Hastings, which ran from 2002 until 2007 was a ratings success. The programme was so popular that protests against its demise led to a seventh series being commissioned for 2010. *Foyle's War* was a detective series set against the backdrop of the Home Front, while a recent, September 2010, drama, *Joe Madison's War*, starring three popular actors – Kevin Whately, Robson Green, and Sir Derek Jacobi – was built around the Home Guard on Tyneside. Although the success of *Foyle's War* and the one-off *Joe Madison's War* had a good deal to do with the writing talent, Anthony Horowitz and Alan Plater respectively, and the casts of the programmes, the Home Front settings of both clearly resonated with a sizeable element of the viewing public. The popularity of re-enactment and living history events set during the war years is also testimony to this phenomenon. For example, the small North Yorkshire market town of Pickering, which is home to the North Yorkshire Moors Railway (a steam railway that features in many period television and film productions), has run a wartime weekend for nearly two decades. The 2010 weekend, held from 15–17 October, was attended by over 40,000 visitors and the entire town was taken over by the event, with much of the town centre transformed to provide a theatrical and historical backdrop for the visitors.[38] The event is of interest in that people attend from various living history and re-enactment groups, not only dressed in the uniforms of combat troops, but also in Home Front uniforms, for example, Women's Land Army, Air Raid Precautions, Auxiliary Fire Service, Boy Scouts, Police, and, of course, the Home Guard. Very few of the visitors were old enough to remember the events being celebrated, and, to a lesser extent, commemorated, and historical accuracy and understanding often seemed to be lacking. The atmosphere was one of happy nostalgia combined with national pride. The Pickering event is far from being the only such '1940s' event that takes place in Britain, and there are a number of active Home Guard re-enactment groups that seek to keep alive the memory of the force.

There are, in October 2010, at least nineteen Home Guard re-enactment groups active across England and Wales. The majority of groups seek to portray Home Guard units that were active in their local area, and the dominant intention is to accurately re-create the force, although there are some re-creations of *Dad's Army*; that is, the re-enactment of a re-enactment. This latter tendency is frowned upon by many re-enactors, with, for example, the 'Chatham Home Guard's' mission statement being: 'to research the history of the Home Guard to portray the real "Dad's Army" and to "re-educate" the public'.[39] This group's stated purpose is to 'portray men who were prepared to make the ultimate sacrifice in defence of their country so we have a duty to take our role seriously. At the same time we make living history and re-enactment an interesting and enjoyable experience for our members.'[40] The driving force behind living history and re-enactment has received little attention or examination, but in relation to the recreation of Home Front Britain, it may be that many people see the period as combining a number of elements that they feel are lacking in contemporary life. Despite the historical evidence of the internal stresses and strains that characterised Britain at war, there is still a popular sense that the country was largely unified, homogenous, and characterised by a sense of noble national purpose, and international significance, that is no longer the case in the age of globalisation, the European Union, and a society struggling to come to grips with all the many implications of mass migration. For some re-enactment groups, there is a more overt and conscious political and historical element to their activities. *La Columna*, a small, predominantly left-wing, living history group that portrays British volunteers in the International Brigades, has established itself as a leading educator concerning the role of Home Guard socialists in 1940 at the Osterley Park training school. The group have run several re-enactments of this training school at Osterley Park in Middlesex (now owned by the National Trust), working in collaboration with Home Guard re-enactment groups. For example, in 2007, *La Columna* and the Home Guard group, *The Civil Defenders* ran the sort of weekend camp that was typical of Tom Wintringham's courses,[41] and a more widely reported re-enactment was carried out in the summer of 2010, to mark the seventieth anniversary of the training centre. For the living history group *La Columna*, the clear aim is to preserve the memory of left-wing anti-fascists and their role in the early days of the LDV and the Home Guard. For Home Guard re-enactors, it is likely that they have a less overt political edge to their hobby, which, nonetheless carries with it historical, cultural and national meaning.

Conclusion: 'The object of the exercise'
The LDV and the Home Guard can be seen as being in the long tradition of the defence of one's homeland. The Anglo-Saxon account of the Battle of Brunanburh in 937, when King Athelstan defeated a Viking-Celtic invasion of England, and, in essence, fixed the historic boundaries of the nations of

the British Isles, noted that: 'it was inborn in them from their forbears that they should often, in warfare against every foe, defend land, treasure-hoard and homes'.[42] The Home Guard was, indeed, defending 'land, treasure-hoard and homes', and given this role as a *defensive* force, it held, and still holds, a particular moral strength. Home Guards died and were injured in air raids and training, and were active in the defence of their country against a particularly dangerous totalitarian enemy. In a previous period, the defensive posture of the Volunteers was also held to have been one of the key reasons why that force was held in popular regard. A contemporary piece of verse, by Alfred Richards, entitled 'Our Volunteers', c.1859/60, combined the pride in defence with a cross-class message, both of which applied to the Home Guard:

> *We are not armed to carry war*
> *To near or distant land,*
> *To steep the smiling globe with gore*
> *Or prowl with hostile band.*
> *But we are trained with trust above*
> *To guard our native coast,*
> *Our Queen, our fame – the home we love,*
> *And those we love the most.*
>
> *For this, the noble and the brave*
> *Of gentle birth and name*
> *Ay, and the manhood nature gave*
> *Stand proudly armed the same.*
> *The courtier with the peasant blunt,*
> *Who thinks not 'neath his stave,*
> *And looks as boldly to the front,*
> *And working men are there.*[43]

The Home Guard certainly fitted this model of an army created not for conquest, but for patriotic defence. In the words of William Scroggie, Dundee Home Guard, and officer in the Lovat Scouts, who was blinded and maimed in Italy in April 1945, the Home Guard had one purpose:

> the object of the exercise was to keep Hitler out of the British Isles if we could do so.[44]

And the men and women of the LDV and the Home Guard played their part in that vital exercise.

Notes

Chapter 1: Defending these Shores

1. Only a 325 line fragment of this Early English poem has survived; even the original title is lost, but it is commonly known as 'The Battle of Maldon'. There are various editions; for example, E V Gordon (ed), with a supplement by D G Scragg, *The Battle of Maldon*, Manchester, Manchester University Press, 1976.
2. Lines 100–103 of *The Battle of Maldon*, as translated by Ian P Stephenson, *The Late Anglo-Saxon Army*, Stroud, Tempus Publishing, 2007, p. 126.
3. Ibid., p. 125.
4. The National Archives (TNA), Cab/66/9/44.
5. David R Orr, *Duty Without Glory; the story of Ulster's Home Guard in the Second World War and the Cold War*, Newtownards, Redcoat Publishing, 2008; Austin J Ruddy, *To The Last Round; the Leicestershire and Rutland Home Guard, 1940–1945*, Derby, Breedon Books, 2007.
6. Charles Graves, *The Home Guard of Britain*, London, Hutchinson, 1943; John Brophy, *Britain's Home Guard; A character study*, London, Harrap, 1945; John Radnor, *It All Happened Before; The Home Guard through the centuries*, London, Harrap, 1945.
7. S P MacKenzie, *The Home Guard; A military and political history*, Oxford, Oxford University Press, 1995. Norman Longmate, a Home Guard veteran himself, published a brief and highly readable history in 1974, which drew heavily on Charles Graves work: Norman Longmate, *The Real Dad's Army; The story of the Home Guard*, London, Arrow Books, 1974.
8. One, somewhat pejorative, view of the Stockton Volunteers of the 1798–1808 period, as made in Heaviside's *Annals of Stockton on Tees*, 1865, and quoted by Winifred Stokes in 'Investigating the history of local volunteer regiments: the Stockton Volunteers and the French invasion threat 1798–1808', *The Local Historian*, vol. 37, No. 1, February 2007, p. 27.
9. Geoffrey Cousins, *The Defenders; A history of the British Volunteer*, London, Frederick Muller, 1968, p. 75.

10. The exact implications of the term 'Fencible' varied. The official definition was a volunteer who was full time and paid, and who had enlisted for the duration of the war. In addition, they did not expect to serve outside the country, although, for example, Manx Fencibles served in Ireland in the period. However, in the case of the Fishguard landings, the local Fencibles were part-timers.

11. Norman Longmate, *Island Fortress; The defence of Great Britain, 1603–1945*, London, Pimlico edition, 1991, p. 238.

12. Ibid., p. 238.

13. Ian F W Beckett, *Riflemen Form; a Study of the Rifle Volunteer Movement, 1859–1908*, Barnsley, Pen & Sword, 2007 edition, p. 9.

14. Ibid., p. 9.

15. Lawrence Sondhaus, *Naval Warfare 1815–1914*, London, Routledge, 2001, p. 74.

16. Beckett, *Riflemen Form*, p. 20.

17. Cousins, *The Defenders*, p. 103.

18. MacKenzie, *The Home Guard*, p. 7.

19. From the second circular on the Volunteer Corps, May 1859, quoted by Beckett, *Riflemen Form*, p. 22.

20. MacKenzie, *The Home Guard*, pp. 9–10.

21. Childers' famous novel is still in print, and his life is a good case study of propaganda, nationalism, and irregular warfare in the early twentieth century. See, for example, Leonard Piper, *Dangerous Waters; the Life and Death of Erskine Childers*, London, Hambledon and London, 2003.

22. *The Riddle of the Sands* was published in May, 1903 to immediate acclaim, and 'by the end of the year [it] had gone through three editions, plus a special cheap edition that sold several hundred thousand copies. It was without question book of the year', ibid., p. 72.

23. I F Clarke in the introduction to *The Battle of Dorking* and *When William Came*, Oxford, Oxford University Press, 1997. Clarke has edited two collections of invasion fiction: *The Tale of the Next Great War, 1871–1914: fictions of future warfare and of battles still-to-come*, Liverpool, Liverpool University Press, 1995; and *The Great War with Germany, 1890–1914; fictions and fantasies of the war to-come*, Liverpool, Liverpool University Press, 1997.

24. MacKenzie, *The Home Guard*, p. 12.

25. Quoted by John Bodsworth, 'The Volunteer Training Corps', *The Armourer Militaria Magazine*, issue 99, May/June 2010, p. 59.

26. Ibid., p. 60.

27. MacKenzie, *The Home Guard*, p. 13.

28. Ibid., p. 15.

29. Ibid., p. 16.
30. Robert Stradling, *Your Children Will Be Next; bombing and propaganda in the Spanish Civil War, 1936–1939*, Cardiff, University of Wales Press, 2008.
31. George Orwell, *Keep the Aspidistra Flying*, Harmondsworth, Penguin edition, 1974, p. 21.
32. Jon Mills, *Within the Island Fortress; the uniforms, insignia & ephemera of the Home Front in Britain 1939–1945; No. 1 The Women's Voluntary Services (WVS)*, Orpington, Wardens Publishing, 2005, p. 25.
33. The standard history of the Royal Observer Corps is the encyclopaedic volume by Derek Wood, *Attack Warning Red; the Royal Observer Corps and the defence of Britain 1925 to 1992*, (Revised edition), Portsmouth, Carmichael and Sweet, 1992. An earlier history, focusing on the two world wars, is by T E Winslow, *Forewarned is Forearmed; a History of the Royal Observer Corps*, London, William Hodge & Company, 1948; while Henry Buckton's *Forewarned is Forearmed; an Official Tribute and History of the Royal Observer Corps*, Leatherhead, Ashford, Buchan & Enright, 1993, marked the disbandment of the ROC.
34. MacKenzie, *The Home Guard*, p. 17.
35. David G Williamson, *Poland Betrayed; the Nazi-Soviet Invasions of 1939*, Barnsley, Pen & Sword, 2009, p. 116. Williamson makes the point that the subsequent development of the war and Poland's post 1945 incorporation into the Soviet bloc, has obscured the history of 'what can be called the Second Polish-Soviet War', ibid., p. 120. Williamson provides an account in pp. 120–128 of *Poland Betrayed*.
36. Angus Calder, *The People's War; Britain 1939–45*, London, Jonathan Cape, 1969; Granada Publishing paperback edition, 1982, p. 78.
37. Ibid., p. 79.
38. Will Fowler, *Poland and Scandinavia 1939–1940*, Hersham, Ian Allan Publishing, 2002, p. 70. During the German occupation of Denmark, which, until 1943, was relatively benign, leaving Danish political and civic structures intact, almost as many Danes fought for the German armed forces as had been in the Danish forces in 1940. Denmark did, however, have the distinction of rescuing almost all its Jewish community from the clutches of the Nazis, secretly transporting them to Sweden. For a good, overall account of occupation, collaboration and resistance in Denmark and Norway, see, Richard Petrow, *The Bitter Years; the invasion and occupation of Denmark and Norway, April 1940–May 1945*, London, Hodder and Stoughton, 1975.
39. Will Fowler, *France, Holland and Belgium, 1940–1941*, Hersham, Ian Allan Publishing, 2002, p. 23.

40. MacKenzie, *The Home Guard*, p. 19.
41. Ibid., pp. 24–25.
42. Roderick Jones, *The Times*, 12 May 1940, quoted in ibid., p. 25.
43. Charles Graves, *The Home Guard of Britain*, pp. 13–14.

Chapter 2: Time of Crisis; May 1940–June 1941

1. For example, early in August 1914, Sir Arthur Conan Doyle helped create a local defence force in the village of Crowborough, and the idea quickly spread, with the help of *The Times*. The government, however, were not so keen on unofficial militias, and, instead created the Volunteer Training Corps. See, chapters 1 and 9 here.
2. S P MacKenzie, *The Home Guard; a military and political history*, Oxford, Oxford University Press, 1995, pp. 28–30.
3. Ibid., pp. 34–5.
4. The National Archives (TNA), Cab/65/7/13, 11 May 1940.
5. MacKenzie, *Home Guard*, pp. 28–30.
6. TNA, Cab/65/7/15, 13 May 1940.
7. TNA, Cab/67/6/34, 'Arming the Police, A Memorandum by the Home Secretary'.
8. Ibid.
9. TNA, Cab/66/8/24, 5 June 1940.
10. 'Training Instruction No. 2, 6 June 1940', quoted in MacKenzie, *Home Guard*, p. 41.
11. Imperial War Museum (IWM), Sound Archive (SA), 15803, Colin Cuthbert.
12. Ibid.
13. Ibid.
14. Ibid.
15. TNA, Cab/65/7/65, 17 June 1940.
16. Ibid.
17. John Langdon-Davies (ed.), revised by General Sir A Godley, *The Home Guard Training Manual*, London, John Murray and the Pilot Press, 1940, p. 11.
18. John Langdon-Davies, *Fifth Column*, London, John Murray, 1940, p. 5.
19. Richard Thurlow, 'The Evolution of the Mythical British Fifth Column, 1939–46', in *Twentieth Century British History*, vol. 10, No. 4, 1999, p. 478.
20. The Germans broadcast a range of radio stations into Britain aimed at different sections of the population. Some purported to be clandestine stations operating from within the UK. See, W J West, *Truth Betrayed*, London, Duckworth, 1987, especially Part 3, pp. 173–244.

21. Thurlow, 'Evolution of the Mythical British Fifth Column', p. 484.
22. TNA, Cab/66/7/33, 10 May 1940.
23. Ibid.
24. Ibid.
25. TNA, Cab/66/7/33.
26. Ibid.
27. Ibid.
28. TNA, Cab/66/10/1, 19 July 1940; also Cab/66/8/2.
29. TNA, Cab/66/7/48, 25 May 1940.
30. TNA, Cab/65/7/23, 18 May 1940.
31. Ibid.
32. TNA, Cab/65/7/18, 15 May 1940.
33. A W B Simpson, *In the Highest Degree Odious*, Oxford, Oxford University Press, 1992; Stephen Cullen, 'Fascists Behind Barbed Wire; political internment without trial in wartime Britain', *The Historian*, No. 100, Winter 2008, pp. 14–21.
34. TNA, Cab/66/9/35, 6 June 1940.
35. IWM, SA 9341, Francis George Codd.
36. Peter Fleming, *Invasion 1940*, London, Rupert Hart-Davies, 1957, p. 68, note 2.
37. MacKenzie, *Home Guard*, p. 59.
38. TNA, Cab/65/7/65, 17 June 1940.
39. Ibid.
40. TNA, Cab/67/6/31, 17 May 1940.
41. TNA, Cab/67/7/3, 15 June 1940.
42. Thurlow, 'Evolution of the Mythical British Fifth Column', p. 492.
43. TNA, Cab/66/8/29, 12 June 1940.
44. On 3–4 September 1939, following a botched anti-Polish armed rising in the town of Bydgoszcz, Polish forces massacred around 1,000 ethnic German Polish citizens. This was followed by German Army reprisals against Polish civilian militia on 5–9 September. See, David G Williamson, *Poland Betrayed; the Nazi-Soviet Invasions of 1939*, Barnsley, Pen and Sword, 2009, pp. 83–4.
45. MacKenzie, *The Home Guard*, explores the struggle over the title of the force, pp. 47–51.
46. Charles Graves, *The Home Guard of Britain*, London, Hutchinson, 1943, p. 16.
47. TNA, Cab/65/8/11, 10 July 1940.
48. Ibid.
49. Ibid. The issue is examined in this book in chapter 6, 'Home Guard Lives'.

50. IWM, SA 12400, John Rayner Bone.
51. National Army Museum (NAM), 8902-200-3.
52. TNA, Cab/66/9/16, 30 June 1940.
53. William Foot, *Beaches, fields, streets and hills ... the anti-invasion landscape of England, 1940*, York, English Heritage, Council for British Archaeology, 2006, p. 9.
54. TNA, Cab/66/9/16, 29 June 1940.
55. The question of the LDV/Home Guard's function in maintaining morale is examined by David K Yelton, 'British Public Opinion, the Home Guard and the Defense of Great Britain, 1940–1944', *Journal of Military History*, vol. 58, No. 3, 1994, pp. 461–480.
56. TNA, Cab/65/8/2.
57. MacKenzie, *The Home Guard*, p. 45.
58. Quoted in MacKenzie, ibid., p. 50.
59. Ibid., p. 50.
60. Ibid., p. 45.
61. TNA, Cab/66/9/44, 18 July 1940.
62. Ibid.
63. Ibid.
64. Ibid.
65. Ibid.
66. Bernard Lowry, *Discovering Fortifications; from the Tudors to the Cold War*, Princes Risborough, *Shire Publications*, 2006, pp. 114–115.
67. TNA, Cab/66/13/1, 15 October 1940.
68. TNA, Cab/65/9/6, 6 September 1940.
69. John Warwicker, *Churchill's Underground Army; A History of the Auxiliary Units in World war II*, Barnsley, Frontline Books, 2008, p. 49.
70. Ibid., p. 49.
71. IWM, SA 7396, Colonel Malcolm Ernest Hancock.
72. Quoted by Warwicker, *Churchill's Underground Army*, p. 51.
73. IWM, SA 15758, Jack French.
74. David Lampe, *The Last Ditch*, London, Cassell, 1968, p. 94. Note, too, the photographs of surviving OBs, and re-enactors playing the part of Aux Unit personnel, in Arthur Ward, *Resisting the Nazi Invader*, London, Constable, 1997, pp. 39–50.
75. Warwicker, *Churchill's Underground Army*, p. 73.
76. Yelton, 'British Public Opinion', p. 469.

Chapter 3: The Long Haul; June 1941–December 1944

1. Anon, *'We Also Served'; the story of the Home Guard in Cambridgeshire and the Isle of Ely 1940–1943*, Cambridge, Privately Printed, 1944, p. 18.

2. An official memorandum from early 1941, quoted in Charles Graves, *The Home Guard of Britain*, London, Hutchinson, 1943, p. 126.
3. William Foot, *Beaches, fields, streets, and hills; the anti-invasion land-scapes of England, 1940*, York, English Heritage, Council for British Archaeology, 2006, p. 14
4. Ibid., p14.
5. Ibid., p. 435.
6. The National Army Museum (NAM) archives, NAM 2000-02-115. Note that all subsequent detail on David Roberts come from this collection, the Roberts' papers, at the NAM.
7. Imperial War Museum (IWM), Sound Archive (SA), 16084 Edward Norman Kirby.
8. Ibid.
9. Ibid.
10. The National Archives (TNA), Cab/65/28/30, 27 Nov 1942.
11. David R Orr, *Duty Without Glory; The Story of Ulster's Home Guard in the Second World War and the Cold War*, Newtownards, Redcoat Publishing, 2008, pp. 214–5.
12. Note that the term 'manpower' is used here to include both women and men.
13. S P MacKenzie, *The Home Guard; A Military and Political History*, Oxford, Oxford University Press, 1995, p. 150.
14. Ibid., p. 109.
15. Ibid., p. 109.
16. TNA, Cab/66/31/36, War Cabinet minutes, 28 November 1942.
17. See TNA Cab/65/20/23, December 1941; Cab/67/9/150, 15 December 1941; Cab/67/9/144, 27 November 1941.
18. The Secretary of State for War at a War Cabinet meeting of 15 December 1941, TNA Cab/67/9/150.
19. TNA Cab/65/25/19, 9 February 1942.
20. Quoted by MacKenzie, *The Home Guard*, p. 118.
21. Charles Graves, *The Home Guard of Britain*, p. 147.
22. Craig Armstrong, 'Tyneside's Home Guard Units: An Able Body of Men?', *Contemporary British History*, vol. 22, No. 2, June 2008, p. 271.
23. The papers of Lt-Col. Herbert Leslie Allsopp, held at the National Army Museum (NAM), 8902-200.
24. MacKenzie, *The Home Guard*, p. 117.
25. By September 1943, 48,950 women were serving in Anti-Aircraft Command. In November 1944, one of the mixed units, 139 (Mixed) Heavy Anti-Aircraft Regiment was deployed to NW Europe to counter German V1s being targeted against the port of Antwerp; Martin Brayley,

World War II Allied Women's Services, Botley, Osprey Publishing, 2001, p. 9.
26. TNA, Cab/66/36/11, 26 April 1943.
27. Ibid.
28. See chapter 6 'Home Guard Lives' here for women in the Home Guard.
29. MacKenzie, *The Home Guard*, p. 147.
30. Ibid., p184.
31. David K Yelton, 'British Public Opinion, the Home Guard, and the Defense of Great Britain, 1940–1944', *The Journal of Military History*, vol. 58, No. 3, July 1994, p. 476.
32. Mike Osborne, Defending Britain; *Twentieth-Century Military Structures in the Landscape*, Stroud, Tempus, 2004, p. 24.
33. Ibid., p27.
34. John Brophy, *Britain's Home Guard; a character study*, London, George Harrap & Co, 1945, p. 41.
35. See chapter 7, 'Rifles to Rockets' here.
36. TNA, Cab/66/34/24, 20 February 1943.
37. See chapter 7 here, 'Rifles to Rockets'.
38. School cadet corps were re-designated 'Junior Training Corps' (JTC) in the autumn term of 1940; prior to then they had been known as the OTC, like the university corps.
39. Allsopp, NAM 8902-200.
40. Ibid.
41. MacKenzie, *The Home Guard*, p. 91.
42. Ibid., p. 121.
43 For further details of these weapons and equipment, see chapter 7, 'Rifles to Rockets'.
44. Stephen Cullen, *Home Guard Socialism: A vision of a People's Army*, Warwick, Allotment Hut Booklets, 2006. See also chapter 9 here, 'It All Happened Before'.
45. Graves, *The Home Guard of Britain*, p. 139.
46. Roberts, NAM 2000-02-115.
47. Ibid.
48. MacKenzie, *Home Guard*, pp. 123–124.
49. Allsopp, NAM 8902 200.
50. Ibid.
51. See note 2 above.
52. Graves, *The Home Guard of Britain*, p. 164.
53. Austin J Ruddy, *To The Last Round; the Leicestershire and Rutland Home Guard 1940–1945*, Derby, Breedon Books, 2007, p. 105.
54. TNA, Cab/65/34/6, 12 April 1943.

55. Ibid.
56. TNA, Cab/66/36/22.
57. David K Yelton, 'British Public Opinion, the Home Guard, and the Defense of Great Britain', note 65, p. 476.
58. Ibid., p. 476.
59. Allsopp, NAM 8902-200.
60. Roy Rowberry, *We You Salute*, Privately printed, 1990.
61. MacKenzie, *The Home Guard*, p. 152.
62. Ibid., p. 152.
63. From the papers of David Roberts, NAM, 2000-02-115-186.
64. Ibid. 2000-02-115-187.
65. Allsopp NAM, 8902-200-41.
66. J D Sainsbury, *Hazardous Work*, Welwyn, Hart Books, 1985, p. 77.

Chapter 4: Playing Fields and Factory Yards

1. The Officer Training Corps (OTC) was divided into two divisions. The senior was based in universities, and the junior in schools. Until the Autumn term of 1940, both were known as the OTC. After that, the school division was known as the Junior Training Corps (JTC), while the university corps remained the OTC. For simplicity, the term OTC is used for both the junior and senior divisions in this book. Today, the junior division is known as the Combined Cadet Force (CCF), and, interestingly, Eton's CCF is still known, in the school, as 'The Corps'. This also reflects the school's much older volunteer tradition, which stretches back to the Napoleonic period. It is said that the main quad of the college buildings was cobbled (badly) for the volunteers of the period to parade on.
2. Geoffrey Cousins, *The Defenders; A history of the British volunteer*, London, Frederick Muller, 1968, p. 159.
3. For example, student numbers at Oxford University fell from 4,500 (including 850 women) in 1938 to 2,500 in 1944 (including 800 women); see, Chris Sladen, 'When War Came Again', in *Oxford Today*, vol. 22, No. 1, Michaelmas 2009, p. 19.
4. James Hugh William Lowther, Imperial War Museum (IWM), SA (SA) 15733.
5. James Lowther, IWM, SA, 15733.
6. Ibid.
7. Harold James Strickland 'Jimmy' Taylor, IWM, SA, 13714. In later years, the school responded to the nuclear threat of the Cold War by building nuclear shelters.
8. James Lowther, IWM, SA, 15733.

9. 'Jimmy' Taylor, IWM, SA, 13714.
10. Ibid.
11. Michael Bendix, IWM, SA, 18570.
12. James Lowther, IWM, SA, 15733.
13. Charles Graves, *The Home Guard of Britain*, London, Hutchinson & Co. Ltd., 1943, p. 65.
14. Michael Bendix, IWM, SA, 18570.
15. See chapter 6 here, 'Home Guard Lives'.
16. 'Jimmy' Taylor, IWM, SA, 13714.
17. Fred Archer, *When Village Bells Were Silent*, Gloucester, Alan Sutton, 1987 paperback edition, p. 64.
18. 'Jimmy' Taylor, IWM, SA, 13714.
19. Michael Bendix, IWM, SA, 18570.
20. S P MacKenzie, *The Home Guard; a military and political history*, Oxford, Oxford University Press, 1995, p. 106.
21. Hugh Slater, *Home Guard for Victory!*, London, Victor Gollancz, 1941, chapter IV, 'How to Defend a Factory'.
22. Maurice Giles 'Peter' Bradshaw, IWM, SA, 12958.
23. 'Peter' Bradshaw, IWM, SA, 12958.
24. Hawtin Leonard Mundy, IWM, SA, 7285.
25. Ibid.
26. Ibid.
27. Graves, Charles, *The Home Guard of Britain*, pp. 68–9.
28. Hawtin Mundy, IWM, SA, 7285.
29. Graves, *The Home Guard of Britain*, p. 53.
30. Ibid., p. 54.
31. Ibid., p. 81.
32. War Office circular, cited in Graves, *The Home Guard of Britain*, pp. 80–1.
33. Stanley Brand, IWM, SA, 27347.
34. Ibid.
35. Frederick George Richard Cardy, IWM, SA, 11350.
36. Graves, *The Home Guard of Britain*, p. 82.
37. Robert James Branscombe Nosworthy, IWM, SA, 10658.
38. Ibid.
39. J D Sainsbury, *Hazardous Work; an account of the decorations and commendations awarded to members of the Home Guard in recognition of acts of gallantry performed on duty 1940–1944*, Welwyn, Hart Books, 1985.
40. Robert Nosworthy, IWM, SA, 10658.

Chapter 5: Celtic Defenders

1. S P MacKenzie, *The Home Guard; A Military and Political History*, Oxford, Oxford University Press, 1995, pp. 84–5.
2. David Orr, *Duty Without Glory; the Story of Ulster's Home Guard, the Second World War and the Cold War*, Newtownards, Redcoat Publishing, 2008.
3. Brian D Osborne, *The People's Army; Home Guard in Scotland 1940–1944*, Edinburgh, Birlinn, 2009.
4. This was the slogan on an Ulster Home Guard recruiting poster; Orr, frontispiece.
5. Charles Graves, *The Home Guard of Britain*, London, Hutchison, 1943, p. 169.
6. Her Majesty's Stationary Office (HMSO), *Land At War; the Official Story of British Farming 1939–1944*, London, The Stationary Office, 2001 facsimile edition, p. 84.
7. Material relating to the Ulster Home Guard in this chapter draws heavily on David Orr's work. I am most grateful for his help and advice in preparing this chapter.
8. Just as not all Protestants were/are not Unionists, neither were/are all Roman Catholics Nationalists or Republicans. On the history of Catholic Unionists see, for example, John Biggs-Davison, and George Chowdharay-Best, *The Cross of Saint Patrick; the Catholic Unionist Tradition in Ireland*, Bourne End, The Kensal Press, 1984.
9. Orr, *Duty Without Glory* p. 22.
10. Ibid., p. 22.
11. Ibid., p. 23.
12. Ibid., p. 45.
13. Ibid., pp. 34–5.
14. Thomas Bartlett, and Keith Jeffrey, *A Military History of Ireland*, Cambridge, Cambridge Universiity Press, 1996, pp. 433–34.
15. Orr, *Duty Without Glory* pp. 55–6.
16. Ibid., p. 90.
17. Ibid., p. 95.
18. Ibid., p. 98.
19. Ibid., p. 121.
20. Donal MacCarron, *'Step Together!' Ireland's Emergency Army 1939–46; as told by its veterans*, Dublin, Irish Academic Press, 1999, pp. 3–4; and Donal MacCarron, *The Irish Defence Forces since 1922*, Oxford, Osprey, 2004, pp. 14–21.
21. Orr, *Duty Without Glory* pp. 101–02.
22. Ibid., pp. 214–15.

23. An unpublished account exists, in two, differing versions. The first typescript, probably written in late 1944, is held by the Manx Aviation and Military Museum (MAMM), Ronaldsway, and is entitled, 'Isle of Man Home Guard History'. In all probability, this TS was written by Major S.W. Corlett MBE. Corlett was the author of another version of the TS, held by the Manx National Heritage Museum Library (MNH), Douglas, entitled, 'History of the Manx Home Guard'; reference, MS06639 (MD475), with an acquisition date of 1969.

24. Bertram E Sargeaunt, *The Royal Manx Fencibles*, Aldershot, Gale and Polden, 1947.

25. Paul Francis, *Isle of Man 20th Century Military Archaeology, Part 1; Island Defence*, Douglas, Manx Heritage Foundation, 2006, pp. 15–20.

26. *Isle of Man Examiner*, 11 December, 1936, MNH, B114.

27. Francis, *Isle of Man 20th Century Military Archaeology*, pp. 93–7.

28. Isle of Man Government Circular, No. 1919, December 1938, MNH B114/IX.

29. 'Isle of Man Home Guard History', TS, 1944, p. 1.

30. Ibid., p. 2.

31. 'History of Manx Home Guard', TS, 1969, p. 3.

32. 'Isle of Man Home Guard History', TS, 1944, p. 3.

33. Ibid., p. 3.

34. MacCarron, 2004, pp. 15–6; and MacCarron, 1999, pp. 65–8.

35. 'History of Manx Home Guard', TS, 1969, p. 6.

36. Francis, *Isle of Man 20th Century Military Archaeology*, p. 132.

37. Francis, *Isle of Man 20th Century Military Archaeology*, p. 130.

38. Cullen, Stephen, 'Fascists Behind Barbed Wire; political internment without trial in wartime Britain', *The Historian*, Winter 2008, p. 20.

39. Francis, *Isle of Man 20th Century Military Archaeology*, p. 130.

40. The noted uniform historian, Philip J Haythornthwaite, notes that a Triskelion badge, with King's crown in brass, was by the Manx Home Guard during the war, and, in white metal, from 1951–57; 'Badges of the Home Guard', *Medal News*, May 1991, p. 24. However, all the photographic evidence suggests that the Manx Home Guard wore the King's Regiment cap badge during the war.

41. 'Isle of Man Home Guard History', TS, 1944, p. 12.

42. 'History of Manx Home Guard', TS, 1969, p. 12.

43. Ibid., p. 21.

44. 'Home Guard exercise briefing notes, issued by Major A R O Mallock, 2 i/c, 1st Bttn., Manx Home Guard, Tromode Drill Hall, 17 June 1944', MNH, TS, 11042.

45. 'History of Manx Home Guard', TS, 1969, p. 23.

46. 'Home Guard History', TS, by Major P D Kissack, OC Southern Coy., p. 4; held by MAMM, Ronaldsway.
47. Graves, *Home Guard of Britain*, pp. 204–05.
48. J D Sainsbury, *Hazardous Work*, Welwyn, Hart Books, 1985, pp. 38–9.
49. Graves, *Home Guard of Britain*, p. 334.
50. William Sydney Scroggie, IWM (IWM), sound archive (SA), catalogue number, 13281.
51. Ibid.
52. Ibid.
53. Ibid.
54. Ibid.
55. Ibid.
56. Ibid.
57. Ibid.
58. Compton MacKenzie's *Whisky Galore* (1947) was filmed in 1949, a features a series of Home Guard set-pieces that, in many ways, foreshadow the comedy of the BBC TV series, *Dad's Army*.
59. Osborne, *The People's Army*, p. 222; his reference is the National Library of Scotland, MS 3821.
60. William Sydney Scroggie, IWM, SA, 13281.
61. Ibid.
62. *The Times*, 18 September 1940, quoted in Sainsbury, *Hazardous Work*, p. 67.
63. Graves, *Home Guard of Britain*, p. 213.
64. Ibid, p. 213.
65. John Stuart Mill, IWM, SA, 11917.

Chapter 6: Home Guard Lives

1. Joseph Flatter, Imperial War Museum (IWM), Sound Archive (SA), 4765.
2. Joseph Flatter, IWM, SA, 4765.
3. Peter Gillman, and Leni Gillman, *'Collar the lot!'; how Britain interned and expelled its wartime refugees*, London, Quartet Books, 1980. Stent, Ronald, *A Bespattered Page?; the internment of His Majesty's 'most loyal enemy aliens'*, London, Andre Deutsch, 1980. Stent gives a total figure for German origin British residents in 1940 as 76,000, pp. 259–60.
4. A W B Simpson, *In The Highest Degree Odious; detention without trial in wartime* Britain, Oxford, Clarendon Press, 1992. Stephen M Cullen, 'Fascists behind barbed wire; political internment without trial in wartime Britain', in *The Historian*, Winter 2008–09.
5. Joseph Flatter, IWM, SA, 4765.

6. Connery Chappell, *Island of Barbed Wire; internment on the Isle of Man in World War Two*, London, Robert Hale, 1984.
7. Joseph Flatter, IWM, SA, 4765.
8. Peter Hariolf Plesch, IWM, SA, 15324.
9. Ronald Stent, *A Bespattered Page?;* p. 262.
10. Helen Fry, *The King's Most Loyal Enemy Aliens; Germans who fought for Britain in the Second World War*, Stroud, Sutton Publishing, 2007.
11. Joseph Flatter, IWM, SA, 4765.
12. Peter Hariolf Plesch, IWM, SA, 15324.
13. Cyril Punt, IWM, SA, 12245.
14. Ibid.
15. Edward Hillson, IWM, SA, 9581.
16. Cyril Punt, IWM, SA, 12245.
17. Ibid.
18. Ibid.
19. Edward Hillson, IWM, SA, 9581.
20. Penny Summerfield, and Corinna Coniston-Bird, *Contesting Home Defence; men, women, and the Home Guard in the second World War*, Manchester, Manchester University Press, 2007, pp. 73–4
21. S P MacKenzie, *The Home Guard; a military and political history*, Oxford, Oxford University Press, 1995, p. 83
22. *The Times*, 12 November 1941. Cited in, Summerfield and Coniston-Bird, *Contesting Home Defence* p. 67.
23. MacKenzie, *The Home Guard*, p. 127.
24. Summerfield, and Coniston-Bird, *Contesting Home Defence*, pp. 65–66.
25. Ibid., note 124, p. 99.
26. MacKenzie, *The Home Guard*, p. 147.
27. From the papers of Lt.-Col. Allsopp, National Army Museum, 8902-200-20.
28. Summerfield, and Coniston-Bird, *Contesting Home Defence*, p. 77.
29. Mary Warschauer, IWM, SA, 16762.
30. Ibid.
31. John Warwicker, John, *Churchill's Underground Army; a history of the Auxiliary Units in World War II*, Bradford, Pen and Sword Books, 2008, p. 101.
32. Ibid., p. 73.
33. Martin Brayley, *The British Home Front, 1939–45*, Oxford, Osprey Publishing, 2005, pp. 54–5.
34. Maria Bloxam, IWM SA, 14816.
35. Ibid.
36. Ibid.

37. Ibid.
38. Ibid.
39. Janie Hampton, *How the Girl Guides Won the War*, London, Harper Press, 2010.
40. Bob 'Ping' Shrimpton, IWM, SA, 21735.
41. Ibid.
42. John William 'Chick' Fowles, IWM, A, 18202.
43. Ibid.
44. Ibid.
45. Henry McArdle, IWM SA, 17631.
46. Frank Kellaway, IWM SA, 11283.
47. Ibid.
48. Ibid.
49. Ibid.
50. Ibid.
51. MacKenzie, *The Home Guard*, p. 91.
52. Frank Kellaway, IWM SA, 11283.
53. Ibid.
54. Ibid.

Chapter 7: Rifles to Rockets

1. David Orr, David, *Duty Without Glory*, Newtownards, Redcoat Publishing, 2008, pp. 186–217; Ruddy, Austin, J, *To the Last Round; the Leicestershire and Rutland Home Guard 1940–1945*, Derby, Breedon Books Publishing Co. Ltd., 2007, pp. 166–179.
2. Martin Mace, *Vehicles of the Home Guard*, Storrington, Historic Military Press, 2001; *Britain At War Magazine*, various monthly issues from July 2007 to June 2008.
3. Norman Longmate, *The Real Dad's Army; the story of the Home Guard*, London, Arrow Books, 1974, p. 63.
4. Charles Graves, *The Home Guard of Britain*, London, Hutchison & Co., 1943, p. 32.
5. Orr, *Duty Without Glory*, p. 43.
6. Longmate, *Real Dad's Army*, p. 67.
7. William Albert Weightman, Imperial War Museum (IWM) Sound Archive (SA), 12246.
8. Gerald Patrick Walgate, IWM SA, 11456.
9. Mace, *Britain At War Magazine*, issues of November and December, 2007.
10. Mace, *ibid.*, November 2007, p. 47.
11. Mace, *ibid.*, December 2007, pp. 53–4.

12. Mace, *ibid.*, November 2007, p. 53.
13. John Langdon-Davies (ed.), *The Home Guard Training Manual*, London, John Murray & The Pilot Press, 1940, p. 76.
14. The National Archives (TNA), Cab/65/7/65, 17 June 1940.
15. Ruddy, *To the Last Round*, pp. 166–67.
16. Frank Kellaway, IWM, SA, 11283.
17. Longmate, *Real Dad's Army*, p. 70.
18. *Ibid.*, p. 70.
19. John Brophy, John, *Britain's Home Guard*, London, George C Harrap & Co., 1945, p. 31.
20. Orr, *Duty Without Glory*, p. 191.
21. Ibid., p. 191.
22. Langdon-Davies, *Training Manual*, p. 91.
23. Ibid., p. 91.
24. Orr, *Duty Without Glory*, p. 212.
25. Langdon-Davies, *Training Manual*, p. 103.
26. Many of these weapons, however, fell into enemy hands. The Vichy French paramilitary force, *Milice Française*, benefited from British supplies in this way, being heavily armed with Stens, Brens and SMLEs; see Stephen M Cullen, 'Legion of the Damned', *Military Illustrated*, No. 238, March 2008, pp. 24–31; and Cullen, 'Collaborationists in Arms; the Uniforms and Equipment of the *Milice Française*', *The Armourer Militaria Magazine*, No. 100, July/August 2010, pp. 24–28.
27. Longmate, *Real Dad's Army*, p. 75.
28. Orr, *Duty Without Glory*, p. 211.
29. Ruddy, *To the Last Round*, p. 169.
30. S P MacKenzie, *The Home Guard; a military and political history*, Oxford, Oxford University Press, 1995, p. 91.
31. Ibid., p. 121.
32. Hugh Slater, *Home Guard for Victory!*, London, Gollancz, 1941.
33. Ibid., p. 62.
34. Mace, *Britain At War Magazine*, July 2007, pp. 45–6.
35. Ibid., p. 46.
36. Orr, *Duty Without Glory*, p. 205.
37. Frank Kellaway, IWM, SA, 11283.
38. Orr, *Duty Without Glory*, p. 205.
39. Ibid. p. 206.
40. Ruddy, *To the Last Round*, p. 172.
41. Orr, *Duty Without Glory*, pp. 200–09.
42. Ibid., p. 204.
43. Ibid., pp. 204–5, 207.

44. Ibid., p. 187.
45. Longmate, *Real Dad's Army*, p. 79.
46. Ibid., p. 79.
47. Orr, *Duty Without Glory*, p. 188.
48. Mace, *Britain at War Magazine*, June 2008, p. 52, quoting, *Tactical Employment of the Smith Gun*, 2 December, 1942.
49. Orr, *Duty Without Glory*, p. 209.
50. John William 'Chick' Fowles, IWM, SA, 18202.
51. Mike Osborne, *Defending Britain; Twentieth century military structures in the landscape*, Stroud, Tempus, 2004, p. 79.
52. Mace, *Vehicles of the Home Guard*, pp. 4, 11–12.
53. Ibid., p. 20.
54. Ibid., p. 13.
55. Ibid., p. 17.
56. Ibid., p. 31.
57. MacKenzie, *The Home Guard*, p. 109.
58. Ibid., p. 109.
59. Ibid., p. 122.
60. Ibid., p. 150.
61. Alfred Price, *Britain's Air Defences 1939–45*, Oxford, Osprey, 2004, pp. 6–11.
62. Ibid., p. 31.
63. Roy Barclay, IWM, SA, 13171.
64. Ronald Elliott, IWM, SA, 10167.
65. Joseph Yarwood, IWM, SA, 12231.
66. Ibid.
67. MacKenzie, *The Home Guard*, p. 147.
68. Price, *Britain's Air Defences*, p. 49.
69. Osborne, *Defending Britain*, p. 24.
70. Ibid., p. 24.
71. Lowry, Bernard, *British Home Defences 1940–45*, Oxford, Osprey, 2004, pp. 28–9.
72. William Aikman, IWM, SA, 25272.
73. Ibid.
74. Ibid.
75. Ibid.
76. Lieut.-Col, J Lee, quoted by Longmate, *Real Dad's Army*, p. 63.
77. Bernard Lowry, *Discovering Fortifications from the Tudors to the Cold War*, Princes Risborough, Shire, 2006, pp. 8–19.
78. Brophy, *Britain's Home Guard*, p. 41.
79. Aikman, IWM, SA, 25272.

Chapter 8: Cloth Caps and Steel Helmets

1. William Sydney Scroggie, Imperial War Museum (IWM), Sound Archive (SA), catalogue number, 13281.
2. Norman Longmate, *The Real Dad's Army; the Story of the Home Guard*, London, Arrow Books, 1974, p. 49; and R J Hunt, *Uniforms of the Home Guard*, Pulborough, Historic Military Press, 2002, p. 4.
3. Charles Graves, *The Home Guard of Britain*, London, Hutchison, 1943, p. 35.
4. Cyril Punt, IWM, SA, catalogue number, 12245.
5. Hunt, *Uniforms*, p. 6.
6. Longmate, *The Real Dad's Army*, p. 50.
7. The National Archives (TNA), CAB/65/8/38, minutes of War Cabinet meeting of 14 August 1940.
8. Graves, *The Home Guard of Britain*, p. 86.
9. Longmate, *The Real Dad's Army*, p. 54.
10. For the story of the Home Guard in Northern Ireland, see chapter Five, 'Celtic Defenders', here; and David Orr, *Duty Without Glory; The story of Ulster's Home Guard in the Second World War and the Cold War*, Newtownards, Redcoat Publishing, 2008.
11. Longmate, *The Real Dad's Army*, p. 49.
12. Orr, *Duty Without Glory*, pp. 34–5.
13. Ibid., pp. 168–9.
14. Graves, *The Home Guard of Britain*, p. 290.
15. Graves, *ibid.*, pp. 290–1.
16. Quoted in David Carroll, *Dad's Army; The Home Guard 1940–1944*, Stroud, The History Press, 2009 edition, p. 82.
17. Orr, *Duty Without Glory*, p. 169.
18. Judging by the extraordinary number of UTP cap badges available on the militaria market, they have, in all probability, been widely counterfeited.
19. Graves, *The Home Guard of Britain*, p342.
20. Ibid., pp. 342–3.
21. See chapter 6 here, 'Home Guard Lives'.
22. Mary Warschauer, IWM, SA, catalogue number: 16762.
23. Carroll, *Dad's Army*, p. 89.
24. Penny Summerfield, Corinna Peniston-Bird, *Contesting Home Defence; Men, Women and the Home Guard in the Second World War*, Manchester, Manchester University Press, 2007, p. 89, figure 3.
25. Ibid., p. 245.
26. Martin Brayley, Malcolm McGregor, *The British Home Front*, Botley, Osprey Publishing, 2005, plate G3, p. 39.

27. This table is adapted from Hunt, *Uniforms of the Home Guard*, p. 21.
28. Quoted by S.P. MacKenzie, *The Home Guard; A military and political history*, Oxford, Oxford University Press, 1995, p. 79.
29. Graves, *The Home Guard of Britain*, p. 42.
30. Graves, *ibid.* p. 97 for examples of mass resignations.
31. See chapter 3, 'The Long Haul; June 1941–December 1944', here, on the manpower issue.
32. Quoted in MacKenzie, *The Home Guard*, p. 76.
33. Ibid., pp76–7.
34. Hunt, *Uniforms of the Home Guard*, p. 21.
35. Frank William Kellaway, IWM, SA, 11283.
36. Graves, *Home Guard of Britain*, p. 96.
37. Philip Haythornthwaite, 'Badges of the Home Guard', *Medal News*, May 1991, p. 24. Most of the details of badges are taken from this source.
38. Ibid., p. 25.
39. Graves, *Home Guard of Britain*, p. 125.
40. This example is illustrated in Haythornthwaite, 'Badges of the Home Guard', p. 25.

Chapter 9: 'It All Happened Before'

1. S P MacKenzie, *The Home Guard; A military and political history*, Oxford, Oxford University Press, 1995, p. 45.
2. Ibid., pp. 117 and 128.
3. Ibid., p. 175. It should be noted, however, that MacKenzie's comparisons are weighted in favour of the Home Guard, given that he only included men of working age, and excluded police and civil defence workers.
4. This is the title of the contemporary account of the force by John Radnor, *It All Happened Before; The Home Guard Through the Centuries*, London, Harrap, 1945.
5. I have rehearsed these arguments elsewhere; Stephen M Cullen, *Home Guard Socialism; A Vision of a People's Army*, 2006, Warwick, Allotment Hut Booklets.
6. 'Cato', *Guilty Men*, London, Gollancz, 1940.
7. George Orwell, *The Collected Essays, Journalism and Letters of George Orwell; volume 2, My Country Right or Left*, (eds.) Sonia Orwell and Ian Angus, 1971, Harmondsworth, Penguin, p. 180.
8. Ibid., p. 180.
9. John Brophy, *Britain's Home Guard, A Character Study*, 1945, London, Harrap, portrait in pastels, by Eric Kennington, facing p. 13.

10. Ibid., portraits between pp. 44 and 45.
11. MacKenzie, *The Home Guard*, pp. 68–86.
12. Quoted by Willie Thompson, *The Good Old Cause; British Communism 1920–1991*, 1992, London, Pluto Press, p. 53.
13. J K Hopkins, *Into the Heart of the Fire; the British in the Spanish Civil War*, 1998, Stanford, Stanford University Press.
14. Ibid., p. 227.
15. Ibid., p. 228.
16. George Orwell, *Orwell in Spain*, 2001, London, Penguin, pp. 205–06.
17. Quoted in Hugh Purcell, *The Last English Revolutionary; Tom Wintringham, 1898–1949*, 2004, Stroud, Sutton Publishing, pp. 173–74.
18. Ibid., p. 173.
19. Tom Wintringham, *New Ways of War*, 1940, Harmondsworth, Penguin, pp. 77–78.
20. Orwell, *Collected Essays*, p. 142.
21. Ibid., p. 181.
22. V S Pritchett in 'An Anecdote of the Blitz', Audrey Coppard & Bernard Crick (eds.), 1984, *Orwell Remembered*, London, Ariel Books, p. 167.
23. Author's note in 'Yank' Levy, *Guerrilla War*, 1941, Harmondsworth, Penguin.
24. Wintringham, *New Ways of War*, p. 28.
25. Orwell, *Collected Essays*, p. 42.
26. Quoted in Purcell, *The Last English Revolutionary*, p. 179.
27. MacKenzie, *The Home Guard*, p. 91.
28. John Langdon-Davies, *Home Guard Warfare*, 1941, London, Routledge, p. 29.
29. 'Yank' Levy, *Guerrilla Warfare*, 1941, Harmondsworth, Penguin, p. 26.
30. Orwell, *Collected Essays*, p. 178.
31. Ibid., p. 178.
32. Brophy, *Britain's Home Guard*, pp. 15–16.
33. Ibid., pp. 24–25.
34. Wintringham, *New Ways of War*, p. 9.
35. Levy, *Guerrilla Warfare*, pp. 14–15.
36. Ibid., p. 29.
37. Stephen M Cullen, 'Defending Mussolini', Military Illustrated, No. 263, April, 2010.
38. Stephen M Cullen, 'Collaborationists in Arms', *The Armourer Militaria Magazine*, No. 100, July/August 2010.
39. Hugh Slater, *Home Guard for Victory*, 1941, London, Gollancz, p. 79.
40. Donald Brown, *Somerset v Hitler; Secret Operations in the Mendips, 1939–1945*, 1999, Newbury, Countryside Books, p. 222.

41. Wintringham, *New Ways of War*, p. 118.
42. Ibid., p. 119.
43. Slater, *Home Guard for Victory*, p. 39, emphasis added.
44. MacKenzie, *The Home Guard*, p. 71.
45. This is the figure that Wintringham gave in his book, *Weapons and Tactics* (1943), where he also noted that once Osterley Park came under War Office control, 'several thousand more' Home Guard were trained there; Pelican edition of *Weapons and Tactics*, Harmondsworth, 1973, p. 16.
46. Quoted in David Fernbach, 'Tom Wintringham and socialist defense strategy', *History Workshop*, issue 14, Autumn 1982, p. 76.
47. MacKenzie, in *The Home Guard*, gave a good account of this process in his chapter, 'A People's Militia? 1940–1', pp. 68–86.
48. John Radnor, *It All Happened Before; the Home Guard Through the Centuries*, London, Harrap, 1945, p. 11.
49. Ibid., p. 13.
50. Charles Graves, *The Home Guard of Britain*, London, Hutchison, p. 19.
51. John Rayner Bone, Imperial War Museum (IWM), Sound Archive (SA), catalogue number: 12400.
52. Cyril Punt, IWM, SA, catalogue number: 12245.
53. Hawtin Leonard Mundy, IWM, SA, 7285.
54. Frank William Kellaway, IWM, SA, 11283.
55. National Army Museum (NAM), taken from the papers of Lt.-Col. Herbert Allsopp, OBE, TD; catalogue number: NAM 8902 200.
56. Brian D Osborne, *The People's Army; Home Guard in Scotland, 1940–1944*, 2009, Birlinn, Edinburgh, pp. 226–27.

Chapter 10: Gone but not Forgotten

1. The National Archive, TNA, Cab/66/65/60.
2. The origins of the aircrew who took part in the Battle of Britain are instructive: there were 2,936 men, of which: 2,340 were British, 127 were New Zealanders, 112 were Canadian, 32 were Australians, 25 South African, 13 Irish, 9 Americans, 3 Rhodesians, one each from Newfoundland, Barbados and Jamaica – this was the English-speaking world coming home. In addition, there were, of course, Poles (145), Czechs (89), Belgians 28 and Frenchmen 13.
3. David K Yelton, 'British Public Opinion, the Home Guard, and the Defense of Great Britain, 1940–1944', *The Journal of Military History*, vol. 58, No. 3 (July, 1994), p. 464.
4. Craig Armstrong, 'Tyneside's Home Guard Units: An Able Body of Men?', *Contemporary British History*, vol. 22, No. 2, (June 2008), p. 274.

5. Yelton, 'British Public Opinion', p. 464.
6. William Foot, *Beaches, fields, streets, and hills; the anti-invasion landscapes of England, 1940*, York, Council for British Archaeology, 2006, p. 513; John Goodall, *Pevensey Castle*, London, English Heritage, 1999.
7. Ibid., pp. 434–442.
8. John Stuart Mill, Imperial War Museum (IWM), Sound Archive (SA), catalogue number: 11917.
9. Michael Bendix, IWM SA, catalogue number: 18570.
10. Yelton, 'British Public Opinion, the Home Guard, and the Defense of Great Britain, 1940–1944', p. 464.
11. Quoted in S P MacKenzie, *The Home Guard; A Military and Political History*, Oxford, Oxford University Press, 1995, pp. 154–155.
12. G J Clayton, *The New Zealand Army; A History from the 1840's to the 1990's*, Christchurch [NZ], New Zealand Army, 1990, pp. 130–131. New Zealand was the foremost ally of the UK in both world wars, with a greater proportion of its adult male population serving in the military than in the UK or any Empire or Commonwealth country.
13. Carlos Caballero Jurado, *Resistance Warfare, 1940–45*, London, Osprey Publishing, 1985, p. 18.
14. Nigel Thomas, *Wehrmacht Auxiliary Forces*, London, Osprey, 1992, p. 22.
15. Karl Bahm, *Berlin 1945; The Final Reckoning*, Barnsley, Leo Cooper, 2001, p. 44.
16. Hans Holzträger, *In A Raging Inferno; Combat Units of the Hitler Youth, 1944–45*, Solihull, Helion and Company, 2000, p. 32.
17. Quoted in Tony Le Tissier, *With Our Backs to Berlin; The German Army in Retreat, 1945*, Stroud, Sutton, 2001, pp. 46–7.
18. This was the view of William Rust, the editor of *The Daily Worker* (forerunner of *The Morning Star*) at the beginning of 1948. Quoted in Christopher Andrew, *The Defence of the Realm; The Authorized History of MI5*, London, Allen Lane, 2009, p. 405.
19. MacKenzie, *The Home Guard*, p. 161. This estimate was later revised to 70,000 paratroopers – a figure that was more than likely to have been a gross over-estimation.
20. Ibid. p. 164.
21. MacKenzie noted Swingler as a strong opponent of the reborn Home Guard, MacKenzie *ibid.*, p. 168, and Christopher Andrew exposed Swingler's secret CPGB membership in *The Defence of the Realm*, pp. 412, and 414.
22. MacKenzie, *The Home Guard*, p. 166.
23. David Carroll, *Dad's Army; The Home Guard, 1940–1944*, Stroud, The History Press, 2009 edition, pp. 111–115.

24. MacKenzie, *The Home Guard*, p. 169.
25. Quoted in Carroll, *Dad's Army*, p. 113.
26. Penny Summerfield and Corinna Peniston-Bird, *Contesting Home Defence; men, women and the Home Guard in the Second World War*, Manchester, Manchester University Press, 2007, p. 170.
27. Books on the Home Guard and the Home Front that make reference to the television programme in their titles include: Norman Longmate's *The Real Dad's Army; The Story of the Home Guard*, London, Arrow, 1974; David Carroll, *Dad's Army; The Home Guard, 1940–1944*, Stroud, The History Press, 2002 and 2009; Mark Rowe, *Don't Panic, Britain Prepares for Invasion, 1940*, Stroud, Spellmount, 2010.
28. Summerfield and Peniston-Bird, *Contesting Home Defence*, chapter 6, '*Dad's Army* and Home Guard history', pp. 170–204.
29. IWM SA 7285. Hawtin Leonard Mundy, Great War rifleman with the Oxford & Buckinghamshire Light Infantry, Western Front, and Wolverton Works Home Guard, 1940–45.
30. Robert James Branscombe Nosworthy, IWM SA 10658. Lieutenant in the Home Guard, and Great War veteran of 3rd Bn London Regt (Post Office Rifles).
31. Maurice Giles 'Peter' Bradshaw, IWM, SA 12958.
32. Summerfield and Peniston-Bird, *Contesting Home Defence*, p. 197.
33. This story is told in Mike Osborne, *Defending Britain; Twentieth-Century Military Structures in the Landscape*, Stroud, Tempus, 2004, pp. 7–10.
34. Ibid., p. 9. Much of the information is available on the internet. A good starting point for those interested is the Pillbox Study Group/UK Fortifications Club website, which provides a wide range of information and links: http://www.pillbox-study-group.org.uk/sitemappage.htm ; accessed, 23 October 2010.
35. Taken from the ESELPWP proposal for the project, 2009.
36. http://www.gwag.org/ProjectsDDA.htm accessed 23 October 2010.
37. I am indebted to Andy Brockman, Research Director, DDA, for this statement of the value of the project.
38. *The Press*, Monday, 18 October 2010: http://www.yorkpress.co.uk/news/8458134.Oh_What_a_lovely_war/.
39. Chatham Home Guard website, http://www.home-guard.org.uk/chg/ accessed 22 October 2010.
40. Chatham Home Guard statement on http://www.staffshomeguard.co.uk/J10GeneralInformationReenactmentGroups.htm, accessed 22 October 2010.

41. The website of La Columna, http://www.lacolumna.org.uk/Event_osterley_2007.htm, accessed 22 October 2010.
42. Lines 7/9 of 'The Battle of Brunanburh', translated by S A J Bradley, *Anglo-Saxon Poetry*, London, Dent, 1982, p. 516.
43. Quoted in, Ian Beckett, *Riflemen Form; A Study of the Rifle Volunteer Movement, 1859–1908*, Barnsley, Pen & Sword, 2007 edition, pp. 264–265.
44. William Sroggie, IWM SA, 13281.

Sources

Audio recordings in the Imperial War Museum
Names of interviewees and Sound Archive catalogue number:
Joseph Otto Flatter, 4765
Harold Lewis, 7208
Hawtin Leonard Mundy, 7285
Marjorie Adams, 7295
Douglas Dytham, 7300
Malcolm Ernest Hancock, 7396
Harry Wharton, 8322
John David Carew Graham, 8337
Francis George Codd, 9341
Frederick William Johnes, 9366
Dorothy Margaret Williams, 9440
Edward Hillson, 9581
William Jones, 9926
Ronald Elliott, 10167
Robert James Branscombe Nosworthy, 10658
Barbara Wynne, 11227
Edna Selwyn, 11228
William Frank Kellaway, 11283
Frederick George Richard Cardy, 11350
Gerald Patrick Walgate, 11456
John Stuart Mill, 11917
Joseph Henry Yarwood, 12231
Cyril Punt, 12245
William Albert Weightman, 12246
John Rayner one, 12400
Eric Stanley Child, 12665
Maurice Giles 'Peter' Bradshaw, 12958
Roy Alexander Barclay, 13171
William Sidney Scroggie, 13281
Peter Alix Wilkinson, 13289
Leonard Shaw, 13326

Percy H Clark, 13612
Norman Steed, 13613 & 14753
Richard Stephen Body, 13614
Harold James 'Jimmy' Strickland Taylor, 13714
Robert Chandler, 14752
Jack French, 14756
Sam Osborne, 14755
Norman Field, 14759
Marina Bloxham, 14816
Janet Wise, 14817
Percy Clark, 14818
Arthur W A Gabbitas, 14819
Noel Andrew Cotton Croft, 14820
Michael Thomas William Ford, 15243
Peter Hariolf Plesch, 15324
James Hugh William Lowther, 15733
Colin S Cuthbert, 15803
Arthur B Smith, 15992
Edward Norman Kirby, 16084
Mary Warschauer, 16762
George Pellet, 16911
Henry McArdle, 17631
William Hugh Griffiths, 17506
Michael Bendix, 18570
John William 'Chick' Fowles, 18202
Bob 'Ping' Shrimpton, 21735
William Henry Aikman, 25272
Stanley Brand, 27347
Gordon Henderson, 30629.

The National Archives
Documents held in the following classifications:
Cab 65/7/65; Cab 65/8/11; Cab 66/9/16; Cab 65/8/2; Cab 67/7/27; Cab 65/7/21; Cab 65/57; Cab 66/8/24; Cab 66/8/29; Cab 67/6/34; Cab 65/7/13; Cab 65/7/15; Cab 65/8/38; Cab 65/9/6; Cab 66/11/19; Cab 65/9/7; Cab 66/11/50; Cab 66/9/44; Cab 67/8/10; Cab 66/11/32; Cab 66/13/1; Cab 66/7/33; Cab 65/7/23; Cab 67/6/31; Cab 67/7/3; Cab 65/7/18; Cab 66/7/48; Cab 66/9/35; Cab 65/7/39; Cab 66/10/1; Cab 66/8/2; Cab 65/9/34; Cab 66/36/17; Cab 65/20/23; Cab 67/9/150; Cab 67/9/151; Cab 67/18/31; Cab 67/9/137; Cab 67/9/40; Cab 67/9/144; Cab 66/31/50; Cab 65/25/19; Cab 68/9/17; Cab 65/28/30; Cab 66/31/36; Cab 195/2;

Cab 66/24/18; Cab 65/34/6; Cab 66/36/22; Cab 65/34/13; Cab 66/34/24; Cab 195/2; Cab 65/33/34; Cab 65/34/11; Cab 66/42/33; Cab 66/36/5; Cab 66/38/46; Cab 66/36/11; Cab 65/42/5; Cab 65/43/45; Cab 65/44/5; Cab 65/43/33; Cab 66/58/29; Cab 66/65/60.

Records in the National Army Museum
The papers of:
David Bevan Rutherford Roberts, catalogue number: NAM 2000-02-115
Herbert Leslie Allsopp, catalogue number: NAM 8902-200

Sources for the Isle of Man Home Guard
An unpublished account of the Isle of Man Home Guard exists, in two, differing versions. The first typescript, probably written in late 1944, is held by the Manx Aviation and Military Museum (MAMM), Ronaldsway, and is entitled, 'Isle of Man Home Guard History'. In all probability, this TS was written by Major S W Corlett MBE. Corlett was the author of another version of the TS, held by the Manx National Heritage Museum Library (MNII), Douglas, entitled, 'History of the Manx Home Guard'; reference, MS06639 (MD475), with an acquisition date of 1969. In addition, the MNH holds a range of documents, including, Home Guard History', TS, by Major P D Kissack, OC Southern Coy. For further details, see the notes to Chapter 5 here.

Contemporary publications
Anon, *'We Also Served'; the story of the Home Guard in Cambridgeshire and the Isle of Ely 1940–1943*, Cambridge, Privately printed, 1944
Brophy, John, *Britain's Home Guard; A character study*, London, Harrap, 1945
'Cato', *Guilty Men*, London, Gollancz, 1940
Graves, Charles, *The Home Guard of Britain*, London, Hutchinson, 1943.
The Stationary Office (HMSO), *Land At War; the Official Story of British Farming 1939–1944*, London, The Stationary Office, 1945, 2001 facsimile edition,
Langdon-Davies, John, (ed.), revised by General Sir A Godley, *The Home Guard Training Manual*, London, John Murray and the Pilot Press, 1940
Langdon-Davies, John, *Fifth Column*, London, John Murray, 1940
Langdon-Davies, John, *Home Guard Warfare*, London, Routledge, 1941
Levy, 'Yank', *Guerrilla Warfare*, Harmondsworth, Penguin, 1941
Orwell, George, *The Collected Essays, Journalism and Letters of George Orwell; volume 2, My Country Right or Left*, (eds.) Sonia Orwell and Ian Angus, Harmondsworth, Penguin, 1971

Orwell, George, *Keep the Aspidistra Flying*, 1936; Harmondsworth, Penguin edition, 1974

Orwell, George, *Orwell in Spain*, London, Penguin, 2001

Radnor, John, *It All Happened Before; The Home Guard through the centuries*, London, Harrap, 1945.

Slater, Hugh, *Home Guard for Victory!*, London, Victor Gollancz, 1941

Winslow, T E, *Forewarned is Forearmed; a History of the Royal Observer Corps*, London, William Hodge & Company, 1948

Wintringham, Tom, *New Ways of War*, Harmondsworth, Penguin, 1940

Secondary sources

Andrew, Christopher, *The Defence of the Realm; The Authorized History of MI5*, London, Allen Lane, 2009

Archer, Fred, *When Village Bells Were Silent*, Gloucester, Alan Sutton, 1987 paperback edition

Armstrong, Craig, 'Tyneside's Home Guard Units: An Able Body of Men?', *Contemporary British History*, vol. 22, No. 2, June 2008

Bahm, Karl, *Berlin 1945; The Final Reckoning*, Barnsley, Leo Cooper, 2001

Bartlett, Thomas, and Jeffrey, Keith, *A Military History of Ireland*, Cambridge, Cambridge University Press, 1996

Beckett, Ian, F W *Riflemen Form; a Study of the Rifle Volunteer Movement, 1859–1908*, Barnsley, Pen & Sword, 2007 edition

Bodsworth, John, 'The Volunteer Training Corps', *The Armourer Militaria Magazine*, issue 99, May/June 2010

Bradley, S A J, *Anglo-Saxon Poetry*, London, Dent, 1982

Brayley, Martin, *The British Home Front, 1939–45*, Oxford, Osprey Publishing, 2005

Brayley, Martin, *World War II Allied Women's Services*, Botley, Osprey Publishing, 2001

Britain At War Magazine, various monthly issues from July 2007 to June 2008

Brown, Donald, *Somerset v Hitler; Secret Operations in the Mendips, 1939–1945*, Newbury, Countryside Books, 1999

Buckton, Henry, *Forewarned is Forearmed; an Official Tribute and History of the Royal Observer Corps*, Leatherhead, Ashford, Buchan & Enright, 1993

Calder, Angus, *The People's War; Britain 1939–45*, London, Jonathan Cape, 1969; Granada Publishing paperback edition, 1982

Carroll, David, *Dad's Army; The Home Guard 1940–1944*, Stroud, The History Press, 2009 edition

Chappell, Connery, *Island of Barbed Wire; internment on the Isle of Man in World War Two*, London, Robert Hale, 1984

Clarke, I F, Introduction to *The Battle of Dorking* and *When William Came*, Oxford, Oxford University Press, 1997

Clarke, I F, *The Tale of the Next Great War, 1871–1914: fictions of future warfare and of battles still-to-come*, Liverpool, Liverpool University Press, 1995

Clarke, I F, *The Great War with Germany, 1890–1914; fictions and fantasies of the war to-come*, Liverpool, Liverpool University Press, 1997

Clayton, G J, *The New Zealand Army; A History from the 1840's to the 1990's*, Christchurch [NZ], New Zealand Army, 1990

Coppard, Audrey and Crick, Bernard (eds.), *Orwell Remembered*, London, Ariel Books, 1984

Cousins, Geoffrey, *The Defenders; A history of the British Volunteer*, London, Frederick Muller, 1968

Cullen, Stephen M, 'Collaborationists in Arms; the Uniforms and Equipment of the *Milice Française*', *The Armourer Militaria Magazine*, No. 100, July/August 2010

Cullen, Stephen M, 'Defending Mussolini', *Military Illustrated*, No. 263, April, 2010

Cullen, Stephen M, 'Fascists Behind Barbed Wire; political internment without trial in wartime Britain', *The Historian*, No. 100, Winter 2008

Cullen, Stephen M, *Home Guard Socialism: A vision of a People's Army*, Warwick, Allotment Hut Booklets, 2006

Cullen, Stephen M, 'Legion of the Damned', *Military Illustrated*, No. 238, March 2008

Duckers, Peter, *British Military Rifles, 1800–2000*, Princes Risborough, 2005

Fernbach, David, 'Tom Wintringham and socialist defense strategy', *History Workshop*, issue 14, Autumn 1982

Foot, William, *Beaches, fields, streets and hills . . . the anti-invasion landscape of England, 1940*, York, English Heritage, Council for British Archaeology, 2006

Fowler, Will, *France, Holland and Belgium, 1940–1941*, Hersham, Ian Allan Publishing, 2002

Fowler, Will, *Poland and Scandinavia 1939–1940*, Hersham, Ian Allan Publishing, 2002

Francis, Paul, *Isle of Man 20th Century Military Archaeology, Part 1; Island Defence*, Douglas, Manx Heritage Foundation, 2006

Fry, Helen, *The King's Most Loyal Enemy Aliens; Germans who fought for Britain in the Second World War*, Stroud, Sutton Publishing, 2007

Goodall, John, *Pevensey Castle, East Sussex*, London, English Heritage, 1999

Gordon, E V, (ed), with a supplement by D G Scragg, *The Battle of Maldon*, Manchester, Manchester University Press, 1976

Gillman, Peter, and Gillman, Leni, *'Collar the lot!'; how Britain interned and expelled its wartime refugees*, London, Quartet Books, 1980

Hampton, Janie, *How the Girl Guides Won the War*, London, Harper Press, 2010

Haythornthwaite; Philip, J, 'Badges of the Home Guard', *Medal News*, May 1991

Holzträger, Hans, *In A Raging Inferno; Combat Units of the Hitler Youth, 1944–45*, Solihull, Helion and Company, 2000

Hopkins, J K, *Into the Heart of the Fire; the British in the Spanish Civil War*, Stanford, Stanford University Press, 1998

Hunt, R J, *Uniforms of the Home Guard*, Pulborough, Historic Military Press, 2002

Jurado, Carlos Caballero, *Resistance Warfare, 1940–45*, London, Osprey Publishing, 1985

Lampe, David, *The Last Ditch*, London, Cassell, 1968

Longmate, Norman, *Island Fortress; The defence of Great Britain, 1603–1945*, London, Pimlico edition, 1991

Longmate, Norman, *The Real Dad's Army; The story of the Home Guard*, London, Arrow Books, 1974

Lowry, Bernard, *British Home Defences 1940–45*, Oxford, Osprey, 2004

Lowry, Bernard, *Discovering Fortifications; from the Tudors to the Cold War*, Princes Risborough, Shire Publications, 2006

Lowry, Bernard, *The Shropshire Home Guard*, Hereford, Logaston Press, 2010

MacCarron, Donal, *The Irish Defence Forces since 1922*, Oxford, Osprey, 2004

MacCarron, Donal, *'Step Together!' Ireland's Emergency Army 1939–46; as told by its veterans*, Dublin, Irish Academic Press, 1999

Mace, Martin, *Vehicles of the Home Guard*, Storrington, Historic Military Press, 2001

MacKenzie, S P, *The Home Guard; A military and political history*, Oxford, Oxford University Press, 1995

Mills, Jon, *Within the Island Fortress; the uniforms, insignia & ephemera of the Home Front in Britain 1939–1945; No. 1 The Women's Voluntary Services (WVS)*, Orpington, Wardens Publishing, 2005

Orr, David, R, *Duty Without Glory; the story of Ulster's Home Guard in the Second World War and the Cold War*, Newtownards, Redcoat Publishing, 2008

Osborne, Brian D, *The People's Army; Home Guard in Scotland 1940–1944*, Edinburgh, Birlinn, 2009

Osborne, Mike, *Defending Britain; Twentieth-Century Military Structures in the Landscape*, Stroud, Tempus, 2004

Petrow, Richard, *The Bitter Years; the invasion and occupation of Denmark and Norway, April 1940-May 1945*, London, Hodder and Stoughton, 1975

Piper, Leonard, *Dangerous Waters; the Life and Death of Erskine Childers*, London, Hambledon and London, 2003

Price, Alfred, *Britain's Air Defences 1939–45*, Oxford, Osprey, 2004

Purcell, Hugh, *The Last English Revolutionary; Tom Wintringham, 1898–1949*, Stroud, Sutton, 2004

Rowberry, Roy, *We You Salute*, Privately printed, 1990

Rowe, Mark, *Don't Panic; Britain Prepares for Invasion, 1940*, Stroud, Spellmount, 2010

Ruddy, Austin J, *To The Last Round; the Leicestershire and Rutland Home Guard, 1940–1945*, Derby, Breedon Books, 2007

Sainsbury, J D, *Hazardous Work*, Welwyn, Hart Books, 1985

Sargeaunt, Bertram E, *The Royal Manx Fencibles*, Aldershot, Gale and Polden, 1947

Simpson, A W B, *In the Highest Degree Odious*, Oxford, Oxford University Press, 1992

Sladen, Chris, 'When War Came Again', in *Oxford Today*, vol. 22, No. 1, Michaelmas 2009

Sondhaus, Lawrence, *Naval Warfare 1815–1914*, London, Routledge, 2001

Summerfield, Penny, and Coniston-Bird, Corinna, *Contesting Home Defence; men, women, and the Home Guard in the second World War*, Manchester, Manchester University Press, 2007

Stent, Ronald, *A Bespattered Page?; the internment of His Majesty's 'most loyal enemy aliens'*, London, Andre Deutsch, 1980

Stephenson, Ian P, *The Late Anglo-Saxon Army*, Stroud, Tempus Publishing, 2007

Stokes, Winifred, 'Investigating the history of local volunteer regiments: the Stockton Volunteers and the French invasion threat 1798–1808', *The Local Historian*, vol. 37, No. 1, February 2007

Stradling, Robert, *Your Children Will Be Next; bombing and propaganda in the Spanish Civil War, 1936–1939*, Cardiff, University of Wales Press, 2008

Thomas, Nigel, *Wehrmacht Auxiliary Forces*, London, Osprey, 1992

Thompson, Willie, *The Good Old Cause; British Communism 1920–1991*, London, Pluto Press, 1992

Thurlow, Richard, 'The Evolution of the Mythical British Fifth Column, 1939–46', in *Twentieth Century British History*, vol. 10, No. 4, 1999

Tissier, Tony Le, *With Our Backs to Berlin; The German Army in Retreat, 1945*, Stroud, Sutton, 2001

Ward, Arthur, *Resisting the Nazi Invader*, London, Constable, 1997

Warwicker, John, *Churchill's Underground Army; A History of the Auxiliary Units in World War II*, Barnsley, Frontline Books, 2008

West, W J, *Truth Betrayed*, London, Duckworth, 1987

Williamson, David G, *Poland Betrayed; the Nazi-Soviet Invasions of 1939*, Barnsley, Pen & Sword, 2009

Wood, Derek, *Attack Warning Red; the Royal Observer Corps and the defence of Britain 1925 to 1992*, (Revised edition), Portsmouth, Carmichael and Sweet, 1992

Yelton, David K, 'British Public Opinion, the Home Guard and the Defense of Great Britain, 1940–1944', *Journal of Military History*, vol. 58, No. 3, 1994

Index